Caught Between
A Review of Research into the Education of Pupils of
West Indian Origin

Caught Between

A Review of Research into the Education of
Pupils of West Indian Origin

Monica J. Taylor

NFER – Nelson

Published by The NFER-Nelson Publishing Company Ltd.,
Darville House, 2 Oxford Road East,
Windsor, Berks. SL4 1DF

First Published 1981
© NFER, 1981
ISBN 0-85633-231 3
Code 8084 02 1

Printed in Great Britain.

This book is sold subject to the standard conditions
of the Net Book Agreement.

Distributed in the USA by Humanities Press Inc.,
Atlantic Highlands, New Jersey 07716 USA

Contents

Foreword

The Committee of Inquiry into the Education of Children from Ethnic Minority Groups was established in March 1979 and was asked to produce an interim report on the educational needs and attainments of West Indian children. It was clear to the Committee that there was already in existence a considerable volume of research on the attainment of West Indian children which should form part of the background to the Committee's interim report. In the early part of 1980 therefore the Committee commissioned the NFER to undertake an evaluative survey of the research evidence relating to West Indian children in schools in this country.

This review formed an important part of the Committee's deliberations for its interim report and the Committee is indebted to the NFER for producing such a valuable document, which evaluates evidence in a very wide field in a clear and fair way. The Committee is particularly grateful to Monica Taylor for the conscientious and professional way in which she has carried out her work and hopes that the review will be widely read by everyone with an interest in the education of West Indian children in our schools.

David Halliday
Secretary to The Committee of Inquiry into the
Education of Children from Ethnic Minority Groups

April 1981

Acknowledgements

This review was undertaken under the supervision of Dr. S. Hegarty of the NFER to whom I am grateful for criticism of the text and advice, particularly on statistical interpretation and especially in respect of Section 9.

During the course of collecting material for review I was fortunate in being able to discuss the education of pupils of West Indian origin with Dr. Christopher Bagley at the University of Surrey and Mr. M. Purushothaman just before the closure of the Centre for Information and Advice on Educational Disadvantage at Manchester. The review has benefited in several places from their experience and insights. A visit to the Runnymede Trust in London was also of assistance, as was a telephone conversation and some correspondence with Mrs. Christine Mabey at the ILEA. In response to inquiries several researchers, too numerous to name individually, were kind enough to send me information on their higher degree work or research in progress, and advance copies of articles reporting recently completed research which have since been published in the period which has intervened. I trust that they will find accurate references to their work in the following text.

No review of research can be undertaken without considerable recourse to library facilities and I should like to express my thanks to all the library staff at NFER for their assistance and in particular to Janet May and Sarah Gerrard for their ready help and patient support. Other members of Editorial Services willingly co-operated during the time in 1980 when I was released from my usual duties to undertake this work and assisted materially in many ways. In particular I wish to thank Mary Dyer for her sterling work in transcribing an entire first draft from tape in record time and Ann

Adlam for typing a recognizable bibliography at short notice. Hilary Hosier had the unenviable task of retyping the revised draft into a final manuscript which she accomplished with rapid and cheerful competence.

Finally, of course responsibility for textual compilation and interpretation rests with the author who has attempted to faithfully represent all the data which came to light and were available for inclusion at this time.

MJT
April 1981

Part One

Background

Section 1: Introduction

Children of West Indian origin have been present as pupils in schools in Britain for over three decades. Over the last 15 years, as their numbers have increased, there has emerged a growing recognition that their needs, potential and aspirations might not be adequately realized by means of existing educational provision. Indeed, the under-achievement of the pupil of West Indian origin has become almost a stereotype. The aim of this book therefore, is to review the currently available research evidence on the performance in school of pupils of West Indian origin. Does research bear out the image of under-achievement? What influence do attitudes of parents, peers and teachers have on performance? How can the position of the West Indian child in the education system best be explained?

Although the last few years have given rise to a considerable amount of concern about and research into ethnic minorities in general, perhaps rather less is known in particular about people of West Indian descent now in this country. More specifically, even though much of the evidence about the education of West Indian pupils remains at the level of hearsay, anecdote or, at best, description, there is reason to believe that there is widespread and growing concern amongst the black community about the quality of education which their children are receiving (Mack, 1977; Mabey, 1980). This, however, is hardly new. As long ago as the late 1960s the West Indian community in London was voicing concern about the apparent generally low performance of their children and the high proportion of them in schools for the educationally sub-normal (see

Tomlinson, 1978), fears which were subsequently given fervent expression in a polemical pamphlet written on their behalf by Coard (1971). Teachers, too, have been no less aware of the difficulties and in 1974 a report of a London working party of teachers and lecturers concluded that on average black children were doing less well than white: they obtained lower status jobs, or none at all, and fewer exam passes; they were less likely to go on to higher education; more likely to be described as backward, poor readers, or slow learners, and that many were disillusioned, uncooperative or unhappy. More recently, a joint working party of local teachers and West Indian parents in Redbridge (Black People's Progressive Association and Redbridge Community Relations Council, 1978) united to investigate an apparent under-achievement in the borough and their resulting report relates their findings locally to evidence on a national scale.

That same document charts chronologically the official reports which have warned of difficulties experienced by West Indian children in education over the last decade. Mention might briefly be made of the following most important expressions of governmental concern. In 1969, the Parliamentary Select Committee on Race Relations and Immigration (Great Britain, Parliament, House of Commons, Select Committee on Race Relations and Immigration, 1969) noted ambivalent reports about the behaviour of West Indian children in schools. This was followed by a report by the National Foundation for Educational Research (NFER) which drew attention to the difficulties with language which many West Indian children experienced in schools and the urgent need for provision to be made for special teaching (Townsend, 1971). In the same year the Department of Education and Science (DES) Education Survey 13 (Great Britain, DES, 1971 b) referred to evidence of disproportionate numbers of immigrant pupils requiring education in schools for the educationally sub-normal (ESN). A yet later Government White Paper which made observations on the report of the Select Committee on Race Relations and Immigration (Great Britain, Parliament, House of Commons, Select Committee on Race Relations and Immigration, 1973) recognized that whilst many of the children of ethnic minorities shared with some indigenous children of older urban and industrial areas 'the educational disadvantages associated with an impoverished environment', they would, in addition, have a diversity of need. Specifically, it referred to the need of some West Indian children for special language teaching and the necessity to approach such provision tactfully with parents. In addition, it recommended that '. . . all local education authorities with a sizeable immigrant child population should make plans to provide by an early date special facilities in ordinary schools to overcome the linguistic and adjustment problems of immigrant children with a level of ability higher than the general run of pupils in special schools for the educationally sub-normal' (Great Britain, Parliament, House of Commons, 1974, Recommendation 19, p.12). What effect such Government reports have in fact had on local education authority policies is difficult to determine, but in 1976 in evidence to the Select Committee on Race Relations and Immigration the Community Relations Commission (CRC, 1976) stated that 'the situation of West Indian children in schools is, if anything, getting worse, not only in terms of cognitive skills, but also in social adjustment' (p.1). More recently the then Government observed in its White Paper *The West Indian Community* (Great Britain, Parliament, House of Commons, 1978) that it was 'aware of the results of surveys already made which indicate that taken as a group West Indian pupils fail to achieve their full potential in comparison to other groups in tests administered in schools' (Para.24, p.7). In consequence, it recommended an inquiry into the under-achievement of West Indian children which, in March 1979, resulted in the establishment of the Committee of Inquiry into the Education of Children from Ethnic Minority Groups (Rampton Committee), of whose work this review forms part.

Section 2: Plan of the Research Review and Evaluation

The National Foundation for Educational Research (NFER) was commissioned by the Committee of Inquiry into the Education of Children from Ethnic Minority Groups (Rampton Committee) to undertake in April–June 1980 'an evaluative survey of the important research evidence relating to the under-achievement of West Indian children in schools in Britain'. During this limited, three-month period it was proposed to survey the published research evidence, concentrating largely on attainment and performance and, where time permitted, to consult related, more general, educational evidence. Initially it was planned that the review should encompass research undertaken within the last decade, and, depending on the volume of material identified and the time available, it should, if possible, reach back to earlier years. Subsequently, it was decided to include research spanning the previous five years from 1965–70 as well, since, despite important changes in the educational situation of pupils of West Indian origin in this country over the entire period (see Section 3 on Statistics and Terminology, pp.8–14), the earlier studies had a considerable influence on the nature and development of the work in this field undertaken in succeeding years. Moreover, from time to time reference is made to research dating back to the 50s, as for example the notable work of Edith Clarke (1957) whose studies of family life in Jamaica are still illuminating and authoritative. Some relevant on-going research, from sources indicated in two major registers of research (NFER, 1979; CRE, 1980) were also taken into account and are indicated in the review.

It is perhaps necessary to explain the meaning given to 'important research evidence' as mentioned in the brief for this review. Although it was the Committee's wish that 'important' should be interpreted as large-scale research, which, in turn, was defined by the sample of pupils involved in the study, it was noted that the findings of some large-scale investigations were already well known and that efforts should be made to discover work of a smaller scale in order to compare trends indicated. Accordingly, a number of higher education theses and research reports on particular aspects of the education of pupils of West Indian origin have been included in the review, although time did not permit a systematic or comprehensive evaluation of such documents.

The research techniques utilized in this review consisted of searches through the literature and bibliographies as well as computer searches using data bases which included American source material. A number of individuals and organizations were also approached for information and visits were made to interview and discuss the achievement of pupils of West Indian origin with researchers having particular expertise in the field of ethnic minorities and to organizations professionally concerned with multicultural education (see Acknowledgements). Attempts were also made to contact black community organizations for information on research carried out by West Indians on West Indian pupils, but few studies were reported.

The following review of research concentrates on research in

Britain. Though it had been the intention to take account of American studies, where these appeared relevant, a computer search of American sources suggested, however, that such material was inappropriate. More importantly, there were several indications in the British research literature (see, for example, Thomas-Hope, 1975; Little, 1975) that direct comparisons with the American situation would be ill-advised. Although much work in this country derives its inspiration and instigation from America and Canada, the position of pupils of West Indian origin in the Americas is both qualitatively and quantitatively different – a difference which is historically and contemporarily so great as to call into question the applicability of research evidence on ethnic minority groups in those countries to a British situation.

In support a number of factors can be outlined briefly here. First, there are obvious differences in migration patterns. As Foner (1977) points out, the tradition of migration from the West Indies to America began much earlier and people of West Indian origin have been established in the United States over a much longer period of time. There was, moreover, a greater tendency for West Indian women to emigrate to America, and it has been claimed, they were those women with higher educational and professional qualifications (Thomas-Hope, 1975) and more often from an urban environment. An interesting comparison of the lives of two sisters, one who migrated to New York, the other to London, is drawn by Seabrook (1980). Though sources differ (depending on the time when figures were collected and the fluctuating responses to job vacancies) on whether migration to this country was led by men whose womenfolk and children followed later, as especially from Jamaica in the 50s (Foner, 1977), and whether it took place from urban or rural environments, the balance of opinion with respect to migration from Jamaica would seem to suggest that it was predominantly rural migration characterized by a high proportion of women, often alone (Peach, 1968; Bagley, 1977). Secondly, there are huge numerical differences between the proportions of blacks in America and the UK. Little (1975) suggests that whereas one in eight or nine of Americans are black, blacks form only one in 50 of the population of Great Britain. He cites figures for 1971 which show that even though two out of three West Indian children in Great Britain are in schools in Greater London very few schools have concentrations of blacks similar to those in the USA.

Cultural differences between the blacks in the two countries are also great. Often children of West Indian origin are not differentiated from those of other ethnic groups in the American educational research literature. There is a much greater homogeneity in the United States immigrant population whereas in Great Britain the different communities are quite distinct. Differences in the language base of the black population in America and this country may be noted in particular: Southern Jamaican is spoken by people of West Indian origin in the States, whereas the more Africanized, Standard Jamaican or Jamaican Creole are the languages of the West Indians in Great Britain. Finally, as Little points out, the institutional frameworks of the two countries are vastly dissimilar: differences in relations between central and local government entail different social arrangements at all levels including, most importantly, systems of education.

For all these reasons the American research literature on the achievement of West Indian pupils was judged to be inappropriate and no attempt was made to consider it in detail. Nevertheless, during the course of this book references to American research will be made in passing, and on these occasions it is important that the above caveats be borne in mind.

Moreover, in view of the time constraint imposed it was not possible within the ambit of this review to draw detailed comparisons with other ethnic minority groups, although some observations of this kind occur incidentally when studies whose samples drew on a wide range of ethnic groups are reported.

Despite these restrictions the scope of this review is broadly defined in educational terms. Its major focus is on the performance of pupils of West Indian origin throughout the entire age range covered by formal schooling. Although this means that the review concentrates on education at primary and secondary levels, account is also taken of influences in early childhood and prospects for school leavers as well as other significant 'factors outside the formal education system relevant to school performance'.

The range of educational research methods which come under review is also wide as it was a particular intention to consult not only the strictly psychometric research evidence but also to seek out more descriptive, phenomenological or analytical accounts. The body of the text provides the main thrust of evidence and summaries of salient work. Where evidence appears to conflict with this trend it has been subjected to more detailed critical analysis, but, it is hoped, not disproportionate treatment. Particular attention was paid, at the Committee's request, to a number of aspects of research on which specific information was required. It was thus hoped to provide an appraisal of evidence on achievement relating to sex, age, length of schooling, size of school, schooling in different locations in the UK and island of origin of West Indian children born in the Caribbean.

The scope and extent of the field under review was both extremely varied and wide ranging so that a comprehensive picture on all aspects of the subject matter could not always be built up. In Parts 2 and 3 the usual format of the review is guided by the following considerations: age of pupil from younger to older age group, chronology of research study and status of research as major or minor. Investigations of particular note are asterisked in the References and Part 4 Overview (pp.210–42) indicates areas in which research is lacking. Indeed, it is worth pointing out at this preliminary stage that any review of research depends very much on the quality of the studies available for consideration, and as a consequence of this assessment it seemed justifiable to devote a separate section of this book to an appraisal of methodological weaknesses of research in this field (pp.210–16). Secondly, such a review can only attempt to evaluate the evidence available for consultation at any one point in time. A number of reports of research highly pertinent to this area have recently been published and the author has reason to believe that other information which it has not been possible to include systematically in this review will be made public shortly (e.g. Verma and Bagley, 1981). Indeed, as concern and interest in this field increases, one or two reviews of research into the education and performance of pupils of West Indian origin have already begun to appear alongside reports of new research (Bagley, 1977; BPPA, 1978; Mabey, 1980, 1981; Tomlinson, 1979, 1981), or in comparison with performance of other ethnic minority pupils (Tomlinson, 1980).

The function of the present review is thus to draw together the research evidence from all previous major studies and to evaluate this as objectively as possible. As a preface to this undertaking something should perhaps be said about the position of evaluation in this context. Jenkins *et al.* (1979) make some pertinent remarks apropos of evaluating educational programmes:

'. . . What any evaluation can tell about an educational programme will be bound to some extent by the cultural background and perspectives of the evaluators. But there is not just one reasonable perspective to take on an educational programme; in multiethnic contexts there is a diversity of expectations about education and a diversity of culturally embedded world views, each with its own rationality. The task for the evaluator is not to arbitrate between these perspectives but to elicit and express them.' (pp.122–3).

It is recommended that an evaluator

'refrain from setting himself up as a judge of achievement or policy and content himself with offering as full a description as possible of the programme in action. The evaluator would not be seen as a person . . . specially qualified to offer criticisms or endorsement. As a "collector of definitions" he would hopefully act as an honest broker between conflicting viewpoints.' (pp.127–8).

This is what the writer has in the main attempted to do.

The remainder of Part 1 deals with some preliminary but pertinent observations about statistics and terminology and briefly delineates the background to social and economic life in the Caribbean, contrasted with that in the UK. In the main body of the text (Parts 2 and 3) which follows research studies on various aspects of the educational performance of pupils of West Indian origin are first described and then the significance of their evidence is evaluated so as to set it in a wider educational context and to present the predominant view or consensus consequent upon the research. Part 4, Overview, embodies a summary of the main findings reexamined from a different perspective and under the headings suggested on p.7, together with an assessment of explanations of under-achievement. Two other sections focus on criticisms of research methodologies of the area and an appraisal of educational strategies. Some personal views are contained in these general conclusions and, at the Committee's request, recommendations for future research and policy which follow from the evaluation are made.

Section 3: Statistics and Terminology
One major problem in making a true assessment of the achievement of pupils of West Indian origin is the lack of accurate statistical information on the total numbers of such children currently in schools. Indeed, the problem dates back to the early 1970s when the DES ceased to collect statistics on immigrant pupils by country of origin in all maintained schools. The absence of such data is thus a factor to be taken into account when considering research which was undertaken during the last decade. In contrast, the early years of the 15-year period covered by this evaluation are those in which the DES's definition of 'immigrant' was fully in operation. The DES defined 'immigrant' pupils as either 'children born outside the British Isles who have come to this country with or to join parents or guardians whose countries of origin were abroad', or 'children born in the UK to parents whose countries of origin were abroad and who came to the UK up to 10 years before the date to which the figures apply'. Children of mixed immigrant parentage were excluded (Great Britain, DES, 1972b, Para. 36, 37, p.xv). Three main groups of pupils were thus covered by the definition whilst it was in operation. They were (1) children migrating with their parents, most of whom had arrived in this country during the 1960s; (2) children joining their parents who were already settled here – again most of these arrivals were in the 60s and were already tailing off considerably as a result of the tightening of the immigration laws by the early 70s; and (3) children born in this country – of whom there were a growing proportion in the early 70s and who now constitute by far the majority of the pupils of ethnic minority origin now undergoing full-time schooling. Even from this bare outline a number of problems in implementing the definition are readily apparent. By the early 70s the definition already excluded children of parents who had been here longer than the 10-year period specified, even though some of them may well have had linguistic and social difficulties associated with first-generation immigrants (Stoker, 1970). The definition also excluded all pupils of secondary school age born in the UK and, in addition, those in their final year of junior schooling and some even younger (Brittan, 1973a). Reference is frequently made in the literature of the period on ethnic minority groups to teachers' difficulties in identifying 'immigrant' children (see, e.g. the retrospective review in Phillips, 1979). The problem is well illustrated by a study undertaken in Bedford

(Brown, 1970) which found that some head teachers gave in their returns the number of all immigrant pupils, regardless of when their parents arrived in this country, since they found no difference in the linguistic and cultural adjustment of children of immigrants who had been in England for over 10 years and that of more recent arrivals. Indeed, it seems that some heads had ceased to employ the term 'immigrant' after the child had been resident in the UK for five years. If such practices were repeated on a national scale the total figures were obviously not completely reliable. On the other hand, some head teachers pointed out that if these Form 7 statistics were used as the criterion for additional resources of staffing, finance or special responsibility allowances, then the apparent size of the need was reduced. Yet others claimed that the very act of counting was in itself divisive and not likely to promote good race relations.

As a result of renewed and sustained criticisms by teachers and administrators that such a definition was not meeting either educational or demographic needs the decision was taken to abandon the collection of numerical information on 'immigrant' pupils. As the Select Committee on Race Relations and Immigration report *Educational Disadvantage and the Educational Needs of Immigrants* (Great Britain, Parliament, House of Commons, 1974) put it 'in the Government's view the main reason for failure was that no general factual definition could answer such need as is felt within the education service for information about the educational needs of immigrants, and that a proper assessment of these needs through the mass collection of national statistics was not feasible' (Para. 4, p.2). When the figures were last collected in 1972 the total number of 'immigrant' children in all maintained schools was 279,872, 3.3 per cent of all pupils. Of these, children of West Indian origin numbered 101, 898, the largest ethnic group, comprising 36.4 per cent of the total. Speculations can only be made about current figures, but a fairly recent estimate (Mack, 1977) suggested 125 – 150,000 children of West Indian origin and Tomlinson (1979) also quotes this figure, though the source was not supplied.

In its response to the 1977 Select Committee report (Great Britain, Parliament, House of Commons, Select Committee on Race Relations and Immigration, 1977) the then Government agreed in a White Paper, *The West Indian Community* (Great Britain, Parliament, House of Commons, 1978) that 'it would be right to make a start on the collection of educational statistics' (Para. 30, p.8) relating to West Indian children entering ESN schools, students of West Indian origin embarking on teacher training courses and the number of West Indian teachers in service. Although it was hoped that for West Indian pupils in ESN schools 'the first returns of information in this form will be made in January 1980' (p.9) it is understood that this process has not started. This Government is understood to be awaiting the views of the Rampton Committee on this matter. This is in spite of the fact that Paragraph 25 (p.7) of the 1978 White Paper clearly stated that 'the Government supports in principle the collecting of statistics on an ethnic basis where these would be of use in establishing facts about how members of the ethnic minority groups are faring in the various stages of the educational system'. Moreover, the majority of those who responded to the Select Committee's consultative document were in agreement with this proposal. Similarly, present soundings suggest that researchers, at least, would be in agreement with the collection of statistics for educational purposes once again. And evidence from the recently reported Schools Council project Studies in the Multi-ethnic Curriculum has indicated that many local education authorities (leas) would also support this. Indeed 17 out of 70 leas said they kept statistics so that they knew how many pupils of ethnic minority origin were present in their schools. Of those authorities with more than 2½ per cent ethnic minority pupils which do not collect statistics at present, half were in favour of doing so and a further quarter neutral. They thought such information would be useful in assessing special educational needs, allocating resources and perhaps in monitoring performance, but emphasized that great care and sensitivity should be exercised in the method of collection (Little and Willey, 1981).

Indeed in 1980 the Assessment of Performance Unit of the DES undertook preliminary discussions with respect to mounting a national monitoring of performance of pupils of West Indian origin in mathematics, English language and science at primary and secondary levels. As a result, its West Indian Study Group, which reported in June 1980, recommended that such a survey be carried out with the collaboration of leas, teachers' unions and the West Indian community. Early in 1981 discussions were in progress with these bodies on whether monitoring of performance should take place, possibly as early as November 1981. However, by April 1981 all interested parties had expressed misgivings and reservations and, as such an exercise was not feasible without the co-operation of the National Union of Teachers, an announcement to abandon it was made by the Secretary of State for Education and Science in May. Criticisms from leas, teachers and West Indian groups focused on the lack of attention to be paid to the child's background, school ethos, teaching styles and indeed the method of sampling as it was not proposed to test all West Indian pupils. Among the detailed issues of survey design and administration which would need to be resolved, not the least would be an adequate definition of 'West Indian' which could easily be put into operation in schools by teachers who would be required to make the initial classification. One definition which included grandparents' country of origin, as was suggested by the then Secretary of State in 1971, might be reconsidered, but a more explicit definition has already been in use in the National Child Development Study (NCDS) (Essen and Ghodsian, 1979). Within that research programme 'immigrant' was defined as 'a child born abroad with at least one parent born abroad' (first-generation immigrant) or 'a child born in Britain to ieast one parent born abroad' (second-generation immigrant).

In the writer's view if data on children of ethnic minority origin were to be ascertained once again it would be necessary to reassure the West Indian community, especially parents, of the importance of such an exercise as a means of helping to establish the correct provision for their children's needs. It may well be the case that very precise information – for example, about the island of origin of families and the kind of environment, whether rural or urban, parental reasons for emigrating to the UK and differences between home and school, especially whether the language of the home is Creole, as well as the more customary indices of socio-economic background – will be necessary to establish a meaningful classification. In addition, Bagley (1980) recommends that pupil performance should be monitored against school ethos and ethnicity in each borough so that the personal and social data on the child may be compared with a similarly detailed appraisal of the school and community. Were such an exercise feasible its magnitude might well pay dividends both in terms of a more accurate assessment of children of West Indian origin and, in addition, by providing much needed up-to-date information on the heterogeneity of the West Indian community.

Note on terminology
One of the difficulties encountered in reviewing research undertaken has been the proliferation of terms used throughout the

literature to refer to children of Caribbean origin. The most commonly and consistently used adjective is 'West Indian' but 'coloured', 'negro' (more particularly in the American literature) and lately, 'black' are all in use. It has also been claimed that 'Caribbean' is most often used self-referentially (Purushothaman, 1978). To some extent, these changes and evolutions of language occur naturally over time, but some usages, it can be argued, are more overtly political, in the broad sense.

As has already been discussed, the distinction drawn in the research literature of the 60s and early 70s between 'immigrant' meaning of West Indian, Asian, African, Mediterranean, etc. origin and 'indigenous' meaning white British, is now no longer tenable. Those immigrants who have given birth to a new, second generation have thereby become indigenous. Thus there are now many second-generation black children in schools who are as indigenous as their white peers. In view of the virtual cessation of immigration in the late 70s any attempt to employ the term 'immigrant' (sic) would connote racialist overtones and even possibly innuendos of repatriation. It is both correct and more accurate to distinguish first- and second-generation immigrants. This, however, for reasons outlined in the preceding paragraphs on statistics (pp.8–12), is relatively rarely done, even in comparatively recent research. An additional difficulty is that in the early research studies a distinction is not always drawn between different ethnic minority groups which fall under the blanket term 'immigrant'. For all these reasons, whilst as accurate a description as possible of the sample under review has been attempted, when referring to research studies *the original terms employed by the authors themselves have in all cases been retained* and hence may give rise to lack of clarity, if not to actual ambiguity.

It is generally helpful when confronted with a piece of research to bear in mind the date of publication, and, where this differs, the time when the research was undertaken, and then to make some allowances for changes in terminology according to fashion and the climate of race relations which obtained when the research was conducted. Most of the research reported includes both first- and second-generation immigrants in its sampling, the later the research the greater the proportion of children of West Indian origin born in this country. To come up to date, the term 'black British', currently in vogue in some circles, may not be either an accurate or acceptable nomenclature (Little, 1975; Hinds, 1980) since it may imply an evaluation and an identity which some adolescents and adults of West Indian descent might not wish to choose for themselves.

In conclusion, it will have been noted that particularly in view of the predominance of second-generation immigrants currently undergoing schooling, this writer's preference is for the term 'of West Indian origin'. This has the merit of indicating ancestry, albeit non-specifically, since it does not suggest whether the Caribbeans are of African or East Indian origin, but then neither does the considerably more long-winded 'American New Commonwealth origin' of the Immigrant Statistics Unit of the Population Statistics Division, and its subtly distinctive 'New Commonwealth Ethnic origin'. The preferred term 'of West Indian origin' is, moreover, not entirely inappropriate for both first- and second-generation immigrants and even children of mixed marriages having one West Indian parent.

Section 4: The West Indians

In any attempt to understand the position of the child of West Indian origin in contemporary British society, and within that the education system, it is essential to consider the historical and socio-economic factors which shaped the conditions of life of such a child's ancestors in the West Indies, and to what extent these forces are still influential. Accordingly, this Section will first look briefly at some of the more important aspects of life in the Caribbean in the 40s to 60s and see how these led up to a pattern of mass migration to the UK at that time. The second part of the Section will then examine and compare some of the central features of the first- and second-generation immigrants' lifestyles in this country, drawing out the implications for schooling which will be taken up in later parts on ability, attainment and achievement and attitudes.

Life in the Caribbean

It is generally agreed that the lands and peoples of the West Indies are far from homogeneous groupings. The geographical area commonly referred to as the West Indies comprises groups of large and small islands and mainland territories, having colonial associations with a number of different countries, and scattered along an arc for 2,000 miles in the Caribbean sea. There appears to be no explicit agreement as to the exact number of countries which together constitute the West Indies, but the following, at least, seem generally to fall under the heading 'British West Indies': Jamaica, Windward Islands including Barbados, Grenada, The Grenadines, The Bahamas, Caymen Islands, St. Vincent and the largely French speaking though also British Colonies of Dominica and St. Lucia, Virgin Islands, Turks and Caicos Islands, Leeward Islands including St. Kitts, Nevis, Anguilla, Antigua, Barbuda and Montserrat, Trinidad-and-Tobago, Belize and Guyana. In what follows most of the comments concerning pupils of West Indian origin are confined to those Caribbean islands which were British Colonial territories and from which the majority of immigrants to Britain came, namely, Jamaica, Trinidad-and-Tobago, Barbados and the largest mainland territory of Guyana.

The Caribbean is an area of great cultural complexity, whose differences in social structure are only rarely related directly to national or geographic boundaries. This means that the area has been a great source of interest to anthropologists and the numerous sources of information, which have generally been consulted at second-hand for this review, are often at variance on matters of detail. Nevertheless, the general consensus in the literature enables two main distinctions to be drawn with profit. First, the peoples of these lands have a diversity of origin. A majority appear to be of African extraction, but there are also a number of East Indians, particularly in Trinidad and Guyana where they form half the populations. It is important to realize that on the whole those of East Indian origin did not suffer the breakdown in family traditions which negroes in the region suffered during slavery. However, research and more general writing have concentrated on West Indians of African origin or else fail to make the distinction. Secondly, this latter group tend also to comprise the lower social classes whose distinct and individual family patterns, deviate in important respects from western standards. The following review of research concentrates on the largest island, Jamaica, both since more information is available on this territory and also as it is the island from which most West Indian migrants to Britain originated. Moreover, much that can be said about Jamaica in particular can also be applied in general to many of the other islands since, despite the differences in origin and class mentioned above, to a large extent the peoples share a common historical heritage. Indeed it is this heritage which has often been claimed as the source for many of the more profound difficulties which children of West Indian origin experience in this country. As Bushell (1973) put it 'the term "West

Indian" therefore extends beyond the frontiers of the islands: it denotes an underlying similarity, a characteristic way of life, grown out of historical events.' (p.82).

Most of the peoples and islands share three features: colonialism, slavery and plantation. The plantation system, a form of overseas capitalism of an industrial kind forced a kind of 'westernization' on the slaves (Pryce, 1979). The cultural life of the African slaves was considerably modified by the social and physical conditions under which the slaves existed. Family life and religious beliefs were radically altered and language became a means of preserving cultural identity in the face of plantation control and the destruction of African culture and social organization (Bagley, 1977). Language is thus of major significance both historically and contemporarily. The Creole which resulted from the experience of plantation was much influenced by African languages, but also depended for its exact orientation on the size and physical features of the islands, which, in turn, were related to the proportion of blacks to whites and the degree of contact between them. After emancipation (c.1830 in Jamaica) many former slaves abandoned the plantations and sought a life of subsistence farming and extreme poverty in the hills. However, the dual cultural system – the modified African culture, as developed under slavery, and the white western orientation, which was greatly valued and an objective for aspiration – continued in parallel. Thus early there was a tension formed between the 'slavery-based sub-structure of values and the defusion of metropolitan values through colonialism' (Pryce, 1979). Over the years, and more recently in particular, the poor villagers have gravitated towards the urban centres in an attempt to find employment and diminish poverty. But the result is often far from the case. It has in fact been characterized as a movement from rural under-employment to urban unemployment (Pryce, 1979).

One of the enduring, central and influential featues of West Indian life is the mother-dominated family. Edith Clarke's book *My Mother who Fathered Me* (1957), probably the most detailed anthropological study of family life, deals with aspects of land tenure, marriage, sex and procreation, household organization and development of kinship roles in three Jamaican communities. From this and other writings there appear to be three main reasons for the matriarchal and matrifocal West Indian family: a tendency to such in African countries of ancestral origin; the reinforcement of this orientation by the conditions of slavery in which legal marriage was not permitted, despite the encouragement to slaves to procreate, any children belonging subsequently to the mother; and, finally, economic conditions in the West Indies after emancipation making legal marriage too difficult to enter into or sustain (Whitehouse, 1973; Pryce, 1979). The varied marriage patterns of West Indian social life have been well documented, but four contemporary patterns appear consistent: Christian marriage; faithful concubinage; companionate or keeper family; and disintegrate family or grandmother household. These are each a function of economic and social status marking a point on a scale of upward social mobility (Evans and Le Page, 1967). The extended family network centred on the mother or grandmother is therefore the traditional pattern, and a number of male/female unions, possibly leading to steady cohabitation and, if economically viable, to marriage in the couple's late thirties or forties, is the norm. The role of the male is considerably diminished and many writers have speculated about the effect on boys' upbringing and behaviour of the absence of the father or father substitute from the home, together with relatively few opportunities for meeting men in the social community and hence the lack of father models as patterns for behaviour. Bagley (1977), in an excellent review of family life in Jamaica, cites evidence that the presence of the father, whilst increasing authoritarianism in the home, has little influence on material and cultural standards. However, several anthropologists have pointed to the tremendous influence which patterns of family life in the West Indies have on economic and social development (see, e.g. Clarke, 1957).

By Western standards descriptions of the home life of the West Indian in the Caribbean make it appear authoritarian, with strict but possibly inconsistent patterns of discipline, which, added to an unstable domestic situation and poverty which often leads to malnutrition, all indicate deprived conditions for upbringing. From time to time writers have conjectured that such environments will tend to produce a type of personality lacking in concentration and a sense of application and behaviour stressing short- rather than long-term goals. This, perhaps, would hardly be surprising. However, it is of interest to note that both girls and boys have many roles and daily tasks which they are expected to perform as a contribution to domestic life. Whereas the girls' jobs centre on the home, the boys' work tends to be in connection with tilling and cultivating the grounds or tending the animals of the homestead. Whereas it is alleged that because of the absence of male figures boys often form a deep attachment with or dependency on their mothers, by contrast, girls appear to be psychologically more mature and have more opportunity to model themselves on their grandmothers or school teachers. Girls tend to assume leadership roles but evidence suggests that they may feel uncertain about males as future partners and that they also tend to develop an over-maternal consciousness. Nevertheless, they nurture early expectations of child bearing and traditionally revolt against their mothers in adolescence (Evans and Le Page, 1967).

There seems to be a general consensus that West Indian society is deeply stratified by class and colour which are, in turn, broadly linked with status as defined by socio-economic group membership (Bagley, 1977; Foner, 1977). The more white a person's skin the more likely he is to belong to a higher social grouping, and conversely, the blacker his skin the more likely he is to be of low social class. Yet there are differences between the rural and urban populations with respect to ascription of status and class based on colour. As Foner (1977) points out, among villagers colour may only be the basis for prestige when combined with other attributes such as income or occupation. However the ascription of status based on colour remains broadly true.

This distinction is reflected also in religious and educational practices. Although there are variations in religious beliefs between the different islands there is a fundamental basis in Christianity. Whereas Trinidad is a secular society of mixed faiths principally Christianity (predominantly Catholicism), Hinduism and Islam, Jamaica, which is basically Protestant, is characterized by cultic diversity which manifests itself in extreme sects, such as Pocomania, which exists alongside almost Victorian Christianity, particularly Pentecostalism.

Similarly, educational arrangements vary from island to island. In his 1977 review Bagley concludes that all the evidence indicates that the quality of education in Jamaica lags behind that of other islands. In Antigua, Barbados and Trinidad, for example, three times as many children complete their education (Cross, 1973). By contrast, it has been estimated that 25 per cent of the Jamaican population is functionally illiterate. Thus it does seem reasonable to suppose that since 60 per cent of West Indian immigrants in this country are from Jamaica they are likely to be less well educated than migrants from other parts of the Caribbean, even when allowances are made for the characteristics of initiative and determination which have to be demonstrated when embarking on the migration process.

Schools in the West Indies undoubtedly reflect the influence of British colonialism. Classes are formal and teacher-centred with an emphasis on rote learning, choral repetition and memorization, as there are few text books. The teacher herself, is likely to be poorly trained, and indeed in rural environments may well not have had any training at all. Corporal punishment is relied upon as an incentive to learning and as a means of control. Until recently schools were limited to all-age primary establishments and secondary education could only be afforded by a paying élite. However, black advancement is now possible but dependent on passing the 11-plus. It is also necessary for children to be bilingual in Jamaican Creole and Standard Jamaican in order to succeed. Despite the disadvantages he suffers the working class Jamaican still exhibits a naïve faith in education as social advancement and recrimination and self-blame attend failure (Bagley, 1977). The same writer points to a variation in success in 11-plus examinations over the 14 parishes which comprise Jamaica, but, interestingly, nearly twice as many girls as boys pass. He observes 'this marked success for girls compared with boys is a feature of many indices of achievement in Jamaican education, and is a reflection of basic features of a social structure moulded by the institution of slavery' (p.11). It is also reported that a study carried out in Jamaica (Manley, 1963) found that in every parish and every type of school girls scored higher than boys on the Moray House tests used to determine entrance to grammar school. Census statistics also show that proportionately more females than males complete secondary education and research in one parish revealed that girls are more likely to be successful when entered for GCE exams (Bagley, 1977).

It is worth including here a reference to two studies which have been carried out in Jamaica. First, a piece of research, relevant to education in the West Indies, which was in fact one of the earliest of all published studies. In 1965 Vernon reported the results of a comparative study of two samples of 50 West Indian boys in the West Indies and 100 English boys in south east England, aged 10½ to 11, on a battery of tests and assessments of non-verbal ability, perception, arithmetic, English and concept formation. He also assessed environmental variables which included regularity of schooling, unbroken home, socio-economic status, cultural stimulus, initiative, male dominance, planning, and linguistic background. The results indicated that overall the West Indian boys did relatively poorly but their performance varied considerably with different tests, being worse on practical and some non-verbal tests and better on perceptual abilities. There was a very strong association between the test performance of both the West Indian and the English boys and the assessed cultural stimulus provided by the homes (Vernon, 1965 a and b).

The second, more recent cross-cultural study directly involving Jamaican pupils is that reported by Bagley (1977) (also Bagley, Wong and Young, n.d.) in which 128 pupils aged 10, in their final year of primary schooling in Jamaica, were tested individually on Schonell's Reading Comprehension Test and Witkin's Embedded Figures Test, primarily a test of perception though having some significant correlations with more conventional tests of achievement. The school had been specially selected for research as, although it was situated in a relatively poor rural area among the sugar estates in the south of Jamaica, it had enjoyed a high reputation, particularly because of the number of its children who were successful in the 11-plus examination. On the reading test the Jamaican children were at least two years behind 88 Jamaican children of similar age who had been previously tested in schools in working-class areas of London together with 103 white middle-class pupils and 45 white working-class pupils (Bagley, Bart and Wong, 1978). This suggests that although Jamaican children in London appear to be under-achieving relative to the norms for both other West Indian children in different parts of Great Britain, and for white English children, the Jamaican children in rural Jamaica were under-achieving dramatically by comparison. The difference between the two Jamaican groups, one in Jamaica the other in London, was much greater than that found between the Jamaican and English groups in the London schools. Although the Jamaican children likewise achieved at a lower level on the Embedded Figures Test compared with their counterparts in London, the authors proposed that differences in socialization practices would largely explain these differentials. Overall these recent findings would indicate that pupils of Jamaican origin in British schools are not performing less well than their peers whom they left behind in the West Indies despite the kind of claim in the Select Committee Report in 1977 (Great Britain, Parliament, House of Commons, Select Committee on Race Relations and Immigration, 1977). On the contrary, Bagley (1977) interpreted the findings as suggesting that exposure to an English educational system may lead quite rapidly to the acquisition of an English standard of achievement and an English cognitive style (see also Ward, 1978).

From the preceding review of life in the Caribbean it is possible to trace a number of factors which, together with a growing population and increasing unemployment, led to a pattern of mass migration which began in Jamaica in the 1940s and continued for over 20 years. Although there is some disagreement about the origin of location of the migrants to this country, the balance of opinion would seem to suggest that they were only latterly from rural backgrounds and that they were in the main 'propertyless, poorly educated masses' (Pryce, 1979, p.21), though they were mainly in employment prior to emigration (Rose *et al.*, 1969). There were undoubtedly several motivating factors. One of these was a desire to escape the rigid stratification which prevented people of African origin from rising in the educational and occupational system, since power and privilege were accorded to those with whiter skins (Bagley, 1977). It is also likely that a background of poverty in Jamaica and an advertised availability of work in this country were primary motivating forces. But many writers (e.g. Alleyne, 1962) have placed equal weight on the migrants' ideological aspirations which, it has been suggested, they hoped to satisfy through education. However, Foner (1977) remarks that few of the migrants whom she interviewed in this country explicitly mentioned such a reason for emigration.

Whatever the true explanation, it was the case that in 1966 approximately twice as many Jamaicans were migrants. The female member of the household would often arrive first, followed later by her children and perhaps husband, common law husband or boy-friend. Many children, however, stayed behind with their grandparents or relatives for several years until subsequently sent for by their mother who might by then have set up home with another man and produced a new family. It has been pointed out by several writers that one of the problems of adjustment for a child who has recently joined his family in this country, having been sent for from the West

Indies, may be that he has come to live in a completely new family situation, often with a new stepfather and several siblings whom he has not previously seen or else with his mother alone – both situations likely to adversely affect educational achievement. Although Jamaican emigration to Britain was continuously characterized by a high proportion of women, in most cases there was just not enough money for the whole family to emigrate together. On the other hand, as in the 50s, when, in response to the labour market, males led migration, some women preferred to stay in Jamaica, perhaps because of child-rearing responsibilities, or their lack of ready knowledge of job opportunities in England. Initially male skilled and semi-skilled workers predominated but later the number of unskilled and farm workers increased (Rose *et al.*, 1969).

Whitehouse (1973) suggests that in the early 60s the migrants expected rapid acceptance by the host society, minimal adaptation and possibly a rich return to the West Indies (see also Thomas-Hope, 1975). Indeed sending money or a wealthy return home may even have been expected by those in the West Indies (Prescod-Roberts and Steele, 1980). However, since the 1968 Race Relations Bill many settled down and few returned. Nevertheless migrants may preserve an idealistic view of life in the West Indies and 'the myth of amassing sufficient wealth to return to the homeland is retained, largely as a psychological support, an emotional lifeline in an alien cultural environment' (Whitehouse, 1973, p.11) especially perhaps when the promises implicit in the experience of migration have not been realized (see Seabrook, 1980). However, it is also increasingly possible that many West Indians who may have been in Britain for many years do not want to be considered British, as one black teacher put it 'One must be confident not only that one belongs but that others accept one's belonging.' (Hinds, 1980.)

Identity was also seen as crucial by Thomas-Hope (1975) who in a comparative study of migrants to London, New York and Toronto, 100 in each category, showed that whereas 41 per cent of the London sample indicated they regretted their decision to migrate, only 12 per cent of the New York sample and 20 per cent of the Toronto group felt that way. Conversely, a much lower proportion of the London group (53 per cent) were satisfied. The number of years spent in the country of residence did not affect the level of migrant satisfaction. In London the unskilled workers were most dissatisfied and men were less well adjusted than women. Fifty-two per cent of the London group were intending to leave Britain and these were almost equally divided amongst those who were satisfied and those who were not. Comparisons between the groups suggested that the migrants to Britain were most disillusioned, possibly because they had higher expectations assuming a welcome as British subjects, and because migration required greater modification of their original goals or the extension of the time-span over which the goals could be realized.

'The regret at having migrated is keenly felt when the result is failure to achieve the goals to which the migrant aspired, and in many cases made great sacrifices. It is only replaced by positive efforts at adjusting to the available opportunities, if there is an accompanying change in the person's attitudes and beliefs. Change in the cognitive structure of an individual's frame of reference tends to take place when the perceptions and aspirations of the group begin to change, or when the individual effectively changes his group membership.' (p.10).

Whitehouse (1973) suggests that the romantic myth of return to the West Indies, or indeed a desire to adjust and stay may seriously affect parents' aspirations for their children's education or indeed the children's own aspirations. However this may be, it is indubitable that the children of these first-generation immigrants, themselves British born, cannot, like their parents, directly compare life in Britain with that in Jamaica, and although they may experience disappointment or dissatisfaction they cannot indulge in the same fantasy of the return home. They are indeed home.

West Indian families in the UK

From the foregoing review it is clear that the patterns of family life in the West Indies are in many ways dissimilar from accustomed patterns in the UK. To what extent then have the West Indian migrants transferred their Caribbean lifestyle to their new home circumstances in this country? How many West Indians are there? How and where do they live? How are they employed? Most importantly, how do they care for and rear their children in the crucial years before school starts? This sub-section will attempt to outline some basic information on these points.

Demographic distribution

Census data in 1971 (CRC, 1975a) showed that of 1,157,170 people born in the New Commonwealth now in this country West Indians formed the largest sub-group of 302,970. Although most of the West Indian immigrants live in urban environments their geographic distribution is uneven. The Census figures on ethnic minorities (CRE, 1978) show that most of the West Indians (168,695) are concentrated in London where they form 6.5 per cent of the population. They are also found in large numbers in Birmingham and the West Midlands (5.1 per cent) and in the major industrial cities of the North and East Midlands. Table 8 of the Commission for Racial Equality (CRE) publication also categorizes the population born in the American New Commonwealth who live in the Greater London Council area and shows that 15,760 came from Barbados, 16,115 from Guyana, 86,820 from Jamaica and 10,100 from Trinidad-and-Tobago.

The DES published statistics from 1966–1972 which included numbers of pupils of West Indian origin who are listed as follows (Great Britain, DES, 1973):

1967	1970	1972
73,605	109,963	101,898

A survey of 146 local education authorities (leas) in England and Wales (Townsend, 1971) found that 46 had more than three per cent of immigrant pupils in their total school population. It also discovered that there were 569 schools in England and Wales in which more than a third of pupils were immigrant. Two hundred and seventeen of these schools had more than 50 per cent immigrant pupils, but only two had more than 80 per cent. It may also be of interest to note that it can be deduced from Table 21 of the CRE's statistics on ethnic minorities (1978) that in 1971 there were both more males and females of West Indian origin aged up to 14 (23 per cent in each group) than in any other ethnic group. Although some members of the latter group will still be undergoing full-time schooling it is appreciated that most of these figures are ten years old and therefore they are unlikely to represent the present position accurately.

Socio-economic circumstances

Housing   Housing conditions of black groups depend to a large extent on government policies, supply of accommodation and racial discrimination in allocation of housing. Following earlier trends (see review by Rutter and Madge, 1976, pp.289–95) the same figures on ethnic minorities (CRE, 1978) show, in Table 17, that apart from Pakistanis, West Indians have the highest number of persons per household per room of all immigrant groups. Moreover, other than African New Commonwealth immigrants West Indians have the highest percentage of shared dwellings (25 per cent). Thirdly, after Pakistanis and African New Commonwealth immigrants, West Indians have the highest percentage of shared dwellings without exclusive use of cooking stove and sink. Although it is only possible to speculate whether these deprivations are cumulative or interactive, it is clear that such figures indicate the likelihood of a child of West Indian origin spending his early pre-school years in a severely disadvantaged home environment.

Such statistics are supported by more detailed findings from a few educational research studies which have also investigated home background. For example, Rutter *et al.* (1975) in their study of the home circumstances and family patterns of immigrants, nearly half of whom were from Jamaica, and non-immigrant families living in one of the inner London boroughs, found that the West Indian families were twice as likely to be living in crowded and poor housing and two-fifths of the 54 West Indian families had to share facilities. Other researchers have found similar evidence of a much higher percentage of West Indians suffering overcrowded living conditions without sole use of basic amenities (Richmond, 1973; Pollak, 1979; Ghodsian *et al.*, 1980). Two-fifths of the 54 West Indian families in the studies undertaken by Rutter and his colleagues were also living in multi-occupied dwellings and less than a third were in council housing. A number of writers have commented on the difficulties which such housing conditions are likely to entail for children attempting to study or read quietly (Fitzherbert, 1967; Holberton, 1977) although the lack of direct research evidence about the influence of poor accommodation on educational achievement means that it would be unreliable to infer a definite correlation.

Early evidence suggested that in the country as a whole the proportion of black immigrants who owned their own homes was much the same as for the rest of the population (Rose *et al.*, 1969). More accurate patterns of tenure may be indicated by localized studies. For example, although it was clear from the reports of parents interviewed by Rutter *et al.* (1975) that when they first arrived in this country many of the West Indians were living in the most appalling conditions in privately rented accommodation, often at exhorbitant rents, a major change had taken place during the years following migration, so that by the time of the investigation nearly half the West Indian families owned their own home, compared with only 18 per cent of the non-immigrant families in the same area of London. Frequent changes of home were also common just after the immigrants arrived but this pattern no longer obtained by the time the West Indian children reached 10. These changes may be influenced by availability of council and private accommodation to rent and the suitability of such property for large families.

To some extent these localized findings are corroborated by an important source of information on a national scale which has recently become available (Ghodsian *et al.*, 1980). This is a set of data from the National Child Development Study (NCDS) which has been reviewing the development of all children born in one week in 1958 at seven, 11 and 16. When the children in this national random sample reached 16 health visitors completed a questionnaire with their parents which included questions on social circumstances and country of birth thereby providing information of particular interest since it was possible to distinguish between first- and second-generation immigrants in the sample. In the survey it was found that similar proportions of both first- and second-generation West Indians rented their houses although there was an indication that more second-generation groups owned their homes and fewer lived in council houses.

A further more detailed indication of housing patterns of West Indians is given in the study by Rex and Tomlinson (1979) of the low housing standards available in the inner-city area of Handsworth in Birmingham. The researchers report that 34 per cent of the West Indians felt that they were acting under some constraint in going to live in Handsworth, often availability of housing finance. In fact 30 per cent reported going to live there because it was convenient to schools or work or near relatives or friends. Yet West Indians were under-represented in council houses. It appeared to the researchers that from the sample of 300 West Indians, 300 whites and 300 Asians that a much higher proportion of immigrants in lower social classes are forced to buy houses than amongst the whites (58 per cent West Indians, 51 per cent Asians, 15 per cent whites). Similarly, a much higher proportion of West Indians had a mortgage (84 per cent compared with about 30 per cent of Asians and whites), especially council mortgages, though they had better levels of mortgage repayments. Somewhat atypically of findings on a national scale, 93 per cent of West Indians in Handsworth, more than in other ethnic groups, had sole use of three basic amenities. On the other hand, although they applied in similar numbers for housing improvement grants they were less successful in obtaining them. Rex and Tomlinson argue, however, that it would be misleading to think that the West Indians did better than other groups: 'For a young population of economically active people with children they needed more in the way of housing than the old white population, so that it still seems reasonable to conclude that these West Indian owner-occupiers were a disadvantaged group, or, compared with comparable white groups, a housing underclass.' (p.148). However, it seemed that the percentage of West Indians drawn into owner occupation because of failure to obtain council houses was small. Of the sample of 182 who rented accommodation in Handsworth 61 were West Indians and 60 per cent of them rented from a housing association. Overall 95 out of 273 West Indians interviewed obtained housing through a housing association tenancy or local authority mortgage and a similar number had building society mortgages. There were no West Indian landlords in the sample. Seventy-five per cent of the West Indians, more than the whites, had sole use of basic amenities in rented accommodation. However, the study found that West Indians were effectively denied access to desirable post-war suburban estates because such housing prevented cheap access to work and would leave West Indians dispersed and isolated from communal ties. In conclusion the researchers claimed that 'the fact of discrimination in housing has given rise to partially segregated areas, and to locally based and relatively effective communal and ethnic organisations, which are useful as a means of protecting the rights of minority groups', and they could only see housing policy changing radically as part of a 'deliberate "high profile" minority rights programme' (p.157).

Employment An outline of patterns of employment of West Indians may also be helpful in establishing a picture of the socio-economic conditions of West Indian family life.

Data from the 1971 Census showed a disproportionate number of West Indians in the lowest status and least desirable jobs. compared with 35 per cent of the population as a whole in 1966 only 10 per cent of West Indians had non-manual employment. This information is substantiated by the educational study of Rutter *et al.*, (1975) in which the main breadwinner of half the West Indian families had an unskilled or semi-skilled job. Scarcely any of the West Indian fathers had a non-manual occupation. In another case, Rex and Tomlinson (1979) in their mid-70s study of ethnic minorities in Handsworth, Birmingham, found among their main sample of 900, equally divided between whites, West Indians and Asians, a similar percentage of West Indian white-collar workers (9.6 : 8 per cent) but a considerable down-grading of skilled (45.8 : 59 per cent) to semi-skilled (44.1 : 32 per cent) workers compared with Smith's (1977) national sample. Although most of the West Indians reported liking their jobs and 68 per cent of the sample had been in their present job for five or more years, they relied mostly on shift work to increase their earnings. West Indians tended to work longer hours but their weekly wage was not necessarily higher than that for whites, e.g. 32 per cent of West Indians worked 40 or more hours per week for less than £50. It is interesting to compare this figure with that reported by the Handsworth Single Homeless Action Group (*The Times*, 11.9.80) who interviewed 500 people under 25, 94 per cent of whom were of West Indian origin and found that, in 1980, of those working, 67 per cent earned less than £40 per week. However, the Office of Population Censuses and Surveys (OPCS) survey of school leavers (1980) undertaken in London and Birmingham found that after five years at work there were only marginal differences in average pay between early and later West Indian immigrants and West Indians were in fact earning slightly more than whites. Smith (1981) has recently reported that among unemployed men the previous earnings of West Indians were distinctly lower than those of whites (£52.8 : £60.6), though they tended to catch up in the higher age group.

Most of the West Indian workers in Rex and Tomlinson's survey were employed in manufacturing metal goods or in transport and communication industries. Other studies have found that male West Indians are over-represented compared with the white indigenous population in manufacturing, transport and communication industries, and yet virtually excluded from sales and clerical employment. A higher proportion of females are employed in hospitals or medical services (Rose *et al.*, 1969; Hepple, 1970). This pattern appears to hold also for young second-generation West Indians in work (OPCS, 1980).

It has been demonstrated by several studies that West Indian immigrants in particular tend to hold a lower status job after immigration than they did in their own country although a majority appear to have come from rural and often agricultural backgrounds (see Rex and Tomlinson, 1979) which may make reassessment in an urban employment situation difficult. For instance, Richmond (1973) discovered that 24 per cent of men from the West Indies were in non-manual occupations before immigration compared with only six per cent in this country. Lack of equivalence between work skills and qualifications in different countries may account for this to some extent, but the Political and Economic Planning (PEP) survey (Smith, 1974) showed that West Indian men tend to have jobs at substantially lower levels than white men with equivalent qualifications.

Over the years much evidence has been built up of racial discrimination in employment and although the Race Relations Act of 1968 made discrimination in many cases of employment unlawful, there have been a number of studies which have suggested that discrimination still exists both with respect to obtaining a job (McIntosh and Smith, 1974) and in practices at the work place (Hepple, 1970; Smith, 1974). In Rex and Tomlinson's study (1979) in Birmingham, for example, twice as many whites as blacks were offered promotion and over one-third of blacks who were not believed this was due to racial discrimination. Similarly, 119 West Indians in their sample who had been interviewed for a job, but not succeeded, thought their failure was due to colour prejudice. However, it appears that there may be some differences in perception of racial discrimination in employment on the part of second-generation immigrants (see Allen and Smith, 1975; OPCS, 1980). Also, in a recent study of the unemployed (Smith, 1981) there was some evidence that of the unemployed ethnic minorities West Indians tended to show a greater awareness of discrimination. Twenty-eight per cent of the West Indian men claimed to have experienced discrimination in employment in 1979 compared with 16 per cent in 1974, and similarly 25 per cent of West Indian women claimed discrimination as against 15 per cent in the job market five years earlier. Eighty-two per cent of West Indian men (73 per cent in 1974) thought some employers discriminate.

Yet from the same data (Smith, 1981) it appears that the unemployed ethnic minorities rarely make an explicit connection between unemployment and colour prejudice (see also Gaskell and Smith, 1981). In 1979, as for whites, an unskilled or semi-skilled black manual worker was at a greater risk of being unemployed than a professional or white-collar worker, though the profiles of the black working population and the unemployed were much more alike. Also the rate of unemployment among ethnic minorities tended to be greater than among whites because more of them became unemployed as a higher proportion of the workforce belong to lower job levels. This means that at times of rising unemployment a higher proportion of the minorities than whites are therefore likely to be affected and the rate will increase more quickly among the minorities.

Commission for Racial Equality (CRE) figures (1978) reveal in Table 36 that in August 1977 the number of unemployed persons born in the West Indies were 20,166, 32.30 per cent of all unemployed ethnic minority workers. This was a much higher percentage than for any other group. Local studies at various times (e.g. Richmond, 1973) have also tended to show that unemployment is more widespread among black workers and it seems likely that in periods of greater unemployment generally disproportionate numbers of West Indian workers will continue to be out of work (Smith, 1981). An example from one area will serve to illustrate how conditions may change. For instance, Rex and Tomlinson (1979) found in the mid-70s in Handsworth that very few of the West Indians in their sample were unemployed and that, although more blacks than whites had been made redundant, long-term unemployment was similar for blacks and whites. Work patterns for the children of this sample aged 16–21 resembled those of the first-generation immigrants. Yet with the recession the picture in the same area appeared quite different in 1980. It was reported (*The Times,* 11.9.80) that it was twice as difficult for black school leavers to get jobs and that, as a result, many left home. In Smith's 1979 survey of the unemployed West Indians 45 per cent were aged 16–24 (Smith, 1981).

Indeed earlier evidence (CRE, 1974) has shown that unemployment for young black males, even in areas of high employment, is likely, as the 1971 Census data showed, to be twice as great as for the general population. Two large-scale investigations undertaken in the 1970s bear this out. Allen and Smith (1975) examined the differential experience of ethnic groups in their occupational aspirations and actual jobs obtained. The researchers interviewed those seeking jobs and in the early years of (un)employment, those placing people in work, and employers in Sheffield and Bradford in 1971. Fourteen thousand school leavers were contacted and a sample of 368 pupils, of whom 24 were of West Indian origin, were interviewed in Bradford, six and 18 months after leaving school, and 300 pupils including 51 West Indians were interviewed in Sheffield. No West Indian or Asian pupil entering the labour market had an A-level. Less than half the total number of pupils had found jobs when they left school and the level of black unemployment was striking compared with that of whites. For example, in Sheffield West Indians had a much higher unemployment rate – 13 per cent males, 25 per cent females – compared with the white indigenous – under three per cent for both sexes.

More recently the latest preliminary report of the OPCS (1980) relating to the fourth interview of a sample of school leavers in London and Birmingham, followed up in 1976, five years after having left school, confirms the trend to greater unemployment amongst young West Indians. They were divided into two groups: 157 'early migrants' who had had at least all their secondary education in Britain and 77 'later migrants' who had had only part of their secondary schooling here. Both groups were of similar social class and matched with a group of 157 indigenous white leavers. There appeared to be a 'startling leap' from six per cent at the third interview in 1974 (OPCS, 1976) to 21 per cent at the fourth interview in the number of unemployed early migrants, whereas the increase for the later migrants was smaller (eight to 10 per cent). The proportion of unemployed whites remained similar to that in the past three interviews. However, if account was taken of all unemployment experienced by each group over the last two years it appeared that there was no difference between the two West Indian groups and that their unemployment was double the duration of that of the whites. Over that time unemployment rates for all three groups had doubled. Most importantly, both West Indian groups consistently experienced twice as much unemployment as whites over the whole five-year period. Similarly, during this time although on average the early and later migrants experienced approximately the same amount of unemployment in total, the later migrants took longer than the early migrants to find another job, so that although both the whites and the later migrants had on average three jobs over five years, it took the later migrants twice as long (six weeks) to find another job. These findings were also consistent throughout the survey from the time of the first interview when it was discovered that West Indian school leavers took longer to obtain a job than the white school leavers (OPCS, 1973) and also that they were more likely to be unemployed in the next two years (OPCS, 1974).

As with the older West Indians in Rex and Tomlinson's (1979) survey these second-generation immigrants in employment tended to be working at the same firm at the third and fourth interviews (50–60 per cent) suggesting perhaps in spite of general difficulty in changing job, increased stability in occupations. There was also an increasing concentration of West Indians in work places where other West Indians were employed. However, there was a slight and continued trend for fewer West Indians to enter manual employment, as when they first left school, so that there was a nearly equal distribution of the proportions of West Indians and whites in manual and non-manual work. The West Indians were also found to have a significantly higher proportion of intermediate non-manual jobs because of the large number of West Indian nurses in the sample (OPCS, 1980).

This finding may be compared with that of Allen and Smith (1975) who reported that on entering work the grade of job obtained by West Indians was lower, mostly Class IV on the Registrar General's Classification of occupations, with the exception of nurses, whereas most whites obtained Class III jobs. Moreover, it seemed as though West Indians with some qualifications were forced to take a lower occupation than those whites with similar qualifications; for example, half the West Indian girls with CSE and O-levels were employed in routine sewing jobs where they were mostly concentrated in the clothing industry. No distinction was made by employers between those who had undertaken CSE or O-level courses unless good passes were obtained. The researchers observed of these second-generation immigrants 'the children are thought of as potentially fulfilling and fitted for the same economic function as their parents. Insofar as they fail to acquire educational success, their use as unskilled labour with little or no prospect for advancement is legitimated' (p.86). Other evidence also indicated that careers officers may underestimate the intelligence of West Indian adolescents compared with white adolescents (OPCS, 1973) and Rutter *et al.* (1975) showed that for a given occupational level black workers tend to have higher educational qualifications or schooling. Similarly Fowler *et al.* (1977) reported that Asian boys with similar qualifications had job opportunities which were markedly inferior to those of whites in Glasgow and despite their wishes many entered work within the immigrant economic infrastructure or undertook further education. The researchers rejected explanations in terms of unrealistic aspirations and inadequate job hunting. However it is interesting to note that in 1976 the OPCS survey (1980) found that after five years the West Indians' jobs had on average a slightly higher status than those of the whites despite the whites having occupations requiring higher basic educational qualifications for entry. The reason for the West Indians having higher ranking jobs was they included more intermediate and non-manual and skilled manual jobs requiring the acquisition of vocational qualifications through on-job training and part-time further education at which they were slightly more successful than the whites.

This is not to say that either West Indians or whites are satisfied with their jobs. In Allen and Smith's survey (1975) when the sample were followed up at the time of the second interview and asked about their perceptions of their first year at work it appeared that only 40 per cent had obtained the job they wanted although many were satisfied to some extent depending on work experience and educational performance, though it has to be remembered that there were comparatively few West Indians in the sample. Nevertheless during their first few months in work 25 per cent had changed job for a variety of reasons and by the time of the second interview 60 per cent had in fact done so. This compares with the early findings of the OPCS survey (1973, 1974) although the number of voluntary job changes decreased over a five-year period. Allen and Smith suggested that an attempt at or an actual change of job sharpens perceptions of job opportunities and brings with it the realization, especially for West Indians, that these are narrowly defined. However, only 10 per cent of the West Indian and Asian sample thought white school leavers had a greater advantage in the labour market and few reported actual instances of discrimination.

These findings may be contrasted with those of the OPCS (1980) which noted a decline in job satisfaction despite higher job status from the third to the fourth interview. Also over five years the relative difference on the satisfaction scale between whites and later migrants was found to have steadily diminished so as to practically converge. This would appear to be associated with degree of satisfaction of original career aspirations, as, although the West Indians by dint of perseverance succeeded in making up for the whites' greater facility in achieving their ambitions, they experienced continuous difficulties which, not surprisingly, left them feeling more discontented. It is of interest that although more than one-third of the West Indians said they had never experienced racial discrimination in any situation, the majority of those who thought they had been discriminated against reported that it had been in connection with employment, especially when seeking jobs. Those interviewed by a West Indian were also significantly more likely to claim that they had encountered discrimination in relation to employment and in other situations.

Thus it would seem fair to observe that both the apparent continuation of racial discrimination in employment and the unemployment rate among young blacks are serious countervailing factors for the future prospects of second-generation immigrants despite evidence of their readiness to attend further education courses (see, e.g. OPCS 1973, 1974, 1976, 1980) and indications that longer residence in Britain is associated with some increase in occupational status (e.g. Richmond, 1973) and probably better acceptance by white colleagues at work (Patterson, 1963).

Finally, it is appropriate to turn from a review of the occupational level and satisfaction achieved by those young second-generation West Indians who have already passed through the education system and entered the labour market, to briefly consider the impact of employment patterns on West Indian family life and particularly the pupil still in schooling, especially since it appears that it is established practice for West Indian mothers to work. For example, an investigation carried out in 1965 on the health and development of one-year-olds in Paddington (Hood *et al.*, 1970) discovered that three times more West Indian mothers than white mothers were working outside the home. A later study by Rutter *et al.* (1975) found that four-fifths of the West Indian mothers in their sample had a job outside the home compared with 53 per cent of white mothers. Moreover, although twice as many West Indian as non-immigrant mothers had taken some form of school examination, and several of those who were working had higher educational qualifications than the white working mothers, they were in lower status jobs. Also a CRC analysis of Census figures (CRC, 1975b) showed that, in all regions except the north, West Indian women are more likely to be at work. Pollak (1979) in a study of nine-year-olds in a London borough also found that the mothers of West Indian children were much more likely to work (87.9 per cent West Indian, 59 per cent white mothers). Earls and Richman (1980) also discovered that West Indian mothers in a London borough were twice as likely to be employed outside the home. Again recently Davey and Norburn (1980b) found that 87 per cent of West Indian mothers in their sample of parents worked, mostly full-time, and more in London than the north had non-manual occupations. Indeed West Indian women may well be the chief wage-earners in their households so that considerable financial difficulties are felt by this group when unemployed (Smith, 1981).

Comparing generations the NCDS found there was a strong indication that more second-generation West Indian mothers are doing paid work (Ghodsian *et al.*, 1980). There was also a gross under-representation of first-generation West Indian children with parents in non-manual employment, and, unlike the Asian parents, there were no great differences in occupational group between first- and second-generation West Indian immigrants. Income per head for both first- and second-generation West Indians was also lower than for indigenous groups. Moreover, a higher percentage of children of West Indian origin aged 16 were receiving free school meals and had families who felt financial hardship. Similarly, a CRC document (1973) reported that 31 per cent of children of West Indian origin received free school meals in the ILEA, compared with only 13 per cent of the indigenous population.

Family patterns
It is not surprising that family migration to this country should be accompanied, at least initially, by the loss of the extended family (BPPA, 1978; Kitzinger, 1978; Rutter *et al.*, 1975). However, whilst this is almost inevitable for first-generation immigrants it will be interesting to see whether it continues into the second generation. Pryce's recent study (1979) of the black community in the St. Paul's area of Bristol supplies some detailed case study information on this question, but it is also pessimistic about what he calls the 'atomistic individualism of West Indians' and 'the fragmented social framework in which West Indian family life takes place' (p.119). He

draws attention to the problem of adjustment of the younger generation of West Indians which he sees as being partly due to a background of poverty, but also 'to the absence of a viable, supportive culture that is independent and capable of tightening family relations to help the West Indian poor carry the burden of their deprivation and impoverishment. The West Indian lower class, both in England and in the West Indies, lacks an indigenous workable class (folk) morality of its own, as is manifested in the deficiencies of the family system.' (p.112). He suggests that sooner or later these deficiencies constitute a predicament for the young West Indians and he is adamant that from his observations in Bristol 'The West Indians lack a group identity and a tight, communal form of group life based on a sense of collective interdependence and mutual obligation among kinsmen.' (p.119).

Another aspect of family life seems to have changed considerably with migration. This is that there appear to be an increasing number of stable monogamous marriages within the West Indian community (BPPA, 1978; Rex and Tomlinson, 1979) and hence nuclear families. To some extent marriage may still be a statement of arrival in the middle class for the West Indian. Rutter *et al.* (1975) judged that there was no difference in the quality of marital relationship of West Indian parents and white parents in their sample, but Kitzinger (1978) has suggested that because of the loss of the extended family network, families here are thrown much more on their own resources (or those of the social services) and hence otherwise unsatisfactory unions may persist long after they would have been dissolved in the West Indies. These can only be matters for speculation.

Despite the noted tendency to the nuclear family, a number of studies have also found amongst their samples a greater proportion of West Indian one-parent families than that found in the population as a whole. One-parent families, are, of course common in the West Indies (Oakley, 1968). Rutter *et al.* (1975) found that 19 per cent of the West Indian mothers in their sample were living alone with their children as opposed to nine per cent of the white mothers. Only two per cent of the mothers in Pollak's 1972 investigation, a similarly localized study, were single parents. However, Ghodsian *et al.* (1980) found that there were significantly more one-parent West Indian families (twice the percentage for other groups) in their national longitudinal study. It seems that findings about the proportion of one-parent families as with other survey information on housing, occupation, employment and income may well depend on the size and range of the sample and the time when the research was conducted. Moreover, research does not appear to provide any direct evidence on the influence of one- or two-parent families on the achievement of pupils of West Indian origin.

There appears to be more consistent information on family size and that children of West Indian origin are more likely to come from families of a large number of children. In the Rutter study of 10-year-olds (1975) 59 per cent of the West Indian children as opposed to 21 per cent of the indigenous children came from families with five or more children. Pollak's 1972 study found that the West Indian children were twice as likely to come from large families. Also 32 per cent of the West Indian families in the sample of parents interviewed by Davey and Norburn (1980b) had five or more children. The NCDS also discovered that, unlike other ethnic minority groups, second-generation West Indians continue to belong to larger families and households (Ghodsian *et al.*, 1980; see also Earls and Richman, 1980).

Care of the child
Coard (1971, Ch.8) was at pains to stress that West Indian parents are very concerned about the general welfare of their children and the parents in the Rutter study were all rated as warm and loving towards their children (Rutter *et al.*, 1975).

It appears that there is little difference between West Indian and white families in the quality of physical care given to their children. One of the few paediatric and social studies (Hood *et al.*, 1970) found that many of the children of West Indian origin in their sample of 101 one-year-olds in Paddington had been delivered in hospital and were not at risk. The children attended health services as often as white British infants up to one year of age and seemed well cared for by their mothers, especially when availability of basic amenities was taken into account. Although there is some suggestion of deficiency in children's diets, no differences in height were found at three years (Pollak, 1972) or nine years (Pollak, 1979) and at 10 years West Indian youngsters were found to be taller (Yule, *et al.*, 1975). Respiratory infections do, however, seem to be more common in West Indian children (Oppé, 1964) and Hood *et al.* (1970) found that the children of West Indian origin in their sample were more prone to minor physical disorders (42 per cent compared with 15 per cent) and more were admitted to hospital (15 per cent compared with two per cent). It has also been noted (Rutter and Madge, 1976) that West Indian children seem to be more prone to deafness and that the proportion of West Indian children in schools for the deaf is exceptionally high (Great Britain, DES, 1973). It is possible that selector bias and other social and linguistic factors (see Jackson, 1975) may be operating here, but in the absence of reports of clinical data it is not possible to make a more accurate assessment. There is also possibly some overlap here with ESN diagnosis (see Section 11, p.124ff).

Although most studies have concluded that West Indian parents have a rate of mental health disorders similar to indigenous parents it seems that for some West Indian immigrant children the 'culture shock' (Triseliotis, 1968) may have been too great, for a syndrome of withdrawal and non-communication has often been noted (Prince, 1967). This may, of course, be one symptom of lack of adjustment, but it has just as often been remarked that the behaviour of children of West Indian origin is as likely to be attention seeking or boisterous as passive in the school situation. More will be said on this also in Section 11.

In view of the evidence that many West Indian mothers work, and in addition the apparently larger numbers of one-parent West Indian families, it is not surprising that many pre-school aged children are given into the daily care of child minders. It seems that a higher proportion of West Indian than white parents rely on substitute care for their children from an early age (Pless and Hood, 1967; Jackson, 1971). Rutter *et al.* (1975) found that more West Indian children had experienced child minding by people other than relatives during the pre-school period. However, the BBPA report (1978) claims that child minding is also widely used by the working class population in Redbridge, similarly both for economic reasons and lack of availability of extended family help, but it was used less by the white working mothers in the CRC study (1975b). Whilst child minding need not involve harm to the child provided there is a continuity of high quality care by someone the child knows well, Fitzherbert (1967) reporting on collaboration between educationists and social workers concerned with West Indians in London, noted that West Indian mothers often left their children with a series of minders, preferably white, and claimed that they did not seem to understand the need of their baby to have an enduring relationship with one adult.

The evidence suggests that choice of minder is more determined by proximity to the home as well as price and willingness to fit in with long hours. Little importance seems to be attached to the number of children in the minder's care; reliability and personal cleanliness are more weighty considerations (Bushell, 1973). Moreover, it appears that the children may be sent to illegal and unregistered child minders as Pollak (1972) found for 71 per cent of the children in her sample who were minded. Such an arrangement is likely to mean there are large numbers of children cared for in an overcrowded room, perhaps in squalid conditions, with little toy provision or adult attention (Jackson, 1975) or even in multi-ethnic child minding situations (CRC, 1975b). All of these deficiencies are likely to contribute to a disadvantageous start to development. Yet there is often little choice for West Indian parents in the absence of local authority provision and the pressing difficulties associated with the overcrowded conditions in which they live.

A CRC study in 1975 investigated the child care needs of working mothers by interviewing officials responsible for day care, child minders and working mothers, of whom 23 out of 71 were black, in Manchester, Leicester, Lambeth and Slough. The report illustrates in some detail the difficulties which working mothers experience in finding satisfactory day care facilities for their children. Although various studies have revealed that women from ethnic minority groups are more likely to be at work and for longer hours the mothers in this group were found to be particularly disadvantaged with respect to child care. In part this disadvantage resulted from a greater degree of need but the CRC survey (1975b) also showed that

'ethnic minority women were less able to get access to the day care provision they most desired, than were white mothers; they had less access to subsidised or free services (day care and nursery schools); they had greater difficulties in finding child-minders near their homes, and found that their choices in minders were restricted by the reluctance of some English minders to take ethnic minority children; there were indications that English minders faced particular difficulties in caring for minority group children due to a combination of language and cultural differences; and minders drawn from ethnic minority groups were particularly likely to be unable to reach as high a standard of child care as they desired, due to environmental deficiencies and a shortage of adequate child minder support services.' (pp.5–6).

Although methods of child care used varied between ethnic groups, child minders were the commonest form of care. More specifically, in contrast to the Asians most West Indian mothers were satisfied with the care their children received from the minder and they sought a new minder least often. Forty-seven per cent of the minders saw play as an important aspect of their work which took up long hours and was less well rewarded than the work of the working mothers. There was some evidence that telling nursery rhymes and playing music was less common amongst black minders (25 out of 39), as was looking at books with children, or reading or telling them stories (75 per cent of black minders, 91 per cent white, 95 per cent Asian). The researchers observed that the service a child minder is able to provide is obviously affected by the quality of the home of the minder and the extent of facilities in the locality. Black minders were least satisfied with available facilities (19 out of 39) and were proportionately more interested in all local authority services. In a smaller pilot survey of a group of minders in Paddington, also reported in the CRC study, it seemed that the West Indian minders had all made conscious effeorts to adapt their child rearing practices as a result of changed circumstances of time and place, and in particular claimed to be less strict.

These findings were to a large extent confirmed by another smaller scale but more detailed observational study of child minding which involved 40 children aged between two and three all placed with registered child minders in four London boroughs for almost 12 months (Mayall and Petrie, 1977). Although the study aimed to concentrate on an indigenous white sample it proved too difficult not to include representatives of different ethnic minority groups, so that West Indians formed seven out of 39 minders and five out of 28 mothers in the sample. Interviews with the minders and mothers and a test of language development taken by the children supplied information on the relationships between mother, minder and child and the quality of care provided. Although this was judged by the researchers to be above average, they noted that more than 40 per cent of the minders in their sample looked after three or more children though they did not appear to be motivated by a concern for children. Only one-third provided an adequate range of toys for children's play and it was observed that minded children received a lack of general attention as instanced by the fact that as many as 16 out of 39 child minders recalled that they had not sat down and read a story to the child on the previous day. Indeed, except on matters of physical care, a considerable lack of interaction between the child and minder was observed during interviews. Whereas the child initiated on average six interactions with his mother during the course of interview he only initiated one and a half in a similar 20-minute period with his minder. Such lack of communication, it was suggested, may contribute to backwardness in language development. The children were found to be 2.3 months below the norm for their age on comprehension and 2.9 months below on expression as measured by the Reynell Developmental Language Scales Test. However, the researchers were sympathetic to the difficulties of the minders' position, a job often done for a short period of time in the midst of other commitments, for inadequate pay, and structured so as to make good relationships with parents difficult. Although 60 per cent of the minders in this study had taken part in a training scheme they were not always adequately supported subsequently by local authority social and health services. As Professor Tizard remarks in the Foreword to the book 'The picture we get from this study is of sad, passive children, of anxious, harrassed mothers and hard-pressed minders insensitive to children's needs and distrustful of the mothers – who are in turn resentful of the minders' (p.11). The conclusion drawn on the basis of evidence from this and other studies was that many thousands of young children, of whom children of West Indian origin form a large number, are by being placed with child minders receiving a low quality of care which is 'detrimental to their well-being, and probably to their future well-being also' (p.13).

However, against the findings of these studies has to be set limited evidence which suggests that children reared by minders did *not* have more developmental retardation (Pollak, 1972) and did not show more psychiatric problems (Rutter *et al.*, 1974) than other West Indian children. But it may be the case that, as Rutter and Madge (1976) comment, this 'does not mean that the pattern of child care provided by minders is satisfactory but rather it implies that in many respects it is similar to that provided by the child's parents' (p.261).

It might also be noted in passing that back in 1967 Fitzherbert made the somewhat alarming report that often the child care service was regarded by the West Indian mothers in her sample of 120 West Indian families in London as an attractive alternative to looking after the child or even to avoiding the expense of placing it with a child minder. She stated that the view that the child would come home as a cultured person often prevailed and there was little appreciation of the psychological factors involved in upbringing. In her experience the West Indians' inability to cope at times of crisis, meant that housing problems and economic privation were liable to increase as was recourse to local authority care, but Fitzherbert also suggested that some parents believed that providing an income was a more responsible kind of motherhood than providing personal care. She explained that nevertheless, a cultural tradition of mothering by relatives and fostering and informal adoption without stigma might also make it easier for West Indian parents to hand over the care of their children to others. It seems likely, however, even if there is any truth in these interpretations, that West Indian mothers will have come to hold a more accurate view of the function of the child care service with their increased length of residence in this country and hence familiarity with British institutions.

Many writers have suggested that although West Indian parents are evidently concerned about their children's development they often do seem to lack understanding of the developmental importance of play, toys, communication and parent-child interaction in the early years. Although this may be attributable to different cultural traditions, values and attitudes, to some extent it is also likely to be a function of economic pressures, poor housing conditions, lack of extended family support and family size. For example, Bushell (1973) suggested that the West Indian parent does not seem to regard the importance of stimulation by conversation or use of toys as part of the function of the baby minder as she does not appreciate their significance herself. Indeed a number of differences in child rearing practices have been noted between West Indian and white families. The study of one-year-olds in Paddington discovered that West Indian children were frequently discouraged from touching and playing with objects (Hood *et al.*, 1970). Pollak's (1972) study of three-year-olds in London found that the West Indian children were much less likely to go on outings, have toys, or play with their parents; indeed, only 16 per cent of their mothers said they found time to play with them. Since the demonstrated importance of mother-child interaction for the young child's personal development, possibly greater than the provision of toys, has been known for some while (Millar, 1968), this may indicate a serious deprivation especially when taken in conjunction with Pollak's (1979) evidence. The follow-up study of the same children at nine years of age found that: the West Indian children tended to play in the streets; were given no fixed time to come home; were less likely to receive regular pocket money and received less; were less likely to have been treated to a special day, and their presents were more likely to have been clothing, rather than toys which they would have preferred; they had fewer holidays, fewer trips and excursions and usually only with the school; and had fewer toys and were less likely to indulge in creative and imaginative play. It is also possible when considering the relation of child rearing practices in the West Indies and the UK that it may well be the case that what has been adequate in one cultural context has been imported into another where it is unsuitable: the toys, treats, trips which a British child expects as part of normal life just may not be needed to the same extent in the West Indian situation. Attitudes to child care and development may be largely culturally determined.

Other studies have generally tended to support Pollak's findings, particularly with respect to the early years. For example, Rutter and Mittler (1972) discovered less conversation taking place between the West Indian parent and her child, and Rutter *et al.* (1975) noted that there were fewer interactions in general between parents and children in West Indian families. It is perhaps not surprising therefore that Pollak's survey in 1972 of the performances of three groups of three-year-olds – 75 English, 75 West Indian and 13 'other' children – on a battery of developmental tests, taken together with a medical history and parental interview and questionnaire, showed that the mean scores of West Indian children were significantly lower than those of the other two groups on tests of language, adaptive and personal and social behaviour. Somewhat controversially she concluded that the variations in developmental performances were due to quality of family life, differences in home setting, composition of family unit and parental attitudes, rather than to social or economic factors. It is significant, but depressing to record that the same children who were found to under-achieve at three remained as under-achievers at nine, particularly on measures of verbal and adaptive abilities and in spite of four years of schooling (Pollak, 1979).

In contrast to the lack of verbal communication between parent and child often noted, observers have remarked on the strong parental discipline often found in the West Indian home. It has been suggested that discipline may be mixed and inconsistent but there appears to be only anecdotal evidence to support this view. Rutter *et al.* (1975) found that the West Indian children were more disciplined than their peers in the home and were more restricted in their choice of friends and less free to go out. It seems that West Indian children are traditionally expected to assist more with household tasks. The same study discovered that three times as many West Indian children as white children helped in the house and were also more independent in looking after themselves. It also discovered that girls, more often than boys, were expected to help with domestic tasks (see also Kitzinger, 1978) and were doing so more frequently than their white female peers. Bagley (1975b) using similar (if not the same) data to the Rutter *et al.* study, also noted that West Indian children took more domestic adult responsibility at an earlier age than their peers and were thus more 'self-reliant' in their home environment. (Further aspects of family life relating to expectations, attitudes, values and perceptions are discussed in Part 3 on Home and School, pp.142 ff.).

Such, then, is the natural family background of the child of West Indian origin starting school. No such review, however, can match the vivid description evoked by Jackson in his (1979) report of the home life of the, in many ways typical, West Indian boy, Beauregard, living in Huddersfield, in the last few weeks prior to his introduction to a multi-ethnic school. This tends to support the consensus of research evidence and other sociological writings which over the years have repeatedly indicated that, despite their love and concern for their children, many West Indian parents may not have fully appreciated the crucial formative importance of play, toys, conversation and parent-child interaction in general for their child's development. For example, the strong evidence of these deficiencies noted by Stoker (1969) in a report for the Schools Council which in 1967-8 surveyed 11 leas with significant immigrant populations gave rise to a chapter (Ch.6) devoted to the difficulties of the infant's transition from home to school. It is fair to point out, however, that such appraisals may not have gone unheeded by the West Indian community, and have even been acknowledged in a joint report by West Indian parents and teachers in Redbridge (BPPA, 1978). The importance of the foundation for schooling begun in the home cannot be too greatly stressed.

In conclusion, looking at the adaptation of West Indian migrants to life in Britain it can be seen that the early studies such as those of Patterson (1963) and Hood *et al.* (1970), followed by those of Pollak (1972, 1979) and Rutter *et al.* (1975) carried out in London, and therefore concerned mainly with West Indian immigrants from Jamaica, who comprise 60 per cent or more of West Indians in the capital, have all pointed to many changes which have taken place gradually amongst West Indians in their family life as they establish themselves here. Yet a recent attempt at a typology of West Indians in Bristol (Pryce, 1979) as 'hustlers, teenyboppers, proletarian respectables, saints, mainliners and in-betweeners' has shown that West Indians are a far from homogeneous ethnic minority group. Moreover, despite considerable adaptations, perhaps the most notable of which have been the greater tendency, revealed by some studies, to monogamous marriage and the norm of the nuclear family, evidence suggests there remain important and distinctive differences between the West Indians and white British, concerning employment, housing, family size and child rearing. Yet here a word of caution should be sounded. Although West Indians are obviously subject to grave setbacks, even perhaps injustices within the community as a whole, the assumption should not be made that to be of West Indian origin is to be automatically disadvantaged or deprived. Whilst it is true that many West Indians will suffer the hardships and difficulties associated with membership of the lower socio-economic groups, there are, it should not be forgotten, other West Indians with more middle-class lifestyles and standards of living. The problem is to avoid seeing social, economic and cultural deprivation purely in Western terms, and yet, at the same time, to remember that the West Indians are participating members of our Western society. From the preceding review of research evidence it would appear that many of the economic benefits which motivated their original migration to this country have so far eluded them. It remains to be seen (in subsequent sections) whether their educational aspirations, which have also been claimed as a motivation for emigration, have been more adequately satisfied.

Part Two

Ability, Attainment, Achievement

The main purpose of this review is to examine the evidence on the educational achievement of pupils of West Indian origin. Having given a simplified account of the background to migration from the Caribbean and outlined some of the main features of the home life of the pupil of West Indian origin in this country, it is appropriate to turn now to more strictly psychometric interpretations of educational achievement in a school context. Other factors influencing achievement will be considered and an appraisal of levels of performance put forward in later parts of this review (Part 3 Home and School, pp.142 ff and Part 4 Overview, p.210 ff).

It is important at the outset to be reasonably clear about what is implied in a psychometric assessment of ability, attainment and achievement. Whereas ability may be defined as 'capacities which are not so much specifically taught as picked up by children in the course of the interaction with the home, school and wider environments', attainment refers more specifically to 'concepts and skills which depend more on direct instruction and on the child's interest and industriousness in the particular subjects studied' (Vernon, 1958). It is usual to measure attainment by standardized tests, of known reliability and validity, e.g. of English, particularly of reading, or of mathematics. Later, in secondary education, nationally validated examinations are also used as measures of attainment. Hence it is possible to draw comparisons between an individual's attainment and his ability in order to make statements about his achievement. In this way, provided there is a realistic assessment of an individual's potential, judgements may be made as to whether an individual can be described as under-achieving or over-achieving in relation to a criterion of average achievement for a particular population.

This over-simplified account of the concepts involved in assessment obscures the difficulties involved in such a process. When the nature of assessment of ability and attainment is considered in relation, not only to the mainstream white population but also to the education of children from ethnic minority groups it will be readily appreciated that this is no mean undertaking. Not only are there the difficulties involved in actually measuring potential, learning ability, and comparing performance by children of ethnic minority groups with white children on tests of certain skills, but these assessments also have to be seen in the wider context of their connection with the learning of language, and other cultural, social and economic factors. Moreover, these abilities, and in particular intelligence, are not fixed but evolving and dynamic; they are as Vernon (1969) has defined them 'a set of developed skills with which the person learns to cope with any environment'.

Scientific racism
Over the last 25 years methods of assessment of ability and performance have been considerably refined. On the other hand, the population to whom tests are administered has become much more heterogeneous so that tests which have been developed with the mainstream white child in mind may no longer be appropriate. In particular this may be the case with respect to tests of intelligence when these are applied to a minority group population within the total population. But apart from such considerations, to which reference will be made again in what follows, mention must be made of one particular debate concerning the intellectual potential of black children, in relation to which much research activity and emotional energy have been expended in the 70s. Although this is not the place to discuss at length different views of the intellectual potential of blacks and whether genetic or environmental factors have the greater influence on the development of intelligence, or, indeed, whether specific programmes can provide equality of educational opportunity, it is important to note the basic arguments of what has been called the scientific racist account in order to see this in the context of the testing and education of ethnic minority pupils. More detailed and lengthy reviews can readily be found, in particular by Rutter and Madge (1976, pp.281–4) and in Volume 14 Number 1 of *Educational Research* for 1971.

It will be recalled that it was Jensen's (1969) article in the *Harvard Educational Review* which asserted that there is an average difference of 15 IQ points between black and white Americans in the United States and that this is due mainly to genetic factors. Thus Jensen advanced the following propositions:

A) individual differences in intelligence are attributable to genetic differences;

B) IQ differs among people from different social class backgrounds;

C) there are well established differences amongst racial groups in the distribution of educationally relevant traits, particularly IQ.

Hence Jensen made the claim that black people were of lower intelligence than whites and that this was a genetically inherited trait. In a further article Jensen (1971) gave a detailed analysis of tests administered and results of an elaborate experiment comparing a large control sample, of negro, white and Mexican pupils aged five to 19 in segregated schools in the United States. Although no appreciable differences in scholastic achievement or evidence of cumulative deficit between minority and majority pupils were found, some differences in overall levels of ability and patterns of abilities between the three ethnic groups were pointed out. As a result Jensen hypothesized two broad hierarchical classes of levels of ability: Level I Associative Ability depending largely on digit memory, rote learning, and paired-associate learning and Level II Conceptual Ability involving abstract reasoning processes such as concept learning and problem solving. Jensen noted that different social classes and ethnic groups show different modal patterns of ability (p.25). As a result of a series of studies he found that children of low socio-economic status, especially ethnic minority children show little or no deficiency on Level I abilities but were about one standard deviation below the general population mean on tests of Level II ability.

Not surprisingly, a furore ensued and much repetitive experimentation and research was undertaken. Some important criticism also emerged, in particular the notable scholarship of Jencks (1973) who estimated that about half of the variance on intelligence test scores is attributable to genetic factors and that environmental influences are therefore still powerful. One of the main criticisms of Jensen's account was just that he minimized the effect of environment on intellectual development. In addition, it was obvious that he had argued erroneously from individual variations in ability to claim that these differences occurred for groups as a whole. Moreover, he confused differences within groups and between groups. Indeed, it was later shown that the data on which Jensen calculated the heritability of IQ were questionable and the failure of compensatory education in America, which he also cited as evidence in favour of his arguments, was by no means so proven. Finally, his many opponents argued that he had equated intelligence with IQ in an over-simplified manner. Subsequent debate on the nature–nurture controversy, which inevitably polarized into the geneticist or environmentalist camps, showed that Jensen had reached premature conclusions on inadequate evidence. Verma and Bagley (1975, pp.349–52) list some of the major writings which contributed to the academic discussion. But Jensen's statements also had a considerable influence on teachers and others in day-to-day communication with black children, as the BPPA (1978) investigation discovered.

More recently, it has been argued by Bagley and others in connection with West Indian children that the arguments in favour of scientific racism fail, not only because the genetic evidence on which they base their case is unreliable, but because of the failure to consider adequately other social influences upon IQ. For example, a new study on the transracial adoption of black children and carefully matched groups of black and white children reared in children's homes (Bagley and Young, 1979) suggests that environmental factors may have a much greater importance on the development of intellectual ability than Jensen's account credited. The fairest conclusion at present would seem to be that insufficient evidence is available to resolve the question. Whilst the possibility that there may be a genetic component in the difference in mean IQ between blacks and whites cannot be excluded, there is equally no convincing evidence in favour of the proposition. It is certain that some of the difference can be accounted for in terms of environmental influences, but what is still not known is to what extent interactive environmental variables do account for differential intellectual development.

Testing

Irrespective of this debate intelligence and other tests developed with mainstream white pupils in mind have continued to be used in schools by teachers and educational psychologists requiring information on attainment and for diagnostic purposes. Indeed, in the absence of other assessment materials it had to be assumed that objective tests, no matter how much their objectivity was impugned, would be of assistance in complementing teachers' more 'subjective' judgements.

A DES survey (Great Britain, DES, 1971a) into the practice of and opinion on the assessment of pupils from overseas in 10 leas noted that the testing of immigrant children and the methods and materials in use were frequently inadequate. Theoretically dubious testing in infant and junior schools was also supplemented by a teacher's subjective judgement, although transfer procedures usually involved standard test results in addition. Nevertheless, it was recognized that these were barely relevant in assessing intellectual potential. Teachers felt that better methods of assessment could be developed which could identify the problems and assess the cultural, social and linguistic progress of non-immigrant children as well, and the report recommended that teachers should be assisted to devise objective measures of assessment in their own localities. Mention was particularly made of the need to be able to assess a child's linguistic readiness to work full-time in an ordinary class situation.

The extent to which objective tests were employed in conjunction with subjective assessments when ethnic minority pupils were concerned was also revealed in Townsend and Brittan's survey of a sample of 230 multiracial schools (1972). Over half the 132 primary schools used objective tests of ability and only five restricted their use to non-immigrants. Almost half the 98 secondary schools also used such tests to provide an assessment of ability and attainment within their schools. Only two used them for non-immigrants alone and two for immigrants only. Teachers in those schools which did not employ the tests were aware that they were not reliable for immigrants. Objective tests of attainment in English, mathematics and verbal reasoning were also used by over a half of the primary schools and a third of the secondary schools. Many heads mentioned that they added a subjective element when judging the results. Most of the schools naturally used the results as a basis on which to form groupings, sets or streams.

However, there was then and until very recently there still has been no other way in which teachers could assess the potential of a pupil of ethnic minority origin other than, as Vernon (1975) counselled by 'clinical judgement based on present achievement on

English tests, the child's reported rate of progress in the school, available results on tests given in his native language and a case history to evaluate the degree of cultural deprivation.' But, as Section 6 on language (pp.68 ff) shows, tests on the child's native language are not so applicable or possible in the case of children of West Indian origin.

As Coard (1971) suggested in relation to the use of tests to diagnose educationally sub-normal pupils, teachers, parents, and researchers have increasingly been seriously concerned that test scores for ethnic minority children might be entirely misleading. The concern is a focus for several different issues. One of these is the problem associated with testing children who are not fluent in standard English. All the tests are based on the assumption that a child will understand the language used by the tester. Clearly, if the child does not, then his test score will reflect his lack of fluency rather than his intellectual performance. This is an issue which has obvious application in the case of pupils of West Indian origin whose use of words, pronunciation and intonation may well differ from those of the tester. A second main area of difficulty in testing is that certain differences in the life experiences of the testee may well suggest to him that the IQ test items have different implications from those intended. Information required to answer a test question may not be part of the natural stock of knowledge of a child from a different culture. Alternatively, such a child may give an answer which is correct in terms of his own cultural orientation, but technically wrong in terms of prescribed answers in the test manual.

It is appropriate therefore as a prelude to an evaluation of assessment procedures in use with black pupils to consider a number of criticisms which have been made in relation to testing, particularly tests of IQ, but which are often germane also to other testing contexts in which black children are involved. These criticisms, as has already been seen to some extent, tend to fall into two main categories: first those which criticize testing in general, or the choice of specific tests, especially IQ tests; and, secondly, criticisms of the testing situation. Those problems which exist with respect to testing in general are obviously heightened and, in addition, fresh problems develop, when the testing of pupils from ethnic minority groups is contemplated or undertaken. Nevertheless, it remains the case that teachers are interested not only in the individual and his capabilities and performance, but also as to how these relate to those of his peers, both black and white. Teachers also need to know how objective measures of abilities and attainments are likely to be influenced by teaching strategies.

Criticism of tests
In a sense IQ tests which were originally designed to assess a child's likely response to education, i.e. his potential, tend to measure performance. This performance in itself reflects biological endowment and experience and, as Hegarty and Lucas (1978) have argued, successful performance depends very much on prior learning and hence the opportunity to learn. A number of researches (reviewed in Taylor, 1974) have indicated the influence of cultural factors on test performances. In particular, Vernon's (1965 a and b) research, in which he compared a sample of 50 West Indian boys with 100 English boys on a series of tests and assessments showed that, although the West Indian children did relatively poorly overall, the deficit varied considerably for different tests, being most noticeable for practical and some general intellectual non-verbal tests and much less for educational attainments and various perceptual abilities. There was a strong implication in the analysis of the test results that intellectual development and environmental handicaps, especially socio-economic cultural and linguistic environments, were linked.

In the light of these and other substantive criticisms doubt has been cast on whether intelligence tests will show the likely response to future education of the child of ethnic minority background, and opinion has been divided on whether IQ even measures an operational capacity at a certain point in time. A number of attempts have been made, theoretically at least, to devise 'culture free' or 'culture fair' tests which would try to avoid some of the difficulties associated with intelligence testing with immigrant pupils. The idea of a culture fair test is that it can be attempted equally by people of diverse backgrounds – socio-culturally deprived white children or black children – without any advantage or detriment because of the background. Yet such a definition says nothing of a possible need to take account of cultural differences and one potential approach to culture fair assessment would be to leave it to the tester to discount the effects of ethnic and cultural differences in interpreting test scores. As Hegarty (1976) points out, such an approach would seem to be an extension of good testing procedure, but in practice it is scarcely realistic in view of the diversity of cultural factors involved. It would be unreasonable to expect psychologists to be conversant with all the cultural differences which might be encountered in relation to test performance. The alternative is to attempt to devise tests which will minimize the effects of cultural differences. But, if it is intended to devise a culture free intelligence test, this is, as Anastasi (1968) has argued 'to criticize tests because they reveal cultural influences' and 'to miss the essential nature of tests. Every psychological test measures a sample of behaviour. Insofar as culture affects behaviour its influence will and should be reflected in the test.' Such attempts appear to be aiming to assess 'innate ability' but Vernon (1969), for one, has advanced many sound arguments for rejecting the claim. In addition, Hegarty and Lucas (1978, Ch.1) have pointed out in an excellent review of culture fairness in assessment, that culture fairness has proved a more complex notion than it appears at first sight, and although at least five different psychometric models have been produced, it has become extremely difficult to give a sufficiently coherent meaning to the notion of culture fairness to make it acceptable in a way in which tests could be widely used. Another, but trivial, solution would be to construct tests especially for minority groups, but this would be unrealistic in a society with many small groups and would only be relevant if the aim was to set up separate educational objectives for those particular children and provide segregated education. This points to the main difficulty in devising culture fair tests since assessment is part of the entire educational process and cannot be viewed outside the context of the aims of education as a whole. Thus the difficulty with culture fair assessment is not primarily technical, in devising tests to meet the requisite criteria, difficult though that may be, but the more philosophical problem of deciding what those criteria should in fact be.

As early as 1966 Goldman and Taylor, in their review of research and literature on the educational problems and potential of immigrant children in Britain, pointed to the need to determine the potential of immigrant pupils. As an alternative to the difficulties attendant upon intelligence tests and culture fair testing Haynes (1971) began to investigate the possibility of constructing tests of learning ability. At the time when Haynes started work in 1967 with the aim of assessing 'the abilities of children from a different cultural background and with a poor knowledge of English' the main approaches suggested were the use of non-verbal tests and the translation of verbal tests. However, as Hegarty and Lucas (1978), who followed up Haynes' work, argue (in agreement with Vernon, 1969), of the available tests, verbal and number tests are in general better predictors of educational achievement than non-verbal tests. Moreover, it is wrong to assume that non-verbal tests are culture free, since non-verbal communication is still culturally differentiated. For example, the arrangement of pictures – a common non-verbal task – may be unfair, not only because of the content of the pictures but also because some children will be more accustomed to handling pictures than others. The other approach which was recommended was the translation of verbal tests. Although this had been found to work well with European and African groups, it was not particularly appropriate in a multicultural situation such as in contemporary Britain where there are many ethnic groups each with their diverse backgrounds, with which many second-generation immigrants may only be partially familiar.

As a result, Haynes concentrated instead on developing tests based on the notion of learning ability. These testing procedures seek to take account of differences relevant to fundamental educational goals and especially differences arising out of cultural background. Tests based on the construct of learning ability provide a sample of learning which can be used to predict a response to certain kinds of instruction. Thus the ability to benefit from teaching rather than attainment as such is measured. In this way, such tests can to some extent equalize the relevant learning background since all children come afresh to the tasks and then, after practice in which their mistakes are corrected, begin the test proper. The structured situation follows the model: teach – practice – test – teach – test. Thus the tests do not look for knowledge of culture-specific information and can be chosen to have minimal cultural dependence. In addition, as they depend on learning ability they also have particular diagnostic use with implications for remedial work. The original learning ability tests, some of which were based on an ability to draw correct geometrical analogies, classify sets of objects according to perceptual attributes and associate familiar objects with unfamiliar names, were administered by Haynes to 125 seven-year-old Sikh children in Southall, West London. They were also given to white English children and a performance scale of the Weschler Intelligence Scale for Children (WISC) was administered at the same time.

In the following year standard school attainment tests were given to 118 children of the original sample. It was found that the new learning ability tests were more accurate in predicting children's attainment than the traditional intelligence tests (WISC) or teachers' assessments. In addition, although the immigrant children did not do as well as the English children on all the tests, they did score better on the learning ability materials than on the WISC. Although the validity of such tests was provisionally established, their superiority over IQ tests and their take-up by teachers and other testers has not yet been assessed, since the tests, in a redeveloped form (Hegarty and Lucas, 1978) have not until recently been available. A review of research using learning ability tests, instead of conventional intelligence tests, with children of West Indian origin is to be found on pp.66–7.

Criticisms of testing context

The second major criticism of testing, particularly in relation to intelligence testing, has centred around features of the testing situation itself. The context in which testing takes place is obviously worthy of investigation to the extent that it alters performance systematically. Usually, standardized tests are administered in a standard format with the aim of allowing examinees to read the instructions in the same way and to deliver their replies and reactions in a similarly standard fashion. This enables comparability across testing samples to be increased and variability of the effect of the tester in such a situation to be reduced. However, such an approach assumes that all those who are being tested bring relevantly similar experiences to the testing situation – a fact which is obviously untrue for black pupils of different cultural background. Moreover, regardless of how explicit and rigid the administration instructions may be, attention may generally not be given to non-semantic and non-verbal characteristics of the test administration. Yet these may well affect the sensitivity of the person being tested and hence his test performance (Boykin, 1977). Other factors which have been pointed out as likely influences on test performance are differences between oral and verbal directions (see Taylor, 1974, p.93), time limits, the physical and geographical context of the place in which the test is being administered, familiarity with testing procedure, personalities, achievement motivation, perceived comparison groups, perceived likelihood of success, perceived status of the examiner, and, indeed, the general climate of race relations in society at large when the test takes place. The state of research is such that in many cases the effect of one or other of these variables is just not known. However, even though some or all of these variables may well not be enough to explain actual differences in test scores they do indicate that standard test procedures are not all what they may seem.

Criticisms of testing situation in respect to testing black pupils in particular have polarized around three main variables which have been hypothesized as likely to affect their test performance. One of these, which is widely believed by the black population to be the main influence on testing, is that of teacher expectation. This is considered in detail in the section on teachers' attitudes in Section 14, p.193 ff. There the conclusion drawn from the review is that although the evidence that the teacher's expectation influences the child's performance to a marked extent is far from proven, it is likely to be significant. However, in this type of circular situation in which it is extremely difficult to disentangle cause and effect it may just as well be the case, as Watson (1970) has suggested, that the child's own expectations and assessment of his ability may have an equal influence on his performance. However, two other criticisms of the testing situation will be considered in more detail here: group versus individual testing and the colour or race of the tester.

As Bagley (1977) has pointed out, evidence on the educational achievement of pupils of West Indian origin in British schools is of two main types: that based on group tests using conventional tests of achievement, and that based on individual testing using conventional psychometric tests. He is of the opinion that in both types of test situation it is rare for adequate conditions for examining ethnic minority groups to be developed. For instance, with individually administered tests there is often no control for the effect of the tester, and with group administered tests there are often no controls for the types of problem to which attention has already been drawn, or for the possible labelling effect of the teacher.

It has been suggested that group tests, such as those used by Little *et al.* (1968) in the ILEA Literacy Survey, are particularly susceptible to environmental influences, including teacher expectation. For example, Kelmer Pringle (1966) concluded that the ability of children from relatively deprived environments was likely to be considerably underestimated if group tests were used. It is claimed that the group situation impairs motivational level so that children from relatively deprived backgrounds will under-function. Against this criticism Mabey (1980, 1981), who worked on the ILEA surveys, makes an interesting comment. Although the ILEA literacy data were derived from group tests, when a 10 per cent sample of the children aged 16 were also tested individually there was both a highly significant correlation overall between the group reading test and the individual testing and also close agreement with the main group testing for immigrants and non-immigrants separately (ILEA, 1972). Mabey suggests, as have Rutter and Madge (1976), that socially disadvantaged white children will be as much affected by a group situation as will black children. Again, it appears that what evidence exists on the question of individual versus group testing is somewhat confusing, but a consensus seems to have emerged that individual testing using verbal rather than non-verbal tests (as was previously discussed, p.54) is a more accurate method of assessment.

Coard (1971) claimed that whenever a white tester gives a test to a black child that child's performance will be worse and he will, in addition, manifest subsequent aggression. He also maintained that black children do better when they do not think they are involved in a testing situation at all, but think they are only playing a game. Although Coard's claims were founded merely on the basis of his own experience as a teacher and in connection with the diagnosis of ESN pupils, and his evidence is, moreover, somewhat anecdotal, these views nevertheless seem to have had a significant influence and currency among the West Indian community. However, the influence of a white tester on adolescents' performance appears to be limited to the test performance situation itself, as Watson's (1970) experiment showed. He tested 500 pupils in a multiracial secondary school in East London in four groups of native whites, immigrant whites, West Indians and Asians with one white and one West Indian tester. When the West Indian group were told by the white examiner that they were to do an IQ test their performance was inferior to that when they were told that they were helping to produce English lessons.

Boykin (1977) has suggested that the mainly American investigations which he reviewed, show that there may be an effect on younger children different from that on adolescents when a white person does the testing. With young children familiarity with the tester may be important. Moreover, it is difficult to be sure when only one black and one white tester are used with young children that it is race *per se* which is influential and not other factors such as personality. Bagley's (1971) study of 50 seven- to 10-year-old West Indians and 50 closely matched English children who were tested on an intelligence test found no difference in performance when either the two black or the two white testers were involved (figures not supplied). Again, Bagley and Coard (1975) found no difference between the white and the black tester when a one in seven sample of white and black pupils in three multiracial infant, junior and high schools were asked about their self-perceptions and image. (In this context it is interesting to compare Milner's (1975) report (see pp.162–4) when only one white tester was employed.) Moreover, a recent research experiment using a group reading test with a class of eight-year-old children and employing one white and one black tester (Anderson and Thomas, 1979) found no difference in the results of the West Indian pupils.

With respect to tests with adolescents it appears that attitudes towards racial differences may influence rapport so that a white tester has the effect of lowering a black adolescent's scores. Some of the most systematic of these studies have been undertaken by Katz (1973), in the United States, who discovered that blacks performed better when a white examiner was co-operative rather than authoritarian. He argued that white experimenters have a higher social status in the eyes of black subjects than do black experimenters and consequently black subjects derive greater positive incentive to good performance in the presence of white testers. On the other hand, there is greater negative incentive if they are unsuccessful. He also found that whether the race of the tester was influential depended very much upon the norm against which the students thought they were working. When they thought they were being compared with white students the blacks performed better for a black tester, but if they thought they were working against a black norm they scored better for a white tester.

There appears to be rather little evidence comparing black and white testers in this country, but a recent report (Thomas, 1978) seems to confirm Katz's observation that black pupils want to do better with a white tester. A sample of 439 white British, 257 West Indian and 154 Asian pupils from a secondary school in a predominantly working class and multiracial area of Nottingham were asked by a white British and a West Indian tester to give information on their attitudes towards school leaving age, job aspirations, effort at school, behaviour towards teachers and spare-time activities. A tendency to claim higher aspirations for jobs and to give an indication of staying on longer was noted in connection with the white tester. The researcher suggested that there was a greater incentive for the black pupils to make such statements as they perceived a greater value in receiving a favourable evaluation from the white tester. That this result is in contra-distinction to that of Watson (1970) highlights the importance of the social context and purpose of such testing.

In general, although the evidence, particularly from British studies, on the effect of the race of tester on black pupils' performance, appears to be inconclusive, there seems no good reason to assume that the white tester necessarily inhibits black performance. The studies so far undertaken indicate that a sufficient distinction has not been made between the effect of the individual personalities of different testers and that due solely to race. In addition, evidence on motivational and social processses involved in testing is very much lacking. Superficially, there does seem to be a difference in performance when blacks perceive different power roles of black and white testers, when they know the ends at which the testing is aimed and when they perceive their performance as being directly competitive with that of whites. The studies reviewed, therefore, have to be seen as preliminary to more sensitive work.

Bearing these reservations in mind when testing, particularly that of black pupils is undertaken, it is necessary to turn now to a consideration of the actual test results found by researchers. These results, on ability and attainment, will be divided into a number of sections. First, on testing of ability, research evidence will be presented in Section 5 both on IQ tests and also verbal and non-verbal tests. The latter have often been referred to and used as if they were IQ tests and hence, as has been seen, have often been subject to the same criticisms. Following this section, results on attainment tests of all aspects of language, especially reading, and maths will be reviewed (Sections 6 and 7). Consideration will also be given to the information available on the 11-plus transfer of pupils of West Indian origin, their performance on GCE and CSE exams and in relation to classification as educationally sub-normal and behaviour.

Section 5: IQ, Verbal and Non-verbal Tests

Some indication has already been given of the kind of ability which these tests are intended to measure. A useful and detailed discussion of the nature of intelligence is contained in Hegarty and Lucas (1978, Ch.2), but it is sufficient for the purposes of this study to understand intelligence as 'the ability to form concepts, grasp patterns and relationships and reason abstractly'. It must be stressed, however, that intelligence tests aim to test a sample of behaviour and not innate intelligence. These behaviours are relatively independent of schooling but provide a prediction of educational attainment – at least on the white mainstream population. They are concerned with general conceptual or reasoning skills. Although verbal reasoning tests are often referred to as 'intelligence' tests, it is more true to say that 'these tests have been designed to give measures of general scholastic ability. The results should not be interpreted as providing in any way a measure of capacity for learning' (NFER, 1980, p.22). At the end of this review of studies which have used intelligence tests, both verbal and non-verbal, to assess black pupils, reference will also be made to the recently developed learning ability tests produced by Hegarty and Lucas (1978) which do attempt to predict ability to learn.

It is somewhat surprising to find that in fact rather few studies have used conventional intelligence tests with West Indian pupils. One of the earliest pieces of research was that by Houghton (1966) who, in a carefully undertaken study, administered the Stanford Binet Intelligence Scale Form L–M to 71 matched pairs of West Indian and English children from 11 infant schools in socially deprived central areas of Nottingham. The children, aged 4.11 to 5.6 years, who had varied nursery school experience included children of West Indian origin who were either born in this country or who had spent a minimum of two years here. No significant difference between the mean scores of the English children (92.00) and children of West Indian orgin (90.09) was found. Both the English and the West Indian girls had higher scores than the boys. It will be noted, however, that the scores were well below the national norm.

Bagley (1971) undertook a partial replication of Houghton's study using two groups of children aged seven to 10, 50 West Indian boys and girls and 50 English boys and girls in 10 London primary schools. His sample was again closely matched for age, sex and father's occupational class, although not for school attended. The children were not told that they were taking an intelligence test. No significant difference was found between the intelligence scores of the West Indian and the white indigenous children of similar home and material circumstances (West Indian mean score 105.7, English 103.2), both of which were well above the norm. Whilst it should be noted that there is rather a large age span between these children, it is possible that since both the studies by Houghton and Bagley seem to have been thoroughly researched (although they differed primarily in that Houghton's sample were socially disadvantaged and Bagley's enjoyed an adequate material standard of living) it may be the case that the Stanford Binet Intelligence Test does not discriminate sufficiently for children of West Indian origin.

Another study by Bagley (1975a) in which he considered the relationship between IQ and the degree of 'European blood' in people of African ancestry is also of relevance here. Fifty-nine black children aged eight to 10 were tested on the Stanford Binet scale and four judges, two African and two West Indian, rated photos of the black children as to whether they were completely African, mixed, more African than European, equally mixed or mixed, more European than African. There was no significant difference between the IQs of the children of pure African (110.3), more African than European (103.9), and more European than African (103.3) blood. In fact, there appeared to be a relationship between IQ and social class. To conclude, Bagley (1975a) proposed a formidable list of potential variables (but not including quality of schooling) which would need to be controlled in a definitive study of race and intelligence on a large random sample of 10-year-olds. Others, (e.g. Phillips, 1979) have pointed to the gargantuan nature of such a task which seems likely to remain a theoretical rather than an empirical exercise.

The results of these studies and another (Bagley *et al.*, 1978) have led to the conclusion that IQ may not be a very useful measure with children of West Indian origin since its scaling is such as to maximize differences between individuals rather than concentrating on the 'cognitive universals' which individuals hold in common, and it is a poor measure of 'competence' or the skills which are essential in the conduct of everyday affairs.

Since, as the following Section 6, Language and Reading, demonstrates, many pupils of West Indian origin have to be considered as bilingual, it is worth noting here the findings of one very early study concerned with the effect of bilingualism on performance on intelligence and attainment tests (Alleyne, 1962). The well designed research using a specially constructed questionnaire on bilingualism and piloted in Wales was carried out by a West Indian with a sample of 102 junior pupils from eight London schools who were either bilingual or monoglot and otherwise carefully matched for age, sex and socio-economic status. All the children of West Indian (Trinidadian) origin and other bilinguals had lived in the UK for at least one year. A variety of verbal and non-verbal tests were administered and it was found that the monoglot groups were consistently superior to bilinguals and the degree of bilingualism had a progressively adverse effect, though to a lesser extent on non-verbal tests (p<.01). Those who were highly or moderately bilingual and had been born outside the UK performed particularly badly. Hence as long as 20 years ago the effect of bilingualism on performance on such tests was adequately demonstrated.

Turning to a consideration of verbal tests, it will be seen that the few studies which have used these have usually administered the verbal component of the Weschler Intelligence Scale for Children. First, however, it is worth observing that in the ILEA study of 11-plus transfer, (Little *et al.*, 1968) it was found that 82 per cent of the 1038 immigrant pupils (of whom 56 per cent were West Indians) fell into the bottom three groups of the seven profile transfer groups when assessed on verbal reasoning tests and teachers' judgements. This result indicated that 81 per cent of the 583 West Indian children were well below average in performance. Even when West Indian pupils had completed most of their primary education in the UK (101) only half as many (eight as opposed to 16 per cent) as in other immigrant groups were in the top two groups for verbal reasoning.

Two studies which are in some ways comparable (McFie and Thompson, 1970 and Yule *et al.*, 1975) used the WISC to assess verbal reasoning. McFie and Thompson gave the WISC to 61 West Indian children aged five to 15 years who were referred to a London child guidance clinic and of whom all except 10 were matched with an English counterpart of the same sex whose age was no more than three months different. It was found that both the performance and the verbal IQ of the West Indian children was lower. On the verbal

IQ West Indians attained 87 compared with English controls of 95. But the West Indians who had arrived in Britain before the age of five did better (91) than those who arrived after the age of five (85) on verbal IQ. Nevertheless, it is to be noted that all scores were lower than the norm. Although this study is modest and is not concerned with a typical group of West Indian children, 10 of whom were not matched with English controls, it is of interest since its findings can be compared with those of a much larger study by Yule *et al.* (1975). This investigation was two-pronged. In the second stage 105 white children aged 11–12 were selected at random from a larger sample of 2000 children in one London borough as a control group. Out of 354 children with West Indian parents in the sample a random selection on the basis of information available to teachers was also made of 49 out of 145 children who had themselves been born in the West Indies and 51 from the UK-born group. The 105 white indigenous and the 100 children of West Indian parentage were then individually tested on a short form of the WISC which includes two sub-tests of verbal ability. Whereas the English mean score was 101.3 for verbal IQ the West Indian Score was 86.9, a statistically significant difference (p<0.1). There was no significant difference on verbal IQ according to place of birth, unlike the findings of McFie and Thompson.

In conclusion to the review of the few researches which have used tests of verbal reasoning it is of interest to note that an inquiry in Redbridge (BPPA, 1978) which monitored pupils in their last year at eight multiracial junior schools in the borough found that on an NFER verbal reasoning test the 66 West Indian children scored 85 compared with the 563 white children's score of 97.7. This is obviously a sizeable difference. The validity and reliability of using verbal tests in the assessment of black pupils has already been discussed (pp.52–5) and whilst it has generally been claimed (see, for example, Vernon, 1965b) that verbal reasoning tests are better predictive instruments for use with children of ethnic minority origin, this recommendation has more recently been severely criticized (see, for example, Hegarty and Lucas, 1978).

Early evidence tended to suggest that non-verbal tests showed greater differences in performance between both first- and second-generation West Indian pupils and white pupils. Vernon (1965 a and b) in his study which compared English boys and West Indian boys in the West Indies found that the West Indian children performed much less successfully on non-verbal materials such as non-verbal Matrices, Kohs' Blocks and Form board, though they were relatively high on perceptual and drawing tests. McFie and Thompson's (1970) study using the WISC found that the children of West Indian origin performed much lower on four of the five sub-tests on the performance or non-verbal scale, obtaining 90 as opposed to 102 by the English control group. This was similar to the finding by Graham and Meadows (1967) also using the WISC on a similar number of children in a child guidance clinic situation. Of particular interest was the difference in the performance IQ scores between those children of West Indian origin who had arrived in the UK before their fifth birthday (94) and those who had arrived after this time (84). McFie and Thompson suggested that these differences, and particularly that between the performance and verbal aspects of the test, probably indicated specific learning difficulties. They recommended that although language more obviously required attention, at least as high priority should be given to teaching with mechanical and constructional objects. Like Vernon, they also pointed to the cultural factors which were operating in these tests.

It is interesting in connection with this, however, to note a small-scale study by Watson (1973) which suggested that performance might increase relatively with length of schooling. He tested 14 West Indian children age seven years on the WISC and found that their IQ was less than 80. After one-and-a-half to two-and-a-half years they were retested and a mean rise of over eight points was noted in comparison with a rise of only .25 points by a control group of non-immigrants, 12 of whom were matched for age, sex and ability. Once again, a comparison in this respect can also be made between the McFie and Thompson study and that of Yule *et al.* (1975). This latter study gives two sources of information on non-verbal tests. On the individual testing on the two performance aspects of the short form of the WISC it was found that the indigenous white children scored 103.9 whereas the West Indians scored 90.4. The West Indian group born in the UK, according to the estimates by their teachers, scored significantly higher on the WISC performance scales than those who had been born in the West Indies. In addition, in the first stage of the study which involved 2281 children in one London borough, of whom 354 were of West Indian origin, a group test of non-verbal reasoning (the

NFER NV5 or BD) was administered. On this 1668 white children had a mean score of 92.38, 201 West Indian children born in the UK scored 85.24 and 143 children born in the West Indies obtained 76.43. In all groups girls tended to score slightly above boys. The differences in scores of the two groups of West Indian children were significant, but, in addition, it will be noted that although the scores of the UK-born children were much closer to that of the indigenous group they were all well below the national norm. From the results of these important studies it can be seen why it was hoped that length of schooling would markedly affect the achievement of West Indian pupils.

A number of other small-scale studies were also undertaken at the end of the 1960s and are worth mentioning in this review of non-verbal assessment. Blair (1969) tested 296 white and 117 West Indian 10–11-year-olds and found that the English children had a markedly higher score on Raven's Progressive Matrices. A study by Payne (1969) supported this finding when tests of coloured progressive matrices were administered to seven- to eight-year-olds. There were three groups of children involved: 99 West Indian, 100 randomly selected British children, and 99 British children individually matched with the West Indian children according to verbal ability. All the groups were matched for socio-economic status. Payne found that the West Indian immigrant children were significantly poorer than the white children on the non-verbal intelligence test but there were no significant sex differences (numbers of girls and boys not given). Another study (Bhatnagar, 1970) also used Raven's Progressive Matrices. He tested 174 West Indian and 200 English pupils in a London secondary school and found that the West Indian pupils had a mean IQ of 90.4 while the English had a mean of 102.3. The author was cautious in his interpretation of these results and suggested that the tests discriminated highly against working-class pupils since their items required abilities usually associated with the nurturing of middle-class homes.

In passing it may be helpful to record that other performance tests which have been used from time to time as secondary measures in researches have been noted as possibly useful though not necessarily 'culture free', in particular the 'Draw-a-man' test (Bagley, 1981; Vernon, 1965b; and Ward, 1978), Porteus Mazes (Vernon, 1965b) and Witkin's Figures on an Embedded Ground (Bagley personal communication and Bagley *et al.*, n.d.).

To conclude this section it is interesting to pay attention to two studies which based their approaches more on that of learning ability than intelligence testing. The first study by Stones (1975) was experimental, using a rather small-scale sample of 30 children of West Indian origin and 30 white children from two junior schools in the inner-ring area of a Midlands city. There were 15 boys and 15 girls aged 10–11 in both groups. Stones examined ways in which performance on Raven's Progressive Matrices could be improved by teaching with instructional materials using the same principles as those contained in the test; pictorial, abstract, numerical and self-instructional. These principles were followed in relation to paired-learning activities on rote learning, concept learning and transfer tests. The results showed that the performance of West Indian children on Raven's Progressive Matrices test did not differ from that of English children provided they were given relevant experience in tasks involving conceptual learning. West Indian children were slightly slower at rote learning, slightly less good on the concept transfer tests, but better at regrouping tests than the white children. It has to be noted that although the numbers in this study were small, there was nevertheless, a trend systematically against performance on the non-verbal tests insofar as both the scores of the West Indian children and their English peers were all lower than the published norms. However, the study may indicate that pupils of West Indian origin are not lower on learning ability.

As has already been outlined (pp.53–5) Hegarty and Lucas (1978) have been working from the basic work by Haynes (1971) to establish tests of learning ability as a fairer way of testing children of ethnic minority groups. These testing procedures aim to take account of differences relevant to fundamental educational goals and especially those arising out of cultural background. The tests relate to other aspects of school work insofar as they indicate the extent to which the child will profit from teaching. They also avoid some of the problems of IQ as they are tests of potential not achievement. It is also claimed that the tests can discriminate between children with uniformly low IQ scores and predict better to subsequent levels of school achievement. Two sets of materials have been produced for individual and group administration, but with a common rationale emphasizing what a child can learn and how easily he can learn it. The individual battery consists of five sub-tests: concept formation, verbal learning of objects, number series, verbal learning of syllables, and analogies. The group battery consists of three sub-tests: concept formation, number series and analogies. These tasks are all administered using the following model: teach–practise–test–teach–test. The individual battery of tests was administered to a national sample of 386 West Indian and Pakistani children and at the same time a short form of the WISC was given. The battery was also given to a 29 per cent sub-sample 12–18 weeks later in order to obtain reliability data and 12 months later the entire sample was retested on a set of attainment tests. Altogether, 211 West Indian children, 103 boys and 108 girls, most of whom had been born in this country, were drawn from 68 schools in 14 education authorities. Test reliability was established reasonably well and the learning ability test battery was also found to be a better predictor of subsequent attainment than the WISC. The researchers (Hegarty and Lucas, 1978) advocate a change in emphasis in classroom assessment from intelligence testing to measurements of learning abilities which can be used for diagnostic purposes. They are particularly suitable for diagnosis since they concentrate on processes rather than end points and have clear remedial implications, as by identifying patterns of learning differences they point to specific strategies of intervention. It remains to be seen whether in the long run this approach proves to be more useful with pupils of ethnic minority origin but early indications are that it may in fact be so.

This review has to some extent charted the history of IQ testing and followed its progressive refinements over the years. Consideration of the need to assess the ability of children of ethnic minority groups has accelerated these revisions since many of these studies have suggested that test results may be influenced to too great an extent by irrelevant differences, and that there are, in addition, powerful environmental influences to be considered in this field. Although, in general, it can be said that West Indian children tend to score lower than white children on tests of intelligence, in the writer's view it may with some justification be claimed that much of the differences in measured IQ can be accounted for in terms of cultural differences, language handicaps and even emotional difficulties rather than low potential ability. IQ scores may obscure some abilities which are shared by many children and which they may well possess in more equal levels than those implied by IQ scores. They can show that one child can do some things better than another, but this does not mean that the second completely lacks the fundamental skills possessed by the first. Thus it seems as if IQ tends to focus on differences rather than similarities and may well not give a true picture of potentiality. There may well be, as Bagley (1977) has suggested, other measures of intelligent behaviour – such as adaptation to an urban environment – which may be more crucial for a pupil of West Indian origin.

Section 6: Language and Reading

Until recently relatively little attention has been paid to the role which language plays in the achievement of pupils of West Indian origin. Moreover, what interest has been shown has tended to concentrate on speech rather than comprehension. However, it seems reasonable to argue that an ability to read is much more fundamental to educational performance since it is also required by most assessment procedures be they tests or examinations. The intention in this section of the review is therefore first to consider general questions of language which arise in connection with pupils of West Indian origin, both in as far as they relate to their home environment and the school, and to examine whether special provision for language teaching might be necessary in schools. In the second part of this section (pp.82–101) the evidence from research inquiries into reading standards and reading abilities of different kinds, presented by studies at local and national level, will be reviewed.

Language

As is well known, many second- and even third-generation West Indians speak a dialect form of Standard English which can loosely be described as Creole. As a preliminary to subsequent evaluation it seems important to attempt to ascertain to what extent Creole influences are still a feature of second-generation immigrants' language, how Creole is and should be regarded in schools, and to what extent it affects the reading attainment of pupils of West Indian origin.

Many writers have pointed out (see, for example, Evans and Le Page, 1967) that the language problem of West Indian children in this country has been concealed, largely because of the mainly British cultural orientation in their educational background and environment in the West Indies and because of the increasing adoption of British cultural patterns by the West Indians as they settle here. Creole means simply 'locally born' (Evans and Le Page, 1967) or 'things, habits, ideas, native to the West Indies' (Foner, 1977). Most West Indian children are likely to come from families who speak a Creole dialect of English, but less commonly it may be a Creole dialect of French. Creole dialects were acquired under conditions of duress by West African slaves working in the plantations under colonialism. Hence the dialects borrowed extensively both from African languages and from the model language of the European planters. The proportion of Europeans to negroes determined the orientation of the model language so that as Le Page (Evans and Le Page, 1967) explains, in those islands such as Barbados where there was a high proportion of Europeans to negroes the influence of the model language – in this case English – was considerable, and brought the Creole dialect much nearer to it. On the other hand, in those islands, like Jamaica, where Europeans were easily outnumbered by negroes, the influence of the model language was far less. It has been noted, for example, that Creole dialects have traditionally been more conservative in Jamaica where the language shows greatest African influence. This is a point of interest since most of the West Indian immigrants to Britain are Jamaican in origin and it is estimated that they comprise at least half the population of schools in London. In other islands of the West Indies, for example the Windward Islands of St. Lucia and Dominica and in Trinidad, French was the predominant orientation of Creole, and English has only been learnt in the last century from Barbadian schoolmasters (see Alleyne, 1962 for an account of the linguistic situation in the Caribbean with respect to bilingualism).

As Craig (1971) has pointed out, the English language has been an indicator of high social status in Jamaica and it is the language of the dominant upper classes, formal social situations and the medium of education. English pidgin was the common language of the varied slave population and used in communication between master and slave. Later it was modified to form Standard Jamaican and has reached the present as Jamaican Creole. There is thus a range of dialects between Jamaican Creole and Standard English which Craig considers are two separate dialects, so that a person speaking both is really bilingual. Which dialect is used depends on both the context of speech and the social class of the speaker, but the lower classes are more likely to use Creole spontaneously and for any length of time. On the basis of his research in the West Indies with three groups of 105 children, aged six-and-a-half to seven-and-a-half years, drawn from different social classes, Craig (1971) showed how different sets of children have inherited different communicative formats, and, when these were separated from differences in socio-cultural environment and sex, they were found to be associated with differences in the purposes and cognitive content of language. More recently, other research in Manchester which examined the effects of narrative, descriptive and explanatory contexts on the language performance of English and West Indian ten-year-olds found that generally children of West Indian origin used a greater variety of nouns, verbs, adjectives and adverbs than English children, but their language was less complex (Crofts, 1978).

It is now generally considered that Creole is a dialect, i.e. a variety or form of language peculiar to a district or class, though some (e.g. Bagley, personal communication) have gone so far as to suggest that it is a language in its own right. Yet, since, language is constantly changing there are tremendous differences of detail in the dialects spoken by West Indians in this country. Just as there is a continuum from Jamaican Creole to Standard Jamaican in the West Indies, so there is a continuum from Creole to West Indian English in this country. Likewise this is associated with social class so that broad Creole is generally spoken by those of lower social classes. However, each speaker as an individual commands a span on the continuum rather than a point on it, so that the more informal a conversation the more likely it is to be expressed by dialect nearer the lower end of the continuum. As Edwards (1976) has remarked, 'possibly no other dialect of English is so far removed from Standard English either quantitatively in the number of features affected, or qualitatively in their degree and kind.' Such a dialect is obviously extremely complex in structure and as well as having affinities with Standard English it also has certain features which are more in keeping with the African languages from which it derives. Bushell (1973) claims that these African languages have affected the dialect's vocabulary, which is generally accepted to be limited, and possibly too imprecise for the communications of a technological society (Holberton, 1977). Creole is distinguished from Standard English by pronunciation, grammar, character and mood, in which sound plays an integral part supplemented by gesture.

In terms of adaptation to an English school situation a Creole dialect speaker is therefore likely to suffer from hearing difficulties, since his framework of reference of sounds is that of Creole, and not English; difficulties of understanding, since even if his hearing is correct his knowledge of grammar and vocabulary may lead him to assign different meanings; and difficulties of expression as teachers may not understand his dialect and he may not understand theirs (Evans and Le Page, 1967). A better appreciation of these kinds of difficulties has led to what has now widely come to be regarded as misclassification of a disproportionate number of children of West Indian origin as educationally sub-normal or even as deaf. Though, as some (e.g. Wight, 1971) have claimed, initial adaptation in terms of speech may not be too problematic, written English, which is less redundant, uses a greater variety of words and has a higher incidence of constructions, would continue to cause difficulties for West Indian children, as has been demonstrated by Edwards (1976) who has shown that Creole interference leads to comprehension difficulties.

Lest it be thought that the potential difficulties of Creole dialect be over-estimated, attention should be drawn to the findings of a recent survey on linguistic diversity in London schools carried out by the English Department of the University of London Institute of Education (Rosen and Burgess, 1980 a and b). From this sociolinguistic description of the interactions of spoken and written language which confront teachers in London schools there emerges a number of interesting statistics. For example, a total of 55 languages and 24 overseas based dialects were found amongst 4600 pupils aged 11–12 in 28 secondary schools in London. These pupils, 46 per cent boys, 54 per cent girls, represented 14 per cent of their age group in London schools. Thirteen per cent of these children were bidialectal in British and Caribbean dialects, mostly Jamaican Patois, although a smaller proportion of children originated from the East Caribbean (see Table 8, 1980b). The researchers discovered that although the overseas dialect was rarely dominant for second- and third-generation immigrant pupils, relatively greater proportions of pupils of Jamaican origin than East Caribbean origin were estimated by teachers as regular dialect speakers. The dialect typically spoken was found to be London/Jamaican not Jamaican Creole, but in any one speech there could be a tremendous diversity depending on the interaction of a West Indian element derived from any part of the Creole continuum and a London element from any part of the London continuum (1980b, pp. 34–6). Pupils were asked whether they would be significantly interested in reading and writing in their overseas dialect, and whilst 162 pupils of Jamaican origin expressed such an interest, 215 did not and 130 did not respond. Most of these pupils are, of course, less likely to be speakers of Standard English. As rated by their teachers, a much higher proportion of girls of Jamaican origin were thought to be Standard speakers, were assessed as having marked superiority in writing and reading over boys, and even where there were difficulties these were less likely to be significant. Boys, as other studies have confirmed (Trudgill, 1975), are much more likely to be dialect speakers.

Home and school

Evidence has been divided about the importance of dialect to children of West Indian origin and even about the extent to which it is maintained, though Essen and Ghodsian (1979) noted that few respondents in their national sample claimed to speak English at home. The extent to which West Indian parents encourage or dissuade children from speaking Creole in their home can only be a matter for speculation. But Rex and Tomlinson (1979) for example, found that linguistic difficulties did not seem to be acknowledged by West Indian parents; only one per cent of the 227 parents in their sample said that their children had difficulty in speaking English when they started school. Stoker (1969), who observed the difficulties which infant school children were finding in adjusting to the school, suggested that children of West Indian origin need to retain their dialect for home but also need to make a compromise in school between how they speak at home and the 'received pronunciation' spoken by the teacher.

Although this would be disputed by some, others (Bagley *et al.*, 1978) have apparently shown that the language of the West Indian child's home can be handicapping in many ways. In a study of 150 black children aged 10–11 matched with a similar number of white children, from four schools in working class areas of London a number of attitudes to home and school were investigated and parents were also interviewed in the home situation. Whilst for both black and white children factors representing parental authoritarianism correlated significantly with reading ability independent of social class, other variables to do with shared housing facilities, lack of home ownership, schooling and qualifications of father and mother and, significantly in this context, use of Creole at home, were also associated with under-achievement in reading for children of West Indian origin. Following a cluster analysis which produced three distinct groups of pupils with differential achievement it was found that the alienation of West Indian parents from English culture was positively related to the child's reading achievement. It was also discovered that Jamaican parents tended to have children who under-achieved; and that they were uncritical of English society, had fewer years of education and tended to speak Creole rather than Standard English or Jamaican at home. The researchers suggested that it appeared that 'what is educationally handicapping is the language in which parents and children converse, not the language which children use in school. And parents who tend to use Creole at home are those who do not converse with their child in ways which stimulate him to achieve in school.' (p.10). Though this appears to be a carefully carried out study, others of its kind would assist in attempting to build up a picture of the kind of home background variables which assist or hinder the promotion of educational achievement of children of West Indian origin. Until such studies are undertaken on a broader basis its findings must be regarded as tentative in respect of their generalizability to the West Indian home.

Another interesting question, which has generated more opinion than evidence, is the extent to which possession of a language is tied up with ethnicity. To quote Rosen and Burgess (1980a):

'no better example could be found of the relationship between language and identity than the use of London Jamaican by school pupils. There were numerous examples of black London-born pupils whose language differs in no way or very little from that of white London pupils. Many of these pupils, usually when they reach their early teens, learn London Jamaican and are very conscious of the symbolic nature of this act. More remarkably, a few white pupils under the influence of the peer-group have also learnt London Jamaican. ... This phenomenon of learning "to talk black" is the more impressive since it often runs counter to wishes of parents who disapprove of "bad talk". Pupils who have in their repertoire a Caribbean Creole may in the school situation be reluctant to admit that they have it, such are the conflicting feelings and powerful attitudes which adhere to it.' (p.42).

Other writers, for example Edwards and Sutcliffe (1978), have also suggested that the self-esteem of black pupils is closely linked with their dialect which is in turn bound up with their deepest experiences. There is no doubt that dialect has been a force for social cohesion historically and may again be being used as a defence and in resistance to teachers and the school ethos if certain accounts (Holberton, 1977 and NAHT, 1980) are not to be considered overemphasized. Researching with black pupils in Bedford schools, Edwards and Sutcliffe found that second-generation blacks who continued to use fairly broad Creole were discouraged in this practice by their parents, and that teachers' efforts to produce children who spoke Standard English were also in vain. They remark: 'The links between language and identity are so strong that attempts to "correct" non-standard speech are likely to be interpreted by the children as criticism or rejection of themselves, their family and friends.' (p.19). Obviously this is a most sensitive issue. There is evidence to suggest both that there are psychological problems associated with the historical development of Creole which condition the child of West Indian origin and his family 'to resent any suggestion that he has a less than perfect command of English or needs special help' (Evans and Le Page, 1967), and also that many teachers have underestimated the importance of bidialecticism as an asset, or for cultural identification or self-esteem. Any such appreciation by teachers was mentioned by Brittan (1976a) as being completely lacking in teachers' comments on their attitudes towards the language of pupils of Caribbean descent in a national survey undertaken by the NFER in 1972. Neither do teachers appear to have much awareness of the linguistic diversity of the Caribbean and the changes which occur to Caribbean dialects in a British context as Edwards (1979) has demonstrated. Again, it is apposite to quote Rosen and Burgess's remarks deriving from their survey into linguistic diversity in London schools:

> 'However, what is at stake here is much more than merely tolerating the dialect of the pupil. For many pupils speaking the dialect means saying something uniquely. It may mean more. The very act of speaking it is a declaration of who and what they are and wish to be. Further, West Indian dialect speakers are heirs to an almost exclusively oral tradition. Their stories, verbal

wit and songs are a popular aesthetic resource which should not be shut out by teachers who would be the first to claim that they are centrally concerned with imagination, authenticity and the creative use of language.' (1980a, p.176).

As this suggests, and as other writers (Evans and Le Page, 1967; Wight, 1971) have also attested, children of West Indian origin are not just linguistic problems on account of the difficulties which they have as 'semi-linguals' (Trudgill, 1975), but they also have a vividly creative gift with language which can enrich classrooms with its flexibility, humour and motivating force. Sutcliffe (1976, 1978) has ably described the creativity of the speech of children of West Indian origin and Edwards (1979, Ch.6) has provided illustrations of teachers' initiatives with styles of work which capitalize on the creativity of bilingualism. This is demonstrated in detail by the case of Jennifer, as described by Richmond (1978), who, although seen in the school's terms as a disruptive and difficult pupil, devised and stage-managed a play, 'Brixton Blues', which exhibited a control and expertise with language which varied from Standard English, even High Church English, to Cockney, to 'Black South London' to almost impenetrable Patois, with the utmost skill and precision. As a result of the sustained co-operation and attention to detail of Jennifer and another black classmate the transcript of a video-taped form of the play is available in Richmond's article. It conveys not only something of the artistry involved in what must be a relatively commonplace dramatic event for many schools in London, but also indicates something of the scope of the linguistic problem which a teacher in such a school must daily face. A review of lea practice and school policy with respect to such a problem is the subject of the following sub-section.

Special provision

As Goldman (1973) has remarked, it is necessary to make a sharp distinction when considering the importance of language skills between (a) lack of knowledge of the English language; (b) a generalized linguistic deficiency; and (c) problems stemming from differences in dialect or linguistic code. Unlike Asian pupils, West Indian pupils cannot be said to lack knowledge of the English language, but they may suffer from a more generalized linguistic deficiency as well as have problems stemming from differences in dialect. It is likely, as has already been mentioned, that there are social barriers and prejudice involved in the differences between the two language cultures – a no-man's land in which children of West Indian origin find themselves caught. Moreover, as has also been noted, they suffer from social deprivation both more generally in relation to the host society and insofar as they may all be brought up in a home environment in which the parents do not engage in stimulating or meaningful conversation with their children, or do not provide play or toys in their early years, thus impeding language development and impairing subsequent intellectual skills and scholastic attainments. An accurate assessment of these factors is complex for although they almost certainly obtain with respect to some pupils of West Indian origin, it is difficult to judge to what extent many of the educational difficulties associated with these children stem from differences of dialect or from genuine linguistic impairment.

In what ways then have leas and schools attempted to meet the linguistic needs of the pupil of West Indian origin? An early warning of the need for leas to consider the provision which should be made for language teaching was made by Townsend (1971) as a result of a national survey of 146 leas. He found that 10 of the leas with over 500 immigrant pupils did not make special arrangements for English language teaching, and that of the 71 who did make special arrangements for other ethnic groups 12 leas with under 1000 West Indians and 10 with more than 1000 did not do so for these pupils. It was clear that this was because the special linguistic needs of West Indian pupils were not appreciated and Townsend made the following recommendation.

'It seems to research workers that the prior need ... is the recognition on the part of LEAs and teachers that West Indian pupils present a special linguistic need which cannot be met most effectively by placing West Indian pupils in lower streams along-side retarded non-immigrants with different needs, as is the practice at present in a number of schools. It might be that this is where some of them belong on grounds other than linguistic ones, but until the language problem is tackled with something at least approaching the urgency with which many LEAs are tackling the question of Asian, Italian or Cypriot language, there is likely to be an increasingly high proportion of West Indian under-achievers both in school and in employment.' (p.110).

A follow-up report (Townsend and Brittan, 1972) studied the

organization in 200 multiracial schools chosen from the original national sample to include certain proportions of different types of school and pupils from different ethnic groups. It was found that although the majority of multiracial schools saw language teaching as a priority, somewhat inadequate provision had been made for children of West Indian origin whose language differences were less well understood than those of their Asian peers. Four main arrangements for language teaching were found to exist: full-time language centres; part-time language centres; full-time language classes within schools; and part-time language classes within schools. It appeared then that although provision for pupils of West Indian origin varied according to the number of such pupils in a local authority, its philosophy, and the staff and facilities available, most language help given to West Indian children was in the form of remedial tuition. Although it is likely that the situation has changed considerably from authority to authority in the intervening years, a recent report (BPPA, 1978) stated that 46 per cent of the first-year West Indians in a high school in Redbridge were receiving remedial help.

The then Government White Paper, *Educational Disadvantage and The Educational Needs of Immigrants* (Great Britain, Parliament, House of Commons, 1974) also recommended that some West Indian children might need special language teaching and that

'. . . all local education authorities with a sizeable immigrant child population should make plans to provide by an early date special facilities in ordinary schools to overcome the linguistic and adjustment problems of immigrant children with a level of ability higher than the general run of pupils in special schools for the educationally sub-normal' (Recommendation 19, p.12).

Yet a CRC investigation (1977) which canvassed the view of West Indian parents, among those of other ethnic minority groups from eight areas across the country, found that only six per cent of their children had attended special language classes and that the West Indian parents were less likely than Asian parents to think that special teaching would have been helpful.

If it appears that there was some recalcitrance on the part of leas in establishing provision and reluctance on the part of West Indian parents to consider their children in linguistic need, then there was also a certain disinclination on the part of teachers to acknowledge a problem, as Brittan (1976a), who undertook a national survey of teachers' opinions in 1972, discovered. Of 510 teachers in 25 schools with ethnic minority groups ranging from 18 to 84 per cent of the school population just 71 per cent agreed with the statement: 'The English spoken by most West Indian pupils requires special attention for the pupils to benefit from an English education.' But 15 per cent disagreed with this statement, their comments indicating a variety of attitudes towards the language of pupils of Caribbean descent, many suggesting that speakers of Creole were linguistically deprived. Two-thirds of the teachers suggested that English should be taught to non-English speaking immigrants before they were admitted to ordinary schools and some commented in particular on the desirability of including West Indian pupils in language centres, though the researcher noted that none made reference to the importance of Creole for the development of cultural identity. As Brittan observed, there seemed at this time to be a gap between teachers' opinions on the necessity for special language teaching and lea practice since few leas included West Indians in their arrangements for special language teaching. However, a recent lea report (Williams, 1978) has indicated that the arrangements for language teaching of West Indian pupils by leas is now more sensitive to the needs of such children.

One early problem, however, in providing proper provision was the lack of valid techniques to assess both the nature and severity of a child's linguistic difficulties (Stoker, 1969), and it was not until 1975 that the NFER tests of linguistic proficiency were validated as an objective measure (McEwen *et al.*, 1975) (see pp.99–101). During the last decade, however, a whole range of views about the linguistic needs of West Indian pupils have been expressed and no simple solution or policy seems to have been reached. Views range on a continuum from that which was optimistically expressed in the late sixties to the effect that special teaching was unnecessary as children of West Indian origin would pick up Standard English in the course of their interaction with their peers and teachers (Wight, 1971); to views about the most favourable time for second-language learning; to recommendations for structured compensatory teaching; and even to the consideration more recently of the inclusion of black English in the school curriculum.

The view that the West Indian pupil 'provided he has reasonable exposure to the dialect of the teacher and the school, will develop skills of language reception to cope with the contrast between

Creole and Standard English' was the conclusion of the Schools Council project Teaching English to West Indian Children (1970 and Wight, 1971). This view, however, was not held by 25 per cent of a national sample of teachers (Brittan, 1976a). As a result of research undertaken with 90 children aged seven to nine of West Indian parentage the Schools Council project took the view that many of the difficulties suffered by such children were similar to those of white children in inner-city schools, but there were also distinctive problems relating to dialect and social and cultural adjustment. The project therefore aimed somewhere between the two extremes of leaving dialect alone and forcing received pronunciation. It concentrated on written communication, which it argued should be standard, but one of its four units focused on dialect, aiming to help the West Indian child write Standard English and also having the intention of informing teachers about the West Indian child's dialect difficulties (Wight, 1971). However, the approach was criticized by Edwards (1976) who claimed that it was based on merely one test (the Dialect Interference Test) which involved single word stimuli, isolated sentences and short narrative passages only. It would be more correct to say that a whole battery of tests was administered including the Bristol Social Adjustment Scale, (see section on behaviour, pp.137–8) the English Picture Vocabulary Test (see p.95) and a Concept Learning Test (which was inconclusive, but nevertheless in agreement with findings by Stones, 1975 and Payne, 1969). The materials eventually developed (Schools Council, 1972), in particular *Concept 7–9*, were tested by a national sample of teachers and their classes. They were designed for use with whole classes in multiracial junior schools and comprise three units: listening with understanding, concept building, communication, and a dialect kit which concentrates on features of Standard English which present difficulty to Creole speakers.

A somewhat different view of approaching dialect differences was expressed by Craig (1971) who suggested that for a child who speaks Creole special programmes should begin early in his school life, which is the most favourable period for new language learning since it is before the time when the child becomes sufficiently aware socially of the Standard-speaking community and is still motivated to learn Standard speech. Stoker, (1969) also supported the need for early intervention. On the other hand, Edwards, whose research discovered that pupils of 11–12 who had Creole dialects also suffered comprehension difficulties (1976), was not in favour of special language classes for such children, but recommended structured and integrated teaching in ordinary classrooms, provided teachers could be sensitized to the difficulties of dialect differences. She stressed that some pupils appeared to surmount the difficulties and became completely bidialectal while others, although they read with comparable fluency, manifested difficulties in understanding. Hence, compensatory education in connection with word choice, sentence structure and idiomatic expression was advocated. Trudgill (1979) may also be cited in support of this view as he maintains that even the evidence that Creole interference leads to comprehension difficulties

'. . . does not really argue for the teaching of Standard English in schools. The West Indians who have this type of difficulty have problems not simply with Standard English but with British English as a whole. And, except perhaps in the case of new arrivals who might be favourably disposed to such an exercise there would clearly be resistance to attempts to withdraw some West Indians from classes for special attention. Much more helpful would be a recognition, especially by teachers, that some West Indian children in British schools may be faced with what is best described as a semi-foreign language problem. (It is probably also true to say that the main problem is the belief, widely held by West Indians and British people alike, that native West Indian dialects are "bad" or "broken".).' (pp.16–17).

That there are strong links between attitudes towards a language and attitudes towards speakers of that language has been shown by some modest and tentative research by Edwards (1978).

At the other end of the continuum is the view considered by Bloom (1979) that there might be a case for introducing Patois in the school curriculum. He advances this assertion on the basis of somewhat limited trials using materials produced by the Centre for Urban Educational Studies in their Reading Through Understanding project. This aims to promote concepts of cultural pluralism and identity by teaching ethnic minority groups and other children about their various cultural backgrounds in an attempt to promote understanding. Bloom describes an interesting investigation which he conducted with some Jamaican pupils in the West Indies into their ability to read unfamiliar Patois poems and prose with phonetic and standard spelling. He inferred from the fact that all five read

Standard English more fluently, though they normally spoke Patois, that in view of the even greater differences in children of West Indian origin in this country with respect to dialect, there would be no grounds for expecting the reading of a child of Jamaican origin to improve if he were given material written in Patois – even if Patois was normally used in the child's home. Secondly, he concluded that teachers should not expect pupils of Jamaican origin to read aloud unless they were given adequate time to prepare the material as this might otherwise lower their self-esteem.

Finally, in view of the variety of current practices which leas seem to operate with respect to the education of ethnic minorities, it is worth noting the latest Schools Council project Studies in the Multi-ethnic Curriculum, directed and initiated by Alan Little in 1978. This survey was intended to update the work of Townsend and Brittan in 1970–3 and to determine the extent to which leas and secondary schools had responded in recent years to the need for a multicultural curriculum. Questionnaires were sent to 74 leas (70 responded), 525 schools, and 22 CSE and GCE examining boards. Secondary schools were categorized according to the concentration of ethnic minority pupils: 'high' 148 schools with 10 or more per cent, 'medium' 77 with two and a half to 10 per cent and 'low' 300 schools with fewer than two and half per cent ethnic minority pupils. Schools with high and medium concentrations received questionnaires for the head and 15 separate questionnaires to various heads of departments. The questionnaire to the head of the Development of Language Skills (if such a person exists) is of particular interest since it concentrated on pupils of West Indian origin, requesting information on how many such children receive extra lessons in English, the numbers of staff involved in providing these lessons and what special qualifications or training they have. The questionnaire also asked whether there are special facilities for providing extra English lessons to pupils whose families are of West Indian origin; whether any available materials have been particularly effective and what kind of materials need to be developed. In addition, it inquired if contact had been made with curriculum development projects on English for West Indian pupils and what sort of in-service training was found most useful. Finally, it asked whether any children from ethnic minority groups receive supplementary tuition in English outside the school and whether the head of the Development of Language Skills has any contact with such groups. In the preliminary summary of the main findings available in early 1981 Little and Willey observed that there had been little advance in the last 10 years 'in assessing and meeting the particular educational needs of children of West Indian origin' (p.4). The majority of the resources of leas go towards meeting initial first-phase language needs of pupils for whom English is a second language. The researchers found that a real difference of opinion existed about the extent to which West Indian pupils are considered to have special language needs in view of the fact that most pupils are second- and third-generation children. Special provision for language teaching for West Indian pupils has consistently been a low priority and only a few leas have given it attention. Seventy per cent of the heads in schools with 10 or more per cent West Indian pupils said they did not have special language needs and that in any case they did not have resources within the school to cope. Others saw the use of Patois as a rejection of school or an assertion of identity. Obviously the full results of such a survey when available will be of considerable interest, and will most probably lead to further recommendations for the detailed assessment and clarification of the linguistic needs of pupils of West Indian origin and of guidance for teachers. Consideration of the evidence presented in the present review alone would suggest that the pre-school age and the seven- to nine-year-old age group would be appropriate targets for particular linguistic attention (see Trudgill, 1975, and Essen and Ghodsian, 1979).

Reading
The research which has been undertaken into various aspects of the reading and linguistic abilities of pupils of West Indian origin is varied both in terms of assessment procedures used and size of sample, though, as is to be expected, it concentrates mostly on junior-age pupils. Therefore the review is divided into the following sub-sections: research on reading standards, mainly investigations of larger scale, using group-administered reading tests at national level, or with largish samples in London, Birmingham and educational priority area (EPA) schools; reading abilities which are usually examined by means of individual reading tests, often tests of comprehension or what amount to vocabulary tests; also, a certain amount of work on listening skills, writing and speaking which will be treated to some extent separately as well as under the headings of psycholinguistics and linguistic proficiency. Most of these latter studies have been of smaller scale, undertaken by individual resear-

chers working in their own localities or by leas who are interested in monitoring the attainment of the children in their schools. There surely must be more research undertaken by local education authorities but which is not readily or publicly available. Some further information about English, language and literature, is to be found in Section 9 on examinations (p.111ff).

Some of the caveats about testing (pp.49–59) are in general applicable to tests of reading, especially perhaps those which concern group versus individual testing procedures and the possibly marginal effect of colour of tester, but these factors do not seem to have been discussed at length in relation to reading tests, largely, it is supposed because they are tests of skill rather than of intellectual potential. It is of interest to note in passing at this point that only one study (Yule *et al.*, 1975) seems to have been concerned with the extent to which IQ tests predict reading attainment. Although the numbers in the sub-sample were small, it was found that the correlation between the WISC tests and the Neale Test of Reading Ability were lower for those children born in the West Indies than those born in the UK, but not significantly so. Children of West Indian parents born in the UK were indistinguishable from the indigenous population. Another question which can be asked is, how far is reading attainment indicative of achievement? Unfortunately, as will be seen from the paucity of research studies on achievement of West Indian children the question will have to remain largely rhetorical.

Reading standards

A new article (Mabey, 1981 and an earlier more detailed monograph, 1980) gives an overview and an up-to-date account of the longitudinal testing undertaken for the ILEA Literacy Survey with respect to West Indian attainment. This is a major piece of work with respect to reading attainment of children of West Indian origin because it is concerned with a sizeable cohort of 1,500 black children over a number of years. It tends to supersede all previous accounts of this investigation (Little *et al.*, 1968 and various subsequent interim ILEA reports e.g. ILEA, 1972) since it includes data on the final testing of pupils at 15-plus and compares these with earlier attainment at eight and 10-plus, as well as relating these findings to attainment scores for white children at the same ages. The subject of this investigation was a whole cohort of pupils born between September 1959 and September 1960 who originally numbered over 31,000 when they were tested for reading at eight. They were subsequently also tested on verbal reasoning tests, and received teachers' assessments on English and maths in connection with transfer to secondary schools at 11-plus. Testing on reading also took place at 13 and 15 using the NFER Silent Reading Test (which all the tests of reading standards use in common in this section), and a sentence completion test involving silent reading, but no up-to-date national standardization was available at 13 hence this age group was excluded from comparison. A 10 per cent sample was also tested on individual tests at 11-plus and at eight and 13 teachers completed questionnaires on the social and educational background of the children. It is calculated that 75 per cent of the sample of West Indian children in this cohort started school at five or younger. However, nearly a third of the entire original cohort had left ILEA schools by 1976 and absence accounted for a further loss of nearly a quarter of the pupils in that year. Therefore approximately half of the pupils identified in 1968 at age eight as West Indians (52 per cent) and United Kingdom non-immigrants (49 per cent) had complete test data. It is acknowledged that this might have introduced a source of bias, but all the analyses compare scores of groups who have been tested three times. It is also important to note that the analysis deals with average scores and differences and that 'For both the indigenous and West Indian groups the range in achievement was wide and many of the latter scored more highly than some of the former.' (p.85). Also, in all cases, pupils with test information at three dates scored more highly than those scores given in Little *et al.*, (1968) or Little, (1975). In view of this the findings deserve even closer attention.

The first and most important finding about the reading attainment of West Indians included in this longitudinal survey was that their attainment was very low compared with other groups. Whilst it was low at eight years it also remained low at school-leaving age. The mean reading scores were as follows:

Age in Years	UK	WI
8	98.1	88.1
10	98.3	87.4
15	97.8	85.9
N	12,530	1,465

No group at any stage was reading at a level expected for its age on the basis of a national sample. Moreover it appears that the West

Indian group's score deteriorated over time, and when compared with the indigenous group. It has to be assumed that the two tests used do in fact measure the same thing as a different test was employed at 15 from that used when the children were eight. In order to check this an analysis of covariance technique was used to establish whether there was a significant difference between the reading attainment of the West Indians and the indigenous at school-leaving age after taking account of the initial difference in their attainment when they were eight years old. This was undertaken in two different ways and both analyses gave substantially the same results. Whereas the actual mean standard score of the UK group was 97.8 at 15 their adjusted score then became 97.0 and the actual score of the West Indian group which was 85.9 became 93.3. The tabular data above suggested a 10-point difference overall at eight and a 12-point difference at 15 years, i.e. an implied two-point deterioration. However, the analysis of covariance showed that when full account was taken of the eight-year-olds' reading attainment there remained nearly a four-point difference at 15 years. Thus there was found to be a real deterioration over time in the reading attainment of the pupils of West Indian origin relative to that of their white peers.

Mabey examines the factors which have contributed to low attainment. It was originally thought when the children were first tested at eight that length of stay in this country would be relevant to increased attainment since those who had started school at five had markedly higher attainment than those who had newly arrived. However, it is pointed out that at eight comparisons were being made between white children with three years of education and West Indian children with anything from one month to two years of education, whereas at 15 the comparisons are between 10 years and seven to eight years respectively. The results on reading attainment at 15 therefore show that there is a greater gap than at age eight in attainment between those West Indians with full education in the UK and their white peers (from eight points at eight to 11 points at 15). On the other hand, there appears to be less difference in reading attainment between those West Indians who have a full education in this country and those who have a restricted education, although those with less education here maintain the same gap of around 15 mean points between their reading attainment and that of their indigenous white peers at 15. Moreover, it was found that the West Indian group did not make as great an improvement as any of the other ethnic minority groups involved in the investigation over this period of time.

It is of interest to note at this point just what claims were made at the end of the 1960s about the likely effect of length of schooling on attainment. These can be shown by inspecting data on transfer placements at 11-plus, part of the same longitudinal ILEA survey, as reported by Little *et al.* (1968) and Little (1975). Since this discussion is concerned with reading, attention will be given here to transfer placements in English and discussion with respect to verbal reasoning and maths will be found elsewhere (p.62 and pp.104–5). Little *et al.* (1968) relate that whereas half of all the ILEA's pupils were below average performance at 11-plus, 79 per cent of the immigrant pupils, who included 56 per cent West Indians, were placed in the lowest three groups for English. Little (1975) shows that in English only five per cent of the 590 West Indian pupils were placed in the top two groups for English, whereas 58 per cent were in the bottom two groups. Compared with other immigrant groups the low attainment of the West Indian children in school placings was noticeable. However, from the analysis which was carried out in 1968 it was noted that although those pupils who had started school earlier had a much higher performance, the immigrant groups still did not match the attainment of the indigenous groups. It was noticeable that even with full primary education in the UK the 101 children of West Indian origin compared with 108 other immigrant pupils were attaining less well in English, although they had kept up in verbal reasoning and mathematics. Nevertheless, the authors stated in conclusion that

'the evidence on completed primary schooling and immigrant performance is not clear cut, and it would be unwise to conclude that even with full English primary education the performances of immigrant pupils is the same as non-immigrants in these schools. Statistical tests suggest that the differences are not wide enough to be statistically significant, but it would be safe to conclude only that the distribution of scores fits closer to that of non-immigrants the longer the length of education in the UK' (Little *et al.*, 1968, p.452).

Somehow, even this negatively worded and cautious statement was taken in the general literature to imply that length of stay or length of schooling would determine performance (especially as it was supported by a parallel study on Asians (Ashby *et al.*, 1970)). However, as Little (1975), treating the same transfer placements from a different angle, restated it: 'Although the distributions of West Indians with a full education in the United Kingdom were better than the distributions of new arrivals, they were still far from the indigenous.' (p.124). Whereas nine per cent of pupils of West Indian origin were placed in the upper quartile for transfer to secondary schools, 20 per cent of Asians with full education were in the upper quartile, only five per cent less than the indigenous. It seems likely, in the writer's view, that the statements made as a result of the ILEA research, which was the most significant large-scale investigation undertaken by the early 70s, when concern about the performance of pupils from ethnic minority groups was beginning to be expressed, were misleadingly seen as *equally* applicable to all immigrant groups. Not until now when comparisons are available for a whole cohort of this size for a complete period of schooling has the under-performance of pupils of West Indian origin with respect to reading, in comparison both with other ethnic minority and indigenous white pupils, who are themselves under-achieving in relation to national norms, become quite apparent.

Two other surveys (B and C) reported by Little (1975) analysed the 1968 ILEA Literacy Survey results with a view to examining the influence of the ethnic mix of the school (percentage of immigrants on role) and index of multiple deprivation. Survey B, examining the social and ethnic mix of the school, used data on reading attainment from the survey of 32,000 pupils aged eight. Overall the children had a reading age roughly six months behind their chronological age and immigrants, of whom West Indians comprised 56 per cent, were about one year below. There was found to be a fall in attainment in schools with greater than 60 per cent immigrant populations, but, as attainment was variable at the mid-points, this finding was taken as suggesting that it was at the extremes of immigrant concentration that the performance of the indigenous population was affected. Parental occupation seemed to be more relevant to attainment than the percentage of immigrants in the school. A similar result was found for the West Indians who tended to be in schools of high immigrant concentration; their performance was only affected when the schools contained over 60 per cent immigrants. The effect of immigrant concentration on educational performance, it was concluded, was less important than the social class of the child and the degree to which schools were experiencing multiple deprivation.

Accordingly, a comparison of the school performance of immigrants on several measures was made between the eight-year-olds in the ILEA survey and a group of 3,000 children from an educational priority area (EPA) in central London. Here comparisons will be made with reading abilities, see pp.95–6 and pp.97–8 for evidence on English Picture Vocabulary Test (EPVT) and Illinois Test of Psycholinguistic Abilities (ITPA) data. This ILEA study (C; Little 1975) confirmed the results of a previous investigation (Payne, 1974) that West Indian children's reading attainment was lower than that of under-privileged white indigenous children in EPA projects. Whereas the mean score of the white indigenous children on the SRA test was 93.4, that of the West Indian pupils was 89.4. This showed that not only was an eight-year-old black child's reading attainment significantly lower than that of his white peer on a national scale, but it was also lower than that of his white peer in a school in an EPA. It is interesting to note here how this finding confirms those of Payne (1974) who reports on the reading and other attainments of various ethnic groups of children in four areas in England and one in Scotland where EPA action research projects were implemented. In two of the areas, Deptford in London and Birmingham, the attainment in reading of West Indian pupils was found to be significantly lower than that of the non-immigrant groups. A quarter of West Indian children in the London project areas and two-fifths in Birmingham were classed as non-readers. In London 878 non-immigrants aged eight to 10 had a mean reading score on SRA of 93.0, whereas 161 West Indian pupils of similar age group had a mean reading score of 88.1. In Birmingham the scores were even lower, 360 non-immigrants having a mean score of 86.4 and 107 West Indians with a score of 83.5. It was noted moreover, that in each area the test scores of all children in the five- and seven-year-old groups increased, but dropped between the ages of seven and 10, with the scores of the West Indian pupils falling off earlier than that of their non-immigrant classmates and continuing to decline much longer. Larger family sizes, use of Creole and 'school processes' were suggested explanations for lower scores.

In addition, an intensive study of 10–11-year-old children in one London borough (Yule *et al.*, 1975) which used the same NFER/SRA reading test for group testing confirmed the same pattern of attainment as the studies by Payne and Little. Two thousand, two hundred and eighty-one children in the borough, of whom 354 were of West Indian origin, were tested. The scores were as follows: 1,660 white children attained a mean of 94.81 whereas 200 children of West Indian origin born in the UK attained 88.68, as compared with 81.93 for 135 children born in the West Indies. Thus the mean scores of the pupils of West Indian origin was significantly below that of indigenous white children, which was, in turn, below the national norm. It was noted that girls tended to score slightly above boys on the reading test and the difference between the pupils of West Indian origin who were born here and those born in the West Indies was slightly significant.

To return to the ILEA data and the comparisons reported by Mabey (1980; 1981) yet another indication, in even greater detail, can be seen of the multiple disadvantages which children of West Indian origin experience in relation to reading attainment. In addition to being in schools with high proportions of immigrants, often in educational priority areas, and having undergone variable amounts of schooling, as has been shown by the studies reviewed above, it is also well known that children of West Indian origin share other social disadvantages (see. pp. 2–45)–all factors which can be objectively measured. Analyses were therefore carried out by Mabey on the actual reading scores of West Indian pupils to take account of such factors as parental occupation, family size, parent-school contact, free meals, length of education and priority of school attended. The results were as follows:

Ethnic Group	N	Actual Score	Adjusted Score
UK	9,914	98.6	98.1
WI	1,009	88.7	93.8

For these groups of pupils who were tested three times overall ethnic differences amounted to roughly 10 points in actual scores and when adjusted to take account of social background factors there was still a difference of just over four points. Mabey suggested in conclusion that the lower attainment of West Indians cannot be entirely 'explained' by differences in home and school experience since they only account for just over half of the difference between the scores of the two ethnic groups. Whilst it is possible that a more precise measure of social disadvantage might 'explain' more of the difference, it is likely, in the writer's view, that a more complete 'explanation' can only be attempted by a consideration of the social psychological factors appertaining to home and school, as described and discussed in Part 3, pp.142–209.

Finally, however, in this section on reading standards a further and again recently reported piece of research is worth taking into account. Like the ILEA Literacy Survey, this study by Essen and Ghodsian (1979) reported data from a longitudinal investigation, but on a nationally representative sample. These data were derived from information obtained during the National Child Development Study which studied children born in one week in March in 1958 (one year older than the children in the ILEA survey) at birth, seven, 11 and 16. Although the sample was national and random it unfortunately contained relatively small numbers of children of West Indian origin. However, it has the advantages that it distinguished between first- and second-generation children and it also used a more sensitive measure of social disadvantage than that in the ILEA study. As schools were asked to supply data on children born in 1958, children who were born abroad who subsequently entered British schools were also included in the study; this resulted in a new definition of 'immigrant' which was used in the later years of the study and in connection with the data on attainment in reading at 16 which are reported here. A first-generation immigrant was defined as 'a child born abroad with at least one parent born abroad' and a second-generation immigrant as 'a child born in Britain with at least one parent born abroad' (Essen and Ghodsian, 1979, p.424). Although all the first-generation ethnic minority groups had lower scores on the NFER Reading Test, only the West Indians among the second-generation groups had clearly lower scores than indigenous pupils. Unfortunately, it is not possible to compare these scores directly with the other studies reviewed in this section since they are not given as actual mean scores but as transformed scores with a mean of zero and a standard deviation of one. For 41 first-generation West Indian pupils the mean transformed score on the NFER Reading Test was −1.06 and for 58 second-generation West Indian pupils the score was −0.63, which shows that some progress had been made, though they were still behind the performance of the white indigenous group which was 0.06. Since the home circumstances of the different immigrant groups have been shown to differ considerably, both from each other and those of the indigenous pupils (see, e.g. Ghodsian *et al.*, 1980), an adjustment was made by using an analysis of variance to allow for sex, region of the country, family size, social class, receipt of free school meals, crowding ratio, use of amenities in the home, tenure of the home and language spoken at home. As a result of this the differences between the transformed mean test scores of the first-generation (−0.75) and second-generation West Indians (−0.34) and the white indigenous pupils (0.14) were considerably reduced – in fact by 20 and 40 per cent. Yet even when these allowances for home circumstances were made the West Indian pupils clearly performed less well than the white indigenous children. When comparisons with length of time in this country and test scores were made the only clear trend was for the West Indians' reading test scores to be lower the shorter the time they had been in Britain. This evidence lends some support for previous reports (Little *et al.*, 1968) which indicated the importance of familiarity with Britain for children's school performance, but, as the ILEA longitudinal data as a whole show, there may not in fact be a real increase in reading attainment with age (Mabey, 1980, 1981).

Reading ability
The following studies all employed individually administered reading tests, which are generally considered to give a more precise measure of a child's reading ability. They may also be seen as supplementing by more detailed and in-depth observations the information acquired by the investigations drawing on larger populations or wider ranging samples.

One particularly thorough and detailed study (Bagley *et al.*, 1978) which related school attainment, as measured by Schonell's Silent Reading Test, and pupils' and parents' attitudes to home and school, found that reading ability correlated negatively on a principle components analysis with parental authoritarianism, shared housing facilities, lack of home ownership, schooling and qualifications of father and mother, and use of Creole at home. These findings were also confirmed by a cluster analysis which revealed three clusters with distinct characteristics. The second of these, for example, defined a high-achieving group of children whose parents were highly critical of English culture and institutions. The material circumstances of the homes were good and the child had a positive image of himself and had good expectations of his school performance, which were confirmed by teachers.

Secondly, under the heading of individual tests of reading ability, comes a group of studies which used the Neale Analysis of Reading Ability. In 1970 Yule *et al.* (1975) used this individual test in the second stage of their investigation into attainment of West Indian pupils in one London borough. A random sample of 105 indigenous white and 100 West Indian children aged 11–12, were involved. The West Indian sample as a whole were shown to be two years below their chronological age and just over one year below the white indigenous control group who were themselves reading well below the level for their age. These differences were highly significant statistically, both for the accuracy component of the test (indigenous total 115.4, West Indian total 102.9) and for the comprehension component (indigenous 114.9, West Indian 99.6). It is interesting to note that, whereas the indigenous white boys scored higher on both accuracy and comprehension, it was the West Indian girls who scored higher on both these components. Also it was found that the children of West Indian origin born in this country attained significantly higher scores on the two reading scales than those who had been born in the West Indies and received some schooling in the UK. Three other researches also indirectly bear out two findings of this study. Pollak (1979), investigating the reading ability of children of West Indian origin in a London borough adjacent to that where the study of Yule *et al.* was undertaken, found that as measured by the Durrell Analysis of Reading Difficulties these West Indian children were reading less well than the indigenous children. Moreover, McEwen *et al.* (1975) discovered when surveying the language proficiency of a representative national sample of second- and fourth-year junior children that 10-year-old West Indian girls were significantly better than boys at reading. Furthermore Bagley and Verma (1980) in an unpublished paper have reported that West Indian girls have been found to perform slightly better on the Brimer Wide Span Reading Test than West Indian boys, although both groups performed below the level of white pupils. The research was undertaken in 39 urban secondary schools in which 29 West Indian boys attained a score of 15.5, 35 West Indian girls 16.6, 416 white boys 18.3 and 388 white girls 21.4.

   Three other small-scale studies are also worthy of note. Edwards (1976) assessed the reading comprehension test scores of two groups of 40 English and 40 West Indian pupils, who were matched for age, sex, social class and ability. These 11- and 12-year-olds came from three schools with a high proportion of West Indians on the school roll. Each of the two groups was further divided on the basis of the reading ages of the children into three sub-groups for slow, average and good readers. Although there were no significant differences between the reading age and the comprehension age of the slow-learning groups, which, the researcher suggested, indicated that test variables were not operating, it was found that for average and good readers the mean comprehension scores of West Indian pupils were significantly lower than those of English children. The scores also indicated to some extent that there might be quite a difference at about age 12 in West Indian children's reading, for whereas there are some whose comprehension remains low even though they have mastered the mechanical skills of reading, others are completely bidialectal. The author also argues, by the use of detailed illustrations, that dialect interference would probably be a major factor in the low performance of West Indian pupils.

Smolins (1975) used the Neale Analysis of Reading Ability to assess the comprehension skills of two groups of children aged eight to nine, 164 of whom were English and 20 West Indian. The important feature of this assessment was that, as with the study by Edwards, the children were divided into three sub-groups of good, average and poor readers, and each sub-group was given the test in three different ways: pupils reading the passages aloud and answering questions presented by the tester orally; pupils reading the passages and questions silently and telling the tester the answers; and the tester reading the passages and the questions aloud and the pupils answering orally. Apart from the good readers taking the test in the first way there were no significant differences between the test scores of the West Indian and English children.

With respect to both of the foregoing studies it is worth comparing an investigation undertaken by Phillips (1977) involving mixed ethnic minority group children, of whom 39 were West Indian, and also 43 native white children aged seven to eight, in three Manchester schools. Although these children were of rather low ability, the West Indian children performed rather better than the native children on listening and reading tests which involved comprehension skills. This suggests a certain competence in oral understanding, which would be in line with the oral tradition of West Indian culture. Phillips noted that the listening and reading tests, which were in fact taken from the NFER Language Proficiency Tests, were very much 'comprehension' tests of increasing difficulty and involved the same kind of English syntax as that used in the Neale tests. Like those of Edwards, the children in her sample were also matched for reading ability. She suggested that the results indicated that, in view of the somewhat better performance of the West Indian children, interference by dialect did not appear to be affecting comprehension with this age group. A similar pattern was found using the same tests of linguistic proficiency of listening and reading with 21 West Indian pupils compared with 23 Asian pupils aged eight and 10 (Weir, 1980). The Dialect Interference Test devised by the Schools Council Teaching English to West Indian Children project (Schools Council, 1970) also discovered in relation to 90 eight- to nine-year-olds in eight schools in the West Midlands that, though the West Indian group scored lower than the English children in all four sections the greatest gap in performance was due to phonology, especially for those children who were newly arrived from the West Indies. The research studies would therefore seem to indicate that dialect interference, as Edwards has maintained, may manifest itself to a greater extent only in the later years, at about 12.

Two lea studies which are publicly available may also be mentioned here. Perhaps the best known is the investigation undertaken in Redbridge (BPPA, 1978) into attainment in English by the pupils in the borough in their last year of junior school. In this area it was found that the scores for the 66 West Indian children were 10 points below the scores for the 563 white indigenous children (88.6 as compared with 98.7). The same ratio of discrepancy has also been noted in Dudley lea (Williams, 1978) both for seven- to eight-year-olds, of whom 48 West Indian children attained a mean score of 94.04, compared with 103.03 for all the children in the borough, and for 11-year-olds, when, on using the NFER AD Test, it was found that 51 West Indian pupils in five schools had a mean score of 89.05, compared with 312 white indigenous children in the same schools who obtained a mean score of 98.9. The same ratio was noted in the scores of the children aged 10 in the ILEA Literacy Survey, where the West Indian pupils obtained 87.4 and the white indigenous pupils 98.3 (Mabey, 1981).

Listening

A number of researches of large scale have made use, as a secondary measure, of another test, the English Picture Vocabulary Test (EPVT), which is a test of listening vocabulary and verbal ability which is 'functionally independent of reading skill'. The evidence from these tests can therefore be regarded as complementing those findings on both the Neale Analysis of Reading Ability and on reading standards. There are two levels to the EPVT test: Level 1 for infant pupils aged five to seven and Level 2 for junior pupils aged eight to 11. However, reservations about the use of this test to estimate children's true attainment have been expressed (Hegarty and Lucas, 1978).

One investigation which employed this measure was the Schools Council project Teaching English to West Indian Children (Schools Council, 1970) which tested 90 children aged eight to nine who were drawn from eight schools in the West Midlands, 40 per cent of which had populations of over 25 per cent West Indian pupils. It was found that 11 of the 40 test items indicated a difference in performance between the West Indian group, and the English group, but neither of the groups could achieve more than 29 of the items. There were very few differences in performance between those West Indians who were newly arrived in this country and those who were born here and the English group—certainly no significant differences.

By contrast, it may be noted that McEwen *et al.* (1975) in a national survey of second- and fourth-year junior school children in multiracial schools, but using their own specially devised tests of linguistic proficiency, found that the performance of the West Indian children at 10 years old was significantly lower than that of English children on listening (0.1 per cent). However, on tests of listening to 'words' at eight the West Indian group were better than their English peers. The researchers noted that this finding appeared to be linked with length of education in this country as most of the eight-year-old sample of West Indians had all their education in Britain whereas many of the 10-year-olds had only received part of their education here.

The EPVT was also one of the measures used in the large-scale action research projects in five EPAs. Sufficient immigrant children were included in the EPAs in London and Birmingham for test scores to be examined separately but unfortunately not for differences between boys and girls to be noted (Payne, 1974). On the EPVT Level 1 for the five- to six-year-olds 957 non-immigrants in 12 London primary schools obtained a mean score of 97.9 compared with their 298 West Indian peers who attained 86.9 with twice as many West Indian children in the three bottom categories as in the overall national sample. At the same age, however, their peers in six Birmingham schools were performing less well: 342 non-immigrant children attaining a mean score of 89.5 and 96 West Indian pupils 81.6. It was noticeable that in each area the scores had dropped off by the age of seven to 10 when Level II of the EPVT was administered. In London the 1,162 non-immigrants attained a mean score of 92.9 as compared with 84.5 by their 250 West Indian peers. Again, in Birmingham the mean scores were proportionately lower: 86.4 for the 785 non-immigrants and 80.1 for the 209 West Indians. As has already been seen (p.88) the EPVT scores from the London EPA were used in Survey C by Little (1975) to make comparisons with the performance of the children in the ILEA survey and thereby to confirm that reading attainment of West Indian children was not only lower than that of their socially disadvantaged white classmates, but significantly lower than that of their national age peers.

The findings of Payne in Birmingham may be directly compared with other results for Birmingham reported by Phillips (1979) whose data relate to 1969. In the latter research the EPVT Level 1 was administered to a group of 2,400 children, with an average age of seven years three months, comprising an approximately equal number of boys and girls. The mean score for the whole group was found to be 93.5, well below the national norm. The author presents detailed analyses with respect to characteristics of schools in different areas of Birmingham, which as a whole had an exceptionally large concentration of non-white immigrant children, and also with respect to characteristics of children and their families. Comparisons between the West Indian group and the white indigenous group on the EPVT showed even more substantial differences than on tests of reading for which age categorizations were also given. Whereas 1,082 indigenous boys attained a mean score of 97.4, 63 West Indian boys attained only 76.6. Although the difference between the girls' mean scores was a little less it was nevertheless still marked: 1,030 indigenous girls attained 96.2 compared with 76 West Indian girls who attained 79.4. It seems that boys normally score higher than girls on this test. An analysis by family size showed that mean scores declined significantly with increasing family size. Yet although children of West Indian origin tend to come from larger families, in this case family size appeared not to have the same relationship with school attainment as a whole for the immigrant groups as for the non-immigrant groups. When a further analysis was undertaken matching 105 West Indian children with 105 indigenous children for sex, geographical area of Birmingham, number of children in family, position in family, number of terms in present school, type of school, and age the West Indian pupils were shown to have significantly lower mean vocabulary scores on the EPVT (p <.001), the West Indian group attaining 81.4 compared with the mean score of 97.6 for the matched indigenous group. Thus whilst results in London indicated cause for concern it would seem that those in Birmingham, being substantially lower, would suggest an even greater need for attention to be given to reading performance.

Two other studies which used another measure which has close association with listening might also be mentioned here. One of these was again Survey C reported by Little (1975) in the EPA where one of the measures was the Illinois Test of Psycholinguistic Abilities (ITPA), administered individually to a sample of classes with seven- to eight-year-old pupils in some of the schools. The test was used to draw a psycholinguistic profile of the language skills of EPA children. Two reservations must be noted about this study: first that only a relatively small number of West Indian pupils was involved: 101 non-immigrants, 27 West Indians and six other immigrants; secondly, that American norms were used with the test. The results showed that the West Indian sub-group of children had a psycholinguistic profile which differed from that of non-immigrant EPA children when hearing was involved. Five of the 10 sub-tests concentrate on auditory skills and on four of these – auditory reception, auditory association, verbal expression and particularly grammatical closure – the West Indian children had significantly different and lower scores from their non-immigrant EPA peers. These findings are very much confirmed by another study by Barnes (1975) using the same ITPA test in London with 205 non-immigrants, 30 West Indians and 12 other immigrant children, aged eight-plus. Again it was found that the West Indian children were significantly lower on auditory reception, auditory association, expression, grammatic closure and visual closure. Little (1975) commented on the results of the ITPA tests in the London EPA that they suggest that West Indian children are deficient in areas where language must be used as a directive tool, but when visual-motor skills are involved their performance may not differ greatly from that of their non-immigrant peers. It would seem therefore, if detailed attention could be given to comparing the kinds of abilities measured by the ITPA, EPVT and Neale Analysis of Reading Abilities, that some soundly based ideas of how to approach compensatory reading programmes for West Indian children might be devised.

Vocabulary

Although a number of the studies reviewed under the heading of listening and, indeed, reading, involved word recognition, a few generally small-scale studies using individually administered tests are worth recording here in connection with vocabulary.

One initial exception to this, however, is the investigation already described (p.96) undertaken by Phillips in 1969 (Phillips, 1979) in Birmingham which used the Southgate Group Reading Test which the author claims is 'more a test of word recognition than reading'. For this reason it is included in this section, though the findings are probably more comparable with those larger scale studies reviewed in the section on reading standards. Two thousand four hundred children aged about seven were tested and were found to have a mean reading age about two months lower than their chronological age, with girls performing better than boys (p < .01). As previous studies (for example Little 1975; McEwen *et al.*, 1975) have suggested, mean reading ages for the indigenous sample were not adversely affected by a high proportion of immigrants on school rolls. The indigenous boys scored 84.3, compared with a score of 78.4 for the West Indian boys; the indigenous girls attaining 86.9 compared with 82.7 by the West Indian girls. The West Indian groups were about six months below their expected reading age. When a sub-sample of 105 West Indians were closely matched for a number of social variables with the same number of indigenous pupils the difference on reading scores was considerably diminished, West Indians attaining a mean of 92.3, the indigenous 94.3, which was not a significant difference. It is to be noted, however, as the author points out, that this test may be of limited value with this age group as a 'ceiling factor', which would fail to discriminate efficiently among the upper quartile of the distribution of reading attainments, might have been in operation.

Turning to a consideration of individually administered vocabulary tests, three studies may be noted. First that of Payne (1969) who administered the Crichton Vocabulary Scale and the Burt (rearranged) Word Reading Test to three groups of children, 99 West Indian immigrant children, 100 randomly selected British children, and 99 British children, individually matched with West Indian children according to verbal ability. All the groups were, in addition, matched for levels of socio-economic status and were aged seven to eight years. Although figures are not supplied, the author claims that there were significant differences between the two racial groups on both of these tests. Interestingly, however, there were no significant differences between the sexes within either racial group on the Crichton Vocabulary Scale, although on the Burt Word Reading Test the British and West Indian girls both performed significantly better than their male counterparts ($p > .05$).

Two other studies used the Schonell Graded Reading Test. McFie and Thompson (1970) administered the test to 61 children of West Indian parents attending a child guidance in London. The West Indian children attained a score of 77 compared with 82 for their matched English controls which were similar to results found for other maladjusted children (Rutter *et al.*, 1967 and Vernon, 1969). Another study (Bagley, 1971) which used Schonell's Graded Reading Vocabulary Test as part of a battery of tests administered to 50 West Indian children carefully matched for age, sex and father's occupational class, found that their reading age was significantly behind their mental age and to a greater extent than that for their white peers ($p < .001$). The author therefore deduced that black children were under-functioning when their mental age was compared with their attainment on this measure which was administered in normal classroom situations by the children's teachers.

Language proficiency tests

From time to time in this review reference has been made to a major study which investigated linguistic proficiency and devised tests of listening, reading, speaking and writing to be used as aids for teachers in diagnosing individuals requiring special linguistic attention, and also as a means of monitoring progress in learning English (McEwen *et al.*, 1975). The tests are very similar to typical classroom tasks and they were validated by reference to teachers' gradings of pupils' proficiency. Using these tests the researchers surveyed the level of attainment of a representative national sample of second- and fourth-year junior school children in 127 multiracial schools with an average of 29.5 per cent immigrants on the school rolls. The actual number of children involved were 1,510 indigenous eight-year-olds and 285 West Indian children and 1,562 10-year-olds and 363 West Indian children. All these children were given tests of reading, writing and listening and a sub-sample were given a speaking test. The influence of 10 different factors, most importantly age, sex and length of residence in the UK, were examined in relation to the levels of attainment on these measures. The main findings in relation to the performance of West Indian pupils were as follows: at age 10 the West Indian children were significantly better than the eight-year-olds, as might be expected, in all skill areas except speaking, though in these three areas they were performing at a significantly lower level than the English children (0.1 per cent). West Indian girls performed significantly better than boys in writing, particularly at age 10, and at the same age they were also better than boys at reading (at five per cent level of significance). On the speaking measure fewer differences in general were found between the ethnic groups, though the 187 English 10-year-olds were significantly better (0.5 per cent) than the 58 West Indian 10-year-olds, many of whom had only had part of their education here.

More recently two small-scale local replications using these tests of language proficiency have been undertaken and reported by Phillips (1977) and Weir (1980). Phillips administered the tests to 43 white indigenous children and 39 West Indian children, among other ethnic minority groups, in their first year of junior schooling in four Manchester schools. As the numbers of those tested varied progressively with the use of the tests and the results are presented in a broad form it is not possible to make a detailed comparison between this study and that of McEwen *et al.* The author, moreover, notes that the findings have to be regarded extremely tentatively, but there did seem to be few differences between the white indigenous and the West Indian groups. As with the original study however, theoretical difficulties with the speaking and listening tests were also noted. In this connection it is also of interest that the correlations between the teachers' ratings and the test scores were much higher for reading and writing than for speaking and listening. Phillips's comments with respect to tests of listening and reading which resembled the comprehension tests of the Neale Analysis of Reading Ability have already been noted (pp.93–4).

The second study to replicate the work of McEwen *et al.* is that of Weir (1980), again involving rather small numbers, this time 21 West Indian pupils being compared with 23 Asians in the second and fourth years of one junior school in an area populated by several ethnic minority groups. In general the results correlated highly with those in the NFER survey. In listening, reading and writing the West Indians failed to increase their performance markedly by the age of 10, although they were initially better than Asians on writing. They also appeared to be superior on reading and to a lesser extent on listening but the researcher argues that the very unrepresentative sample in the English group accounted for its low performance. Whilst it is commendable that smaller scale replication studies are being undertaken, it is necessary to regard their results with caution.

Overall conclusion
The picture with respect to language and reading attainment and abilities which has been presented is of considerable complexity. A few brief concluding remarks will be made here, but the issues are also considered in relation to achievement in general in the Overview (pp. 227–9). Obviously language is of crucial importance in relation to achievement, but there is no simple explanation of the way in which it is affecting achievement. It appears to be the case that Creole dialects have an influence on linguistic proficiency, even for those children of West Indian origin who are born in this country. A number of studies have also suggested that Creole may be a factor in handicapping achievement in school. It is clear, moreover, that it is very much linked with cultural background, and more particularly with individual identity and self-esteem. Though relatively little is known about its exact function in this respect, nor the extent to which West Indian parents encourage or discourage Creole, it is evident that for those pupils of West Indian origin who are semi-lingual in Standard English their knowledge of Creole could either become a significant asset or a considerable disadvantage. Nevertheless, studies of reading attainment and ability bear witness to the fact that it is use of Standard English which is being measured and which counts towards achievement in schools. Moreover, parental involvement in reading practice can be particularly effective for West Indian pupils. One project by the Thomas Coram Institute has shown (Tizard *et al.*, 1980) how the systematic

co-operation of West Indian parents with their child's teacher in a structured programme of hearing their child read at home, even when they lack full linguistic competence themselves, can lead to significant improvements in reading (see p.238).

The research on reading has shown that a number of factors—proportion of immigrant children in schools, length of schooling, sex differences, and social background—are relevant here. Their interaction, however, is extremely complex and evidence is more clear in relation to some factors than others. For example, it seems reasonably apparent that the number of immigrants on the school roll, except perhaps at the higher and lower extremes, does not influence reading attainment, either for the pupils of West Indian origin, or the indigenous pupils. However, the evidence on length of schooling is not so well defined. Although those pupils of West Indian origin who have been born here do seem to read more proficiently than those who have arrived in this country at some point during their school lifetime, this observation may well be of much less educational significance now that by far the majority of pupils of West Indian origin are in fact second-generation immigrants. What is of far greater importance is that, as one study (Mabey, 1981) appears to demonstrate, reading attainment relative to age may diminish with length of schooling, so that at 15 performance may well be less than at eight. A number of investigations taken together seem to point to the years of seven to nine, as well as the immediately pre-school years, as being vital in establishing a level of ability in linguistic skills if any improvement is to be made in subsequent years. For reasons which are not very clear, but may well be related to social and historical circumstances of the pupils of West Indian origin, as well as the known tendency for girls to perform better in general on verbal tests at an earlier age, it does appear to be the case that West Indian girls often have higher levels of attainment in reading and other measures of linguistic ability than do boys.

Finally, socio-economic factors, which are a popular explanation for relatively low achievement of pupils of West Indian origin, have been shown to be complex in their influence on attainment. Although they go some way to explaining some of the difference in reading performance, they by no means explain it all, since those pupils with whom they are being compared and with whom they share their education often come from similarly socially disadvantaged backgrounds, and yet the performance of West Indian pupils is still at a lower level. Undoubtedly more precise measures of social background would enable firmer conclusions to be reached and particular sources of influence to be detected, yet such investigations would need to be extraordinarily complex, lengthy and detailed and there would have to be both in-depth studies and investigations involving large samples before any generalizations could be made. It may well be the case that socio-economic factors do not operate in quite the same way with respect to pupils of West Indian origin as they do with respect to white indigenous children, or that they may operate in different ways in different geographical locations. But, it has always to be remembered, that the performance of pupils of West Indian origin must inevitably be more or less influenced by one distinguishing factor, that of colour, which is obviously related in the most complex way to social history and cultural conditions, which to some extent are still being carried over into the social lifestyles, linguistic, and hence educational experiences of those children who have been born in this country.

Section 7: Mathematics

Compared with the variety of information available on the attainment and ability of children of West Indian origin on measures of reading there is a paucity of similar information on mathematics. Occasionally mathematical data are cited incidentally since they relate to or support the main measures used in an investigation, as for example in developmental work by Hegarty and Lucas (1978) in which the Young Group Mathematics Test was employed as a validity criterion for the Learning Ability Tests. In other cases, the measures of mathematics which are used are not stated specifically. However, some further information with respect to mathematics is given in the sections on school placement (pp. 106–11) and examinations (pp. 111–22).

Two studies of very small scale which give incidental information on early performance in mathematics are those by Ward (1978) and Phillips (1977). The former reports a systematic observation study which was undertaken for a whole year in connection with 22 immigrant subjects and an equal number of paired controls in Hertfordshire, Buckinghamshire, Brent and the ILEA, and which supplies information on social interaction and adjustment. During the study the Schonell Diagnostic Arithmetic Test was administered to all the subjects, but no significant differences in attainment were recorded between the immigrant group and the English children even with respect to those arriving from overseas and those born in the UK. It is interesting that the researcher remarked that work in mathematics appeared both as a welcome relief to language learning and as a reinforcement of self-confidence for the immigrant children, and hence performance in mathematics made a significant contribution to overall adjustment. The other study (Phillips, 1977), which was primarily an investigation into the linguistic proficiency of first-year junior school children in four schools in Manchester, also provides incidental information on performance in mathematics on the NFER Maths Attainment A test. This appears to show that for 78 pupils of West Indian origin their mean score of 88.61 meant that they were performing slightly better than their 86 white peers who obtained a mean score of 87.68. However, it will be noted that these scores are low when compared with a national norm and the author does point to the low ability of both the West Indian and white groups in general. On the whole because of certain features of both these studies little weight can be placed on the information given on performance in mathematics.

Possibly a little more representative are the scores cited for performance in mathematics of all the pupils in the fourth years of eight multiracial junior schools in Redbridge (BPPA, 1978). In this case the the score of 86.1 for the 64 children of West Indian origin was some 13 points below the score for the 563 white indigenous children who attained 99.6.

More detailed data are available from the ILEA transfer study (Little *et al.*, 1968) when teachers' assessments for attainment in mathematics were utilized. Information on performance in mathematics was available for 1,051 immigrants transferring to secondary education in 1966 from 52 schools in the ILEA where more than one-third of the school roll was immigrant. Seventy-nine per cent of the immigrant group were placed in the bottom three profile groups in mathematics. Moreover, 85 per cent of the 590 pupils of West Indian origin, who constituted 56 per cent of the immigrant sample, were placed in the lowest three groups in mathematics so that the performance of the West Indians was the lowest for all ethnic minority groups. On examination of the data to determine whether length of stay in this country influenced performance in mathematics it was found that there were 219 immigrants with complete primary education in the United Kingdom, 101 of whom were children of West Indian origin and only 11 per cent of them compared with 15 per cent of other immigrants were placed in the top two groups for mathematics, whereas 46 per cent compared with 35 per cent of the other immigrants were placed in the two lowest groups. This generally low performance was also confirmed by some other data on attainment in mathematics reported by Little (1975) in connection with a study of pupils in an EPA who were tested on the Bristol Achievement Tests which evaluate pupil performance in English, mathematics and study skills. Whereas 202 non-immigrant children attained a score of 96.9 for mathematics, the score for the 54 pupils of West Indian origin was 91.0. Once again the data showed that pupils of West Indian origin were performing at a level not only lower than their indigenous peers, but much below their age peers in the country as a whole.

Finally, some research by Essen and Ghodsian (1979) as part of the National Child Development Study reports on the attainment in mathematics of the cohort children aged 16 in 1974. Although the numbers of children of West Indian origin involved in the comparison are relatively small, it is interesting to compare these findings in the light of suggestions about length of stay made in earlier studies. On the NFER mathematics test both the first- and second-generation groups of West Indian children were found to have lower scores than white indigenous children. (The scores were transformed to give a mean of zero and a standard deviation of one.) Although the mean scores for the second generation were noticeably higher (-0.59 for 58 children as compared with -0.90 for 41 first-generation children) they were still much lower than those of the indigenous children (7,185 with a mean score of 0.05). When an analysis of variance was undertaken to match the West Indian pupils with their white peers on home background variables it was found that the differences were considerably reduced (-0.61 for the first-generation, -0.32 for the second-generation West Indians and 0.13 for the white indigenous children). However, the attainment on mathematics of the pupils of West Indian origin was still relatively low. An interesting feature of the mathematics attainment scores in particular was that there appeared to be an unexpected dip in the scores of those who arrived in this country during their junior school years. When attainment on mathematics was considered with respect to length of stay, no clear trend emerged between first- and second-generation groups, so that it was not possible, as with attainment on reading, to state that increased length of schooling would mean increased scores on mathematics tests. However, in view of the small numbers involved in this study and the apparent lack of information on performance in mathematics of pupils of West Indian origin at seven and 11, when monitoring was also undertaken by the NCDS, it is not possible to state categorically that mathematics performance will not increase with length of schooling.

In conclusion, once again it appears that pupils of West Indian origin are performing relatively poorly in comparison with their white school peers and to an even worse extent compared with their age peers at a national level. However, in the absence of more specific and longitudinal data, especially for secondary pupils, these conclusions must remain highly tentative.

Section 8: School Placement

In this section available information on assessment within schools on selection procedures for transfer at 11-plus, streaming and setting will be reviewed in order to see how this complements data on attainment tests in reading and maths and IQ ability tests. Although some of the following figures will be out of date in view of recent trends towards comprehensivization and mixed-ability group teaching, it may be enlightening to examine what is known of the past placement of children of West Indian origin and to inspect one or two lea documents which reveal current streaming and setting procedures. The subject of school assessment of a child as having severe or moderate learning difficulties, since it has assumed such an important place in the literature on children of West Indian origin, will be dealt with in a separate section on ESN (pp. 124ff).

Of particular relevance here are the findings of the study of transfer procedures at 11-plus within the ILEA undertaken in connection with 52 schools having a high proportion of immigrant children numbering 1,068 transferring to secondary education in 1966 (Little *et al.*, 1968). Information has already been given on assessment for selection in the sections on verbal reasoning (p.62), English (p.86) and mathematics (pp.104–5), but it is worth restating that whereas half of all the ILEA's pupils could be termed as of below average performance, approximately four-fifths of the immigrant pupils fell into this category when given an IQ test and were rated by their teachers and headmasters on English and mathematics. However, it has been noted that the assessment for placement in a secondary school or stream placement in a comprehensive school depended on group tests and teachers' estimates of ability, and Bagley (1971) has queried the description given by the researchers of the methods by which children were assigned to ability groups. Little *et al.* (1968) state

> 'Within the school, the head teacher may adjust the number placed in the various groups in the light of information about the school's distribution of attainment ... A pupil's grouping for Verbal Reasoning is also based on the school's cumulative knowledge of the child, ... though the standards in English and maths applied to the school can be related to general standards in the ILEA.' (p.441).

Bagley suggests that the possible effect of self-confirming expectation of teachers in such an inter-ethnic testing situation means that some doubt must be placed on the validity of such assessments. The research findings, nevertheless, as he points out, have been widely accepted and have had an important influence on official policy. Yet, until recently appropriate materials have not been available for assessment purposes and, in any case, teachers' opinions will be involved to some extent. The fact remains that in 1966 clear, consistent and significant differences were found between the performance of immigrants taken as a whole and all pupils in the ILEA. No difference was found between the distributions of groupings for non-immigrants in the sample schools and all ILEA pupils. Indeed, more recent results from one London borough, Redbridge, would appear to bear out the same kind of performance at junior level (BPPA, 1978).

In a national survey of leas undertaken for the years 1967-9 Townsend (1971) found a clear indication that considerably smaller proportions of immigrant pupils than non-immigrants entered grammar schools and that far fewer West Indian immigrants than other immigrants did so. It appeared from the DES January 1970 Form 7 statistics quoted by Townsend and Brittan (1972) that a mere 1.58 per cent of children of West Indian origin were being selected according to their age, ability and aptitude for grammar school secondary teaching, although one in five of their white indigenous peers were so selected. Several reasons have been suggested for such a low proportion: first, it may have been the case, even at the end of the 1960s, that many children of West Indian origin would have lived in areas which even then were not operating selective schooling policies; secondly, it was possible that the DES definition of 'immigrant' then in operation (see p.9) might have reduced the numbers so defined as many of these West Indian children would have been over the age of 10; thirdly, in Townsend's survey it was found that only 11 out of 38 leas with 500 or more immigrants kept records of transfer procedures. Of these leas it is interesting to note that there was very little difference in the percentage of black children selected for grammar school education when there was a high or low percentage of immigrant pupils on the school roll. The researchers remarked that these findings could have reflected the then state of readiness of immigrant pupils to benefit from an academic education, or the unsuitability of selection procedures for multiracial populations.

In a subsequent survey of 230 schools with higher concentrations of immigrant pupils Townsend and Brittan (1972) found that two-thirds of the sample of 132 junior schools transferred some pupils to selective secondary schools in 1970. Although a higher percentage of black children selected for grammar school education groups, were found to have been transferred to selective schools than those in the previous study, only four per cent of children of West Indian origin were selected, about half the number of those from other ethnic minority groups. Some leas offered such pupils a chance of reassessment later at 13-plus. Nevertheless it seems likely, as teachers then recognized, that the procedures of selection and the materials used, which were standardized on non-immigrant populations, were thus inadequate both for the assessment of the ability and aptitude of ethnic minority group children, among them children of West Indian origin, at that point in time and as an indication of their likelihood to benefit from a certain type of education at a future date.

Due to the absence of available statistics since 1972 and the reorganization of secondary schooling in most leas it is only possible to speculate as to whether the proportion of pupils of West Indian origin entering grammar schools on a national level has since increased. However, there is an indication that the under-representation of pupils of West Indian origin in selective schooling appears to have continued throughout the 1970s from Rex and Tomlinson's study in Birmingham (1979). From a total of 1,526 pupils who were children of their Handsworth householders it was discovered that whereas seven per cent of the indigenous children attended the city's seven remaining grammar schools only 1.5 per cent of West Indians and 1.2 per cent of Asians did so.

The national survey carried out in 1970 (Townsend and Brittan, 1972) which sampled 230 schools having larger numbers of immigrant pupils also provides both the earliest and most wide-ranging information on the use of streaming within schools. Whilst less than a quarter of infant schools grouped their pupils by ability, 28 primary schools did so and of these 17 indicated that the West Indian pupils clustered in the lower streams and were generally placed lower than other ethnic minority group children. Similarly, in two-thirds of the 98 secondary schools which had streaming by ability at some stage in the school, immigrant pupils, especially of West Indian origin, were invariably in the lower divisions. Where schools had fewer than 20 per cent of immigrant pupils almost half reported that pupils of West Indian origin and other ethnic minorities clustered in the lower streams. The same applied for West Indian pupils only in schools with higher concentrations of immigrant pupils. Indeed, there was a slightly greater concentration in the lower streams with three-fifths of the schools reporting this distribution, compared with less than one-fifth finding West Indians evenly distributed.

Streaming position has also been found to be related to length of stay in Britain. An investigation in a boys' comprehensive school (Wiles, 1968) found that the percentage of immigrants in the top streams rose and the percentage in the lower streams fell as the length of stay increased. Similarly, the DES (Great Britain, DES, 1972a) reported on the basis of a survey of secondary schools that fewer pupils who had completed at least three years of junior schooling in this country were in the lowest streams. However, the differentiating age was found by Townsend and Brittan's (1972) investigation to be somewhat lower as the headmasters in the schools involved claimed that it was pupils who had entered Britain after the age of five who were concentrated in the lowest divisions.

Two lea documents (BPPA, 1978; Williams, 1978) suggest that pupils of West Indian origin are still similarly placed in the lower sets for English and mathematics. Although the numbers of West

Indian pupils in the one high school involved in the Redbridge inquiry were rather small, it would appear that, in English, for example, in the second year 33 per cent (eight) West Indian pupils were placed in a remedial class and the majority in B and C streams, whereas by the third year only two children remained in the remedial group but the West Indian pupils were concentrated in the C stream (54.5 per cent). This trend appeared to continue into the upper school with only the occasional pupil in the A stream. Setting results were somewhat better for mathematics although in most years the majority of West Indians were again in the lower streams, with perhaps rather more pupils in the B streams than the C streams. Although more pupils (20 per cent) started the first year in the A stream there was a decline in the second and third years so that they were more evenly distributed, even so there were 30.8 per cent (eight) pupils in the remedial form in years one and two. The trend for the majority of black pupils to be in the middle streams continued into the upper school with again only one or two high achievers in the top streams.

Williams (1978) reporting on an analysis of performance and setting in schools in Dudley, shows that starting in the infant school and going right through the secondary school West Indians are continually being placed in lower streams. Reception teachers in seven schools were asked for their opinions on the readiness of children of West Indian origin for learning, and, although the numbers involved were very small, and teachers had obvious and proper reservations about making an assessment on a relatively slight acquaintance with their charges, it appears that none were thought to be above average for the class, and twice as many were rated below average as those who were considered average. Again, at 11 and 12 a pupil was placed in sets for mathematics and foreign languages. The criteria of poor performance were if a pupil was in the bottom set for basic subjects or if his reading performance was at least three years behind the standard for his chronological age. By these criteria two-thirds of the pupils of West Indian origin (40 out of 60) were said to be poor achievers. The setting of pupils of West Indian origin in English and mathematics in the fourth and fifth years of four secondary schools was also investigated. Of the 597 pupils in the fifth year 82 were of West Indian origin and almost half of these were found in the bottom two sets for mathematics and English. Only two of the pupils were in a set designated for O-level

English and six for O-level mathematics. As the researcher noted, this meant that very few pupils of West Indian origin would be leaving secondary schools in Dudley with qualifications necessary for further education and training and by far the majority would leave with no educational qualifications. The overall trend of these placements taken together with measurements of reading over the whole period of schooling indicated that pupils of West Indian origin were achieving lower standards than other pupils at all ages.

In conclusion, although some of the data in this review on selection procedures and school placement may be comparatively out of date, even the more recent information, albeit limited, which is available, tends to bear out the results on ability and attainment tests and confirms the disadvantaged position of pupils of West Indian origin within schools on the basis of the school's own assessment procedures.

Section 9: Examinations

The following section looks at what evidence is publicly available on the performance of pupils of West Indian origin on CSE and GCE examinations. This evidence is extremely limited, and, as will be seen from the detailed analysis of one piece of research which appeared to show contrary trends, the findings can only be regarded with the utmost caution.

In an intensive study of 230 multiracial schools with fairly high numbers of immigrant pupils in 1970 Townsend and Brittan (1972) found that twice as high a proportion of pupils of West Indian origin and other immigrants as that of non-immigrants stayed on for an optional fifth year. However, in these fifth-year forms from one-quarter to one-third of pupils of West Indian origin and other immigrant groups were in non-examination courses as compared with less than one-thirtieth of the non-immigrants. Conversely, there were only six per cent of pupils of West Indian origin undertaking O-level courses. Moreover, it was discovered that over half of the West Indians in the sixth form were working on CSE examinations, compared with one-twentieth of the non-immigrant population. Similarly, only one in five of the West Indian sixth formers were following A-level courses. These findings and others which were similar for other ethnic minority groups prompted the researchers to observe that it might be necessary 'to look closely at this position to ensure that the regard for education of many immigrant pupils and their parents at fifth and sixth form level does not cause them to remain at school until 16, 17 or 18 years of age without the opportunity of obtaining qualifications of a sufficient standard to enable them to secure employment suitable to their greater maturity' (Townsend and Brittan, 1972, p.56).

Evidence of school-leaving qualifications has also been obtained in the context of a study of the employment situation of ethnic minority and white young people (Allen and Smith, 1975). In 1972 the researchers interviewed 368 school leavers in Bradford and 300 in Sheffield but no West Indians obtained A-levels in either town. At O-level/CSE standard only very few West Indian pupils were recorded as passing, more in Sheffield than Bradford, and more girls than boys. Whereas whites overall achieved a mean of 2.8 passes in O-level and CSE, blacks only achieved a mean of 1.9 passes. Teachers cited linguistic problems, lack of discipline and poor home circumstances as reasons for the comparatively low performance of West Indian pupils. A second study (Rex and Tomlinson, 1979) in which a sub-sample of 25 West Indians aged 16-21 living at home (out of 256 children of householders in their Handsworth sample) were interviewed in 1975, found that a majority had their primary schooling overseas and 20 had left school by 16. However, 14 West Indians had obtained 63 CSEs but no O- or A-levels. There appeared to be some resentment among this group that their teachers had not encouraged them to take O-levels. Also, in another (pilot) study inquiring into the participation rate in further and higher education and carried out in 1979 in all the 16 secondary schools in one outer London borough, Craft and Craft (1981) reported that the performance of West Indian pupils in fifth-year public exams was behind that of all other pupils, even when matched for social class.

To some extent these findings are supported by an investigation in the London borough of Redbridge (BPPA, 1978) which concentrated on the performance of pupils of West Indian origin who comprised 10 per cent of one high school, a large comprehensive in South Ilford, having one-third of its catchment drawn from ethnic minority groups. An analysis of examination records for 1977 showed that although the number of GCE O-level and CSE Grade 1 passes averaged 0.7 per student for the whole school, the figure was only 0.3 for the pupils of West Indian origin. The comparative numbers of O-level and CSE passes at all grades were 4.2 and 1.0 respectively. From a more detailed breakdown which was supplied in Appendix C there appeared to be a higher proportion of boys among examination candidates. However, this may have been due to a larger number of boys in the school, though it is not possible to be sure of this from the information provided. Moreover, no pupil of West Indian origin passed an A-level in 1977 in this particular school.

One researcher, Driver, has undertaken what appears to be the only detailed work on examination passes by pupils of West Indian origin. In 1977 he published a preliminary study which reported two main findings: the lower performance of pupils of West Indian origin, which was in keeping with the findings of Townsend and Brittan (1972), and yet the higher persistence level of pupils of West Indian origin when compared with their white peers. The research was limited insofar as it took place in one school in the West Midlands. It was based on an ethnographic approach which tended to focus more on descriptions of extra-curricular activities and teacher-pupil interaction rather than the collection of numerical data. All 66 pupils of West Indian origin, 29 boys and 37 girls from one fourth year were observed in comparison with their 48 white peers. In addition, a sub-sample of West Indian pupils, selected by their teachers as doing particularly well or badly, were interviewed together with their parents. The author describes the challenging classroom atmosphere at the centre of which were the West Indian boys. He argues that when teachers were asked to allocate pupils to three sets and to make assessments and predict CSE grades as a guide for external examiners they allowed the difficulties with social behaviour experienced in classroom situations to influence their assessments unduly, particularly in the case of boys for whom the correlation of assessment for academic ability and social behaviour was twice as high. Thirteen out of 18 pupils in the middle stream, which was oriented towards the taking of three CSE examinations, were West Indian. The author suggests that it is against the background of the account which he gives of relations with parents, peers and teachers, that the school achievements, as expressed in terms of the results obtained in CSE school-leaving examinations by the West Indian pupils, are best understood. In these examinations the 61 pupils of West Indian origin obtained substantially lower results than those of their 46 English peers or 24 South Asian peers. It is interesting to note however, that the West Indian girls persisted with their education to a much greater extent than the West Indian boys insofar as 74 per cent of the girls (22 out of 31) actually attained a CSE qualification of some sort, whereas only 23 per cent (seven out of 30) of the West Indian boys did likewise. This meant that the average CSE results obtained by West Indian boys who began the two-year examination course was less than two passes at Grade IV or V CSE, whereas for the West Indian girls as a whole it amounted to more than five such passes or almost three with substantially better grades. However, the author failed to indicate that the number of mean CSE units obtained per pupil who actually sat the CSE exam was very similar for both West Indian boys and girls. Moreover, although Driver notes that the West Indian girls' overall CSE average was much better than that for the English pupils as a whole, he omitted to point out that, although many fewer English pupils sat the examinations, those who did so obtained significantly better grades than their West Indian peers. The conversion procedure which the researcher used for CSE results is confusing, as is also his failure to distinguish course entrants from examinees, thereby underestimating the mean examination score per English examinee.

A follow-up investigation undertaken by the same author (Driver, 1980a and b) is of especial interest since it runs counter to the main trends indicated by other research. It is the only investigation to consider in detail the performance of West Indian pupils at examination age and to suggest that the examination performance of West Indian pupils was better than that of their white peers. By contrast, other surveys involving pupils of West Indian origin of school-leaving age on reading (Mabey, 1980, 1981) and mathematics and reading (Essen and Ghodsian, 1979) have indicated substantially poorer performance. For these reasons, and, in addition, since the work has received wide public attention in the press (see, e.g., *TES*, 25.1.80) a more detailed analysis has been undertaken in respect of this study which will be considered in two ways since it appeared firstly as an article in the journal *New Society* (Driver, 1980a) and only subsequently as a CRE pamphlet entitled *Beyond Underachievement* (Driver, 1980b). Whilst both writings refer to the same data and make similar claims it is intriguing to observe how such claims can be distorted by over-simplification, as in the case of the magazine article, and that there was subsequently felt to be a need to make more modest claims when more details of the study were supplied.

The investigation was concerned with just over 2,300 16-year-old school leavers of whom 590 were West Indians. They attended five multiracial secondary schools, two of which were in the north of England, two in the Midlands and one in the home counties. Information on the examination performance of these pupils was obtained from records and comparisons of groups were made within the same school and the same year. Ranking by means of the conversion of passes into a unit scoring system also enabled the researcher to indicate trends in examination performance over the five schools. The data relate to the period 1975-8 and examination performance at 16-plus.

In the *New Society* article (Driver, 1980a) the author made the following claims:

1) West Indian girls and boys achieve better results than English girls and boys in examinations.

2) In some cases, West Indian boys and girls overtake their English classmates during secondary schooling.

3) West Indian girls do better than West Indian boys (and vice versa for English boys and girls).

4) West Indians obtain better average results in English language, maths and science.

The author maintained that a positive self-image had influenced the West Indian pupils' performance, so that, although they were achieving less well than their peers at 11-plus, they subsequently pulled ahead to achieve relatively better results with increasing age. Driver suggested that the most important finding was the higher achievement of West Indian girls, and that this could to some extent be related to conditions of upbringing which might not be conducive to parallel development in West Indian girls and boys, and was contrary to socialization practices for English boys and girls. As mention has already been made earlier in this report (p.19) he observed that West Indian girls also tend to perform better in the Jamaican educational system (see Manley, 1963).

A number of criticisms may be advanced with respect to the presentation of the study in the *New Society* article, both generally on educational matters and more specifically in relation to a number of technical and statistical weaknesses.

1) It has been claimed by a West Indian commentator (Colly-more, 1980) that all the schools used in the investigation were situated in suburban areas, (in fact it seems as if three were in outer city locations) whereas most children of West Indian origin live in inner-city environments. But whatever the exact urban location of the schools investigated, as Driver himself points out, this would indicate lack of parity between schools, not primarily between ethnic populations.

2) Although the sample size has also been criticized, it is in fact quite large but, more importantly, there was no evidence that it was chosen in a statistically representative way.

3) Although most of the data obtained relate to five schools, at two points in time data are confined to only two schools.

4) It appeared from, for example, Table 1, that the data concentrated on exam entrants and that the achievement score was based on the average for all pupils registered as members of a two-year examination course, thereby excluding pupils who did not sit for external examinations, particularly Easter school leavers, from the analysis. Indeed the figures supplied by Driver in this article (p.112) showed a significantly higher drop-out rate for English pupils (36 per cent of boys and 43 per cent of girls, compared with only 24 per cent of West Indian boys and 22 per cent of West Indian girls). This means that those English students sitting external examinations would have had to have achieved either higher or more passes for the English groups as a whole to score the same achievement total. Moreover, if the schools involved in the investigation operated differential examination entrance policies then this would mean that only the more able pupils would be entered, since they might have a reasonable chance of success, and this would also influence the examination passes.

5) An important criticism is that Driver failed to provide raw data to support his conclusions. He does not supply information on sub-sample sizes and hence it is not possible to be sure of the relationships between the groups. Ranks are indicated for sub-groups based on a somewhat devious method of totalling exam results, hence it is not possible to look at the *actual* achievement of each group.

6) In addition, no information is given about the size of differences: neither with respect to how great they are, for example

as between one rank and the next, West Indian boy as opposed to West Indian girl, etc.; nor is the reader informed whether differences are significant or not since the sample size and distribution are not indicated.

7) As Mabey (personal communication) has pointed out, although Driver suggests that the theory of progressive deficit is disproved by his findings, he produces no data to prove or disprove it. Although information on reading results at 13-plus is given for one year-group at one school (but not necessarily for the *same* pupils), and on non-verbal test results at 11-plus in another school, progressive deficit can only be tested by examining the progress of the same pupils at different ages.

These criticisms were all made largely as a result of the lack of sufficiently detailed information in the article, acknowledgement of which was also made by the author himself. At this point therefore it was only possible to comment that the study appeared to be of interest but that reservations, especially about the drawing of comparisons, and many qualifications needed to be made. Perhaps the most telling observation concerns the extent to which such publication highlights certain findings at the expense of others in a rather sensational way. It remained to be seen, until the subsequent publication of the CRE booklet, whether these preliminary criticisms would be borne out or could be explained by the support of more detailed data.

When *Beyond Underachievement* was in fact published a few months later (Driver, 1980b) it was immediately apparent that the claims for the investigation were much more modest than had seemed at first sight. As David Lane, Chairman for the Commission for Racial Equality, expressed it in a Preface to the book

'though his study is based on only 5 schools, the findings suggest that in some circumstances and in certain schools minority group children (particularly West Indian girls) are doing rather better than one would have expected from earlier research, and in some cases have higher levels of scholastic attainment than their white contemporaries' (p.5).

It was also noted that generalizations on a national scale could not be made as a result of this study because the pupils involved were not a representative sample since relevant records were often not available, either from a larger number of leas which had initially been approached, or from within the schools themselves. In addition it was admitted that it was not possible to compare one school with another on progressive measures of attainment or even one pupil-generation in the same school with another. Thus the original claims for the findings were seen to have been considerably modified.

In addition to the information supplied in the *New Society* article, Driver gives further details in the booklet *Beyond Underachievement* in that he analyses examination performance with respect to case studies of five individual schools, each of which has a number of similarities and differences in terms of percentage of immigrant pupils, neighbourhood served and degree to which a multicultural curriculum is in force (Driver, 1980b). Driver was particularly interested in persistence and attainment. A percentage of pupils persisting with schooling was derived by dividing the number of course entrants by course examinees. The measure of attainment was given a grading system using the following conversion: GCE and CSE Grade I or II equal three units; Grade III or IV equal two units and Grade V equals one unit. These were summed for each pupil in order to obtain the total examination result. Sixteen-plus examination results were also used to determine pupil performance in critical subject areas, namely, English language, mathematics and science. Results were generally analysed separately for each age group and only in relation to other pupils in the same school for different years. No direct inter-school comparisons were made although trends across the five schools were indicated.

The general findings indicated:

1) In terms of overall school achievement and in the combined results in the critical subjects West Indian girls performed better than West Indian boys. Only in mathematics and physical science did West Indian boys perform better than West Indian girls.

2) West Indian girls obtained considerably better results than their English girl peers except for English language and biology.

3) There appeared to be little difference in the performance of West Indian boys and English boys although English boys tended to do better in the combined critical subjects. When these subjects were analysed separately it was found that West Indian boys performed better in English language,

mathematics, biology and integrated science whilst English boys performed better in physics.

4) West Indian pupils obtained better 16-plus examination results than English pupils. The performance of the West Indian girls was best and their persistence in school work was demonstrated by their low drop-out rate from examination courses and their tendency to obtain better results than the other three groups. It was suggested that this attainment was even more remarkable when the results of those girls at 11-plus were taken into account (Driver, 1980b).

Whilst it is not possible to discuss in detail the figures provided in this report it is appropriate to raise some queries and make several points in criticism.

1) Why are results reported for course entrants and not course examinees? The analysis is based on mean scores per course entrant. There was a typically greater drop-out rate in the English than the West Indian groups. Therefore, mean scores based on numbers of course entrants systematically underestimate the English mean per examinee.

2) If the data are analysed in terms of the means per examinee then the claimed differential in favour of pupils of West Indian origin virtually disappears, for example in Table C1 and C2. Indeed, in many cases, the English sample is seen by this analysis to perform considerably better.

3) Several criticisms can be made with respect to the presentation of and general mode of analysis of data in ranked sub-groupings. Whilst it is a common convention for CSE Grade I to be equated with an O-level pass, it is not standard practice for Grade II to be treated in this way. The effect of this kind of point system is to inflate the value of low-level results and deflate the value of high grades. This means, for example, that if more English pupils are taking and passing O-levels it is likely that they are not taking so many subjects and these factors will not be adequately reflected by this method of analysis. This can be seen by taking a closer look at Columns 8 and 10 in Tables A1, A2 and A3 in the appendix and comparing this with Table 3 on p.24. By inspection of the mean overall score per examinee and mean combined critical subject score per examinee in Table A1 for example, it is only possible to say in the absence of tests of significance and data

on standard deviations that English girls appear to have better overall scores and West Indian girls are worse on critical subject scores, otherwise there are no apparent differences. If such an examination is also made of the same columns in Table A2 and A3 and these findings related to Table 3 p.24 it appears that if real averages are taken a different picture emerges from the summary of the data for the first school which is provided, so that the statements A to D are in fact not true. The point can perhaps be made more simply by saying that since tests of significance are not reported very minor differences are given spurious significance through ranking, for example see Table B2 Column 8. Comparisons are made more difficult by reversing the scores in the rank orderings in the second publication so that e.g. Table 17, C2, C7 (Driver, 1980b) and Table 2 (Driver, 1980a), both dealing with pupil categories for achievement in critical subject areas, appear different.

4) The data are not analysed systematically and the researcher fails to advert sufficiently to counter trends when examining West Indian and English group differences.

5) Data on School D are conflated, it is claimed for statistical reasons, because of the small number of West Indian pupils (it so happens that West Indians are doing less well in School D, see Table 16), but by the same token the data in School B and C should also be conflated because of the small number of Asian pupils involved.

6) There seem to be minor discrepancies in the data especially where specialist subjects are concerned. For example, see Appendix, Tables A1–E2 where there appear to be discrepancies between Column 4, number of examinees taking critical subjects, and Columns 14–18 giving course entrants and examinees in critical subjects.

7) The claim is made (e.g. p.22, para. 2) that West Indian girls are more persistent in their schooling and achievement in that in two out of three years the scores for girls and their levels of persistence as measured by the proportion who eventually obtained positive results, easily exceeded those for the boys. However, if the persistence levels for West Indian boys and girls in School A are taken over three years then it will be found that their persistence is in fact very similar, both sexes averaging 74 per cent.

8) It seems odd to have such a strong bias to science in the critical subject scores, and in particular to include physics which will be restricted to the more able and fewer girls. In addition, there are difficulties in making comparisons since two schools only taught integrated sciences.

9) A query may be raised about the identification of ethnic affiliation: how accurate will a teacher's designation of a pupil as West Indian be in retrospect after the pupil has left the school?

10) The general level of education and attainment of the pupils as a whole may be questioned. This tends to be obscured by the rating of examination performance by unit scores, as, if inspected in greater detail, the figures reveal that the number of passes per pupil is actually very low. This indicates that whether the West Indian pupils are in fact performing better than their school peers or not they are certainly not performing as well as their national age peers. The descriptive evidence about the schools involved suggests that there are fewer more able white children in the school populations and so the full range of West Indian children is being compared with a smaller group of white children who also comprise the school intake. It is only possible to speculate why there is such a high drop-out rate amongst the white pupils in such areas.

Dr. Driver's findings have been analysed in such detail because of the wide attention which they have received in the Press and also since they appeared to contradict other findings. Such an analysis highlights at least two main points. First, an over-simplified presentation such as that in the *New Society* article tends to give rise to further speculations; in this case the findings were interpreted both as supporting geneticist arguments (e.g. Stein, 1980) and as disproving them (e.g. Siriwardena, 1980; Driver, 1980c). Secondly, and more importantly, the analysis shows that in many cases the inexplicit nature of the data and failure to provide sufficiently detailed information do not empower the researcher to draw the kind of conclusions which have been stated. Although, it is true, he acknowledges the limitations of the study and stresses its ethnographic approach, it is also fair to point out that he does draw educational conclusions on the basis of statistical evidence which in many cases is found wanting in statistical terms. Nevertheless, the findings should be seen in context and the study has attempted to provide data, which are absent elsewhere, on the examination performance of pupils of West Indian origin. Moreover, if such a detailed analysis had been undertaken with respect to other research studies it is quite possible that some similiar deficiencies would have been found. In conclusion, the investigation is perhaps most important for drawing attention to the fact that the attainment of ethnic minority pupils in relation to their white peers is a complex matter, since it is clear that not all pupils of West Indian origin are under-achieving and that some are indeed attaining relatively high results. To what extent an examination of the differences between high and low performance can be explained by factors such as quality of schooling, teachers' attitudes, pupils' home backgrounds and pupil motivation, no research has yet been able to determine.

Section 10: Other Curricular Activities

Schools are not merely places for academic learning but also for personal and social development. The contributions of pupils of West Indian origin to the life of a school have often been remarked upon, particularly with respect to their natural sense of rhythm, colour and harmony, which mean that they have frequently been noted for excelling in music, cookery and sport, as is typified by the girl, Phyllis, mentioned by Jeffcoate (1977 and 1979) and other pupils referred to in Giles's (1977) descriptive account of schools in London. In Townsend and Brittan's (1972) survey of the organization of multiracial schools 41 out of 114 primary heads and 52 out of 93 secondary heads commented overwhelmingly favourably about the contribution of immigrant children to school activities, especially music, dancing and performances in school concerts, open days etc. As well as the vigour and courage of West Indian pupils in sport which were singled out, two quotations which specifically mentioned children of West Indian origin are worth repeating again here.

'The simpler domestic habits of West Indians – their emphasis on cleaning, cooking, needlework etc. – are reflected in children's activities and contribute to worthwhile activities with less able children in particular.'

'The warmth and ebulliance of the West Indian character has enriched our school – we seem so *alive*! This helps other children, including some West Indians themselves who are withdrawn and moody.' (Townsend and Brittan, 1972, p.114).

There appear to be relatively few research studies which have specifically investigated the contribution to the school which pupils of West Indian origin do undoubtedly make. In one investigation Sargeant (1972) who questioned 969 boys, 127 of whom were of West Indian origin, all in third-year classes in seven London secondary schools, about their participation in sport found an overwhelming predominance of West Indian boys taking part in soccer, cricket and athletics. He also noted that there was a high correlation between academic ability and participation in sports; both West Indian and white English participation was proportionately higher in the top streams. Jones (1977) in a study reported in more detail in a later section (pp.167–8) noted a similarly high representation of pupils of West Indian origin in school sports, but found that this did not correlate with higher self-esteem. Another study (Driver, 1977) found that for fourth-year pupils in a Midland school, soccer which was played by the higher achievers, was used as a means of transcending ethnicity and was approved of and admired by teachers in the school, unlike Reggae which was used as a means of maximizing ethnicity, as was the illegal playing of dominoes and a West Indian version of cards.

Perhaps the most up-to-date information available, which has the added advantage of giving an overall picture of one particular school where pupils of West Indian origin constitute 10 per cent of the school roll, is that given in the BPPA account of Loxford High School (1978). Pupils of West Indian origin were found to be over-represented in proportion to their numbers in school teams for soccer, and for basketball, which was played by both boys and girls, West Indian girls forming 80 per cent of the school team. Forty per cent of those playing cricket in the lower school as a voluntary club activity were West Indian pupils. Mention is also made of a sports day in another school where there were fewer than five per cent children of West Indian origin on roll but who nevertheless comprised 40 per cent of those participating in the competitions. Again, with respect to music almost a quarter of all West Indians in the lower school were learning a musical instrument and they constituted 40 per cent of the school band. Pupils of West Indian origin were also keen participants in drama (25 per cent) – as is also well illustrated by the case of Jennifer (Richmond, 1978) – and dance (18 per cent). Most importantly pupils of West Indian origin were also taking their full part in exercising the authority roles of the school and were quite adequately represented on tutor group committees and as prefects and librarians.

Though such a description, especially of only one school, is too limited an account upon which to make generalizations, it is heartening to find that pupils of West Indian origin are fully participating in some schools and making their own distinctive contribution to school activities and the social life to be found within the school's premises. It cannot be too obvious to emphasize the especial contribution which such activities may well make in enabling pupils of West Indian origin to come to have a proper sense of their own worth and to encourage them through increased self-confidence to realize their full potential in other, more academic, spheres.

Section 11: Educational Sub-normality and Behaviour

The issues of educational sub-normality and behaviour in respect of pupils of West Indian origin is one which is particularly emotive, embarrassing and controversial. It has certainly been the case, and it is likely that it continues to be so, that children of West Indian families are much more likely than other children to be placed in special schools for the educationally sub-normal. In fact, as Tomlinson (1978) demonstrates, from the point of view of West Indian parents the designation of educational sub-normality has taken on special significance in that it now symbolizes the general underachievement of West Indian children in the English school system. Administratively it has caused embarrassment insofar as the referral and assessment processes in connection with designation of a pupil as ESN are by no means clear-cut, so that it is not possible to give a simple description of an ESN child and what criteria are used for the purposes of classification. There appears to be no normative consensus about ESN, and criteria other than those which are educational are used in assessment (Tomlinson, 1979). The issues surrounding ESN have thus often become a bitter battle-ground for general controversy both about the failure, as many West Indians see it, to incorporate pupils of West Indian origin into the school system, and their supposition that schools for the ESN are for children of low innate intelligence. Whilst a number of variables concerning the education system, the pupil's behaviour and home environment and their interaction are all implicated here, it is necessary to try and determine whether there are any causal links between these three factors and, if so, in what way they impinge upon each other. For example, do behaviour disorders develop as a reaction to academic failure or do they inhibit educational progress?

Educational Sub-normality

An informative article by Tomlinson (1978) charts the chronology of disproportionate placement of pupils of West Indian origin in schools for the ESN. Apparently as early as 1965 the West Indian community became aware that a greater number of pupils of West Indian origin relative to their numbers in the total school population were being placed in schools for the ESN, and that this was especially the case where West Indian children formed a large percentage of the school population.

One of the earliest official sources of placement figures was an ILEA report (1967) which stated that although there were only 15 per cent pupils of immigrant origin in all ILEA schools, they comprised 28.4 per cent of children in schools for the ESN and three-quarters of these pupils were of West Indian origin whereas they were only half the immigrant population in ordinary schools. It seems that about half the headmasters of these 19 schools thought that at least 20 per cent of the immigrant pupils were wrongly placed and the report itself stated 'that where children are suspected as being wrongly placed in the ESN school, this is four times as likely in the case of immigrant pupils' (p.5). Misclassification was thought to be largely due to the lack of culture fair diagnostic tests used in the processes of assessment. Schools also suggested that many of the immigrant pupils were referred to them primarily for behavioural rather than educational reasons. However, the report also stated that only seven per cent of immigrant and four per cent of non-immigrant pupils returned to ordinary schools in the ILEA.

The disproportionate number of pupils of West Indian origin in schools for the ESN may also be seen in the particular case of one borough, Brent, which in December 1966 had 14 per cent of pupils of West Indian origin enrolled in its schools. In 1967 a survey of secondary schools in the borough was conducted (Graham, 1968) and the head teachers in seven schools were asked to give the names of the 30 most backward children in the first and second years. The average age of the pupils was about 12½ years. In all 211 children's names were submitted and 175 of these (73 girls and 102 boys) were group-tested on verbal reasoning, word recognition and 'Draw-a-man' tests. One hundred and twenty-seven of these children were of immigrant origin, and of them 56 were thought to be ESN. After individual testing on the WISC 25 of these children who were West Indian were found to be dull and backward but not ESN, although a further 17 were classified as ESN, making a total of 42 West Indians out of the 56 immigrant pupils. Indeed, because of the disproportionate number of pupils of West Indian origin in schools for the ESN in Haringey the North London West Indian Association made representations to the Race Relations Board which found that there was no evidence of an unlawful act although it suggested the intelligence tests used did not effectively distinguish the educationally sub-normal from the 'educationally deprived'.

Evidence to confirm the picture built up in London boroughs was provided in 1971 by Townsend and Brittan who from a national survey of 146 leas found that, although there were difficulties in ascertaining exact and accurate pictures for the distribution of immigrant and non-immigrant pupils in schools for the ESN, because of both the uneven nature of the distribution of such schools and of immigrant pupils, it was clear that there was a higher proportion of West Indian pupils placed in schools for the ESN than would be expected from the proportion of West Indian pupils in the school population as a whole. DES figures for January 1970, quoted by Townsend and Brittan, showed that there were estimated to be 109,580 pupils of West Indian origin in all primary and secondary schools and 2.33 per cent (2,550) were found in schools for the ESN. In fact, the ratio of pupils of West Indian origin to other immigrant and indigenous pupils in schools for the ESN was found to be in the region of four to one. The excess numbers of West Indians in schools for the ESN were mainly found in 18 leas of which 12 had immigrant school populations with more than 30 per cent of West Indian pupils.

There continued to be little improvement in the position of West Indian children with respect to ESN schooling as in November 1973 the DES sent a circular letter to all Chief Education Officers (CEOs) which indicated in an appendix that in January 1972 pupils of West Indian origin constituted five per cent of all children in schools for the ESN. Difficulties with dialect, discipline and teachers' assessments were mentioned as possible factors contributing to over-representation and an annual review of the placement of immigrant children was recommended. As has already been noted, discussion of actual numbers of immigrant children becomes particularly problematic after the DES ceased to collect statistics in 1972, but tables from DES *Statistics of Education Vol. 1. 1972. Schools.* (Great Britain, DES, 1973) show that while the total number of children in schools for the ESN constituted less than one per cent of the total population in maintained primary and secondary schools (0.6 per cent) in 1972, the figure was nearly three per cent for West Indian children. Moreover, misclassification of many children of West Indian origin was tacitly acknowledged by the Government White Paper (Great Britain, Parliament, House of Commons, 1974) which recommended that

'all local education authorities with a sizeable immigrant child population should make plans to provide by an early date special facilities in ordinary schools to overcome the linguistic and adjustment problems of immigrant children with a level of ability higher than the general run of pupils in special schools for the educationally sub-normal' (Recommendation 19, p.12).

Subsequently, in its response to the 1977 Select Committee report (Great Britain, Parliament, House of Commons, 1977) the then Government, in a White Paper on *The West Indian Community* (Great Britain, Parliament, House of Commons, 1978) recommended that statistics should once more be collected on West Indian pupils in ESN schools. However, lack of up-to-date figures at present means that it is only possible to speculate about the numbers of pupils of West Indian origin still in schools for the mildly or severely educationally sub-normal. For example, whilst the 1976 figures for ESN(M) schools indicate an overall drop of one per cent, as Tomlinson (1978) points out, even supposing the percentage of West Indian children to have fallen correspondingly they would still be over-represented. One estimate (Tomlinson, 1979) suggests that while the proportion of children in the school population in ESN(M) schools is 0.5, the proportion for West Indian children is 2.5. Moreover, the statement quoted by Mack (1977) that CEOs of areas having sizeable immigrant populations had reported clear impressions that the number of children of West Indian origin in ESN schools is declining, has to be regarded as similarly hypothetical. However, actual evidence cited in the BPPA (1978) report on Redbridge does not indicate a down-turn, as although West Indian pupils represented about two per cent of the total Redbridge borough school population, 10 out of 120 children at an ESN school were of West Indian origin. Similar over-representation was observed in remedial units for socially maladjusted children (see also Williams, 1978). These, together with a variety of disruptive units, withdrawal classes and guidance units have developed on an *ad hoc* basis in the 70s, but despite much comment on the numbers of pupils of West Indian origin which they may contain, there is a complete lack of research evidence, and similarly for suspension of pupils.

Townsend and Brittan (1972) in a critical discussion of some of the arrangements used by leas for the assessment of immigrant pupils with respect to educational sub-normality point out the difficulties which educational psychologists face in the absence of valid instruments to measure the ability of pupils of different linguistic, cultural and educational backgrounds. They suggested that there should be a minimum period of schooling for immigrants before assessment takes place and this was also endorsed by Coard (1971) who proposed a two-year period. Such a procedure would appear to be justified by research evidence. Fethney (1972) conducted a survey of 150 pupils, of whom over 70 per cent were of West Indian origin, in nine classes of an ESN school. The pupils were aged between 11 and 16, and of those born in Jamaica all had arrived in the UK when they were at least eight years old. It was found that the sooner after arrival children had been given intelligence tests the lower they had scored. As has already been reported, Watson (1973) found that recent immigrants increased their scores on IQ tests when they were retested after their first 20 months in this country.

What then are the usual processes for classifying a child as ESN? Houghton (1970) and others point out that although there is no standard technique for classifying children as educationally subnormal, common criteria in practice have been that a child should be three years retarded in his school work, take an intelligence test administered by an educational psychologist or a school medical officer, and have an IQ of between 50 and 70. It appears that official statements have always stressed that a child could be classified as ESN on the basis of *both learning and behavioural* problems. Indeed Bagley (1973) has claimed that disobedience in schools is as likely as poor scholastic performance to lead to removal to an ESN school. The following points made by Tomlinson (1978) on classification are worth noting:

'It is perhaps not unfair to comment that by 1969 according to official definition, a child could be educationally backward whether he had a high or low IQ, and he could be ESN without requiring special schooling. No cause needed to be established for a child's retardation, but teachers were expected to distinguish different types of and degrees of backwardness. Definitions of educational sub-normality are supposedly educational, but only medical officers, under the 1944 act, have any statutory powers in the ascertainment procedures. An ESN child was not intended to be a troublesome child, but troublesome children are sometimes referred as being potentially ESN.' (p.239).

Moreover, there was a hint of compulsion about classification as children can be compelled to attend special schools. No doubt it was this and other factors implicit in assessment procedures which caused the following statement to be made to the Select Committee on Race Relations and Immigration by Caribbean educationalists and community workers who claimed:

'Many children are packed off to ESN schools on the basis of very inadequate assessment procedures. Very little consultation between the parents and the authorities takes place. Many parents are given inaccurate information as to the nature and purpose of ESN schools. Many children are wrongly assessed and sent for reasons other than educational sub-normality.' (Great Britain, Parliament, House of Commons Select Committee on Race Relations and Immigration, 1973, p.824).

The suggestion behind these remarks is that the means by which children were ascertained for placement did not discriminate sufficiently between children who were backward because of cultural differences or disadvantages and children who were backward for other reasons. As Hegarty has argued (Hegarty and Lucas, 1978)

'In any case the situation did not make good sense in educational terms. Children whose present level of attainment is low because they have not had opportunities to learn need to be taught in a different way to genuinely slow learners. Placing both groups in the same learning environment is to do a disservice to both unless differential provision can be made within it. It is no slur on the dedicated work done in ESN schools to say that such differential provision is not always available within them. Quite apart from the fact that there are large gaps in our understanding of how best to make up for cultural disadvantage (with the resulting implication that *general* educational enrichment as provided in a good ordinary school may be more to the point), ESN schools have traditionally been enjoined to carry out quite different tasks. Placing such large numbers of ethnic minority children in special schools was not making the best use of either special schools or ordinary schools.' (p.71).

In this respect it is important to note a recent study (Tomlinson, 1979, 1981) which considered the concept of ESN(M) and investigated the context of the decisions of 120 professionals – heads, psychologists, medical officers and teachers in special schools – who had made decisions on 40 children passing through the assessment processes for ESN(M) in Birmingham. Eighteen of the 40 children were of immigrant parentage and nine were of West Indian origin, seven born in the UK and two in Jamaica. The researcher found that the judgements of professionals were crucially related to their own positions and perceptions about social and racial groups. In particular the head teachers' perceptions of the problems of West Indian children in terms of 'natural' slower learning ability, lack of concentration, boisterousness and linguistic difficulties were almost identical with their general referral criteria for ESN(M). The heads felt genuine concern but West Indians, it seemed, were nevertheless more likely to be considered potentially ESN than other groups. Although similar problems were cited by the heads of special schools the researcher judged that in that context pupils were considered more as individuals than as members of ethnic groups. All the professionals made decisions more speedily on 'immigrant' than indigenous children; whereas it took an indigenous child two years on average to pass through the assessment procedures and reach an ESN(M) school, it only took an immigrant child 11.4 months on average. Indeed the pupils of West Indian origin in the study seemed to have been referred for actual or potential disruptive behaviour as well as educational problems, and whilst disruption was often mentioned initially as a reason for referral, retardation was subsequently explained in terms of family, environment and socialization practices. Yet Tomlinson observed that the West Indian pupils appeared to be handicapped by equal treatment with whites in the assessment process although West Indian parents explicitly did not want them to be treated as if they were white disadvantaged low-achieving children.

Perhaps the best known and certainly the most emotive and heartfelt attack on the misclassification of a disproportionate number of West Indian children as ESN was the pamphlet *How the*

West Indian is Made Educationally Subnormal in the British School System, written by Coard (1971), who was himself a West Indian teacher in ESN schools and a member of the Caribbean Education and Community Workers' Association. Coard exhorted West Indian parents to help their children themselves and indicated how this could be done as well as insisting that they attempt to obtain extra assistance from their lea. He maintained that the curriculum and organization of the ESN school was geared to children of below normal academic abilities so that West Indian pupils who were misclassified were not encouraged to perform at their best. He portrayed the misplaced black child as one who is upset, disturbed, refuses to co-operate and participate and hence appears more retarded, thereby *becoming* retarded through mental inactivity as time goes on. Such a child he claimed 'feels deeply that racial discrimination and rejection have been practised towards him by the authorities who assessed him wrongly as being ESN' (p.10). Coard placed the blame for misclassification squarely on the schools and teachers and attributed incorrect assessment to three main factors – differences in culture and social class which he claimed were reflected in tests and teachers, and cases where children are emotionally disturbed. He claimed that West Indian pupils' academic achievement is influenced by low teacher expectation, lack of motivation and a negative self-image due to negative social attitudes. Indeed, he stressed the influence of teacher expectation to the extent that he maintained that the very act of being assessed for placement in an ESN school is seen as such a threatening situation by the West Indian child that he will lose any motivation he possesses since he perceives such a low probability of success. For this reason Coard recommended that West Indian psychologists should be used as testers. Although a review of the evidence on teacher expectation (see pp. 195–208) suggests that it is not possible to conclude that white teachers do necessarily have a demotivating effect on black pupils or that their low expectations are self-confirming, it nevertheless appears from some evidence (Brittan, 1976a and b and Giles, 1977) that teacher expectation may well be a significant feature of attitudes in general towards children of West Indian origin, and, in this particular instance may suggest that initially assessments involving expectations about language, behaviour and family problems may have led to over-referral (see also Tomlinson, 1979).

Coard also stressed that parents should excercise their rights of objection and appeal in the case of classification of their child as ESN and pointed to the importance of the involvement of West Indian parents in schools. Although the general impression is of West Indian parents' anxiety and concern about ESN classification, which they see as a further instance of discrimination, little is known about West Indian parents' views on education specifically with respect to ESN placements. Foner (1975) incidentally mentions that those Jamaican parents whom she interviewed in London who had children in ESN schools seemed both to accept the classification and to appreciate the special help given. Tomlinson reports in her study of the assessment of ESN pupils (1979) that some interest was shown in the process by West Indian parents as measured by the amount of home-school contact. In her interviews with parents she discovered that most know something about their children's schools and special schools, and West Indian mothers in particular seemed quite knowledgeable about certain aspects of the educational system. However, they seemed neither to have been properly informed or consulted and they appeared not to understand the role of the educational psychologist in particular. Tomlinson recommended that there should be more channels of communication between professionals and parents involved in assessment.

Indeed in view of the proportionately large numbers of children of West Indian origin currently in ESN schools virtually nothing is known about West Indian parental involvement with these schools or the extent to which they understand the purpose of such schools and what they are trying to do. It would appear that there is a good case for investigating the involvement of parents and the position of children of West Indian origin in ESN schools in greater detail, possibly on a case-study basis as, for example, in the research on an ESN school in Lancashire (Hunt, 1975).

There have been many attempts to explain the often apparently different behaviour patterns of many children of West Indian origin which it would appear from the little research evidence has been the main factor in evaluation and diagnosis of children as ESN. Several writers have pointed to the 'culture shock' with respect to different social patterns, dress, food etc. which many West Indian immigrant children appear to experience on migration to this country (e.g. Triseliotis, 1968). This may apply in particular to those who arrive after their parents and may come to a new home situation with a different father, and perhaps new brothers and sisters, often living in shared dwellings where there is little chance of obtaining peace and quiet for doing homework. The stresses on such a child are great, since not only does he have the process of adjustment to contend with, but in the English educational system he is seen as responsible for his own learning and self-discipline to a much greater extent. Even those children of West Indian origin born in this country may still experience particularly severe transition difficulties when they leave their homes for the first time and enter the environment of the school. Williams (1978) in her report about the position of West Indian children in Dudley schools mentions that infant teachers saw the majority of West Indian children as requiring above-average attention when they first entered school. On the other hand, Ward (1978) in an observational study of immigrant and indigenous children at the infant level (which seemed to include just a few West Indian pupils) noted that whether the ethnic minority pupils were born in the UK or came directly from overseas they very quickly adopted a set of behaviour patterns as varied in range as those manifested by their peers, and each child developed an individual response to the special climate of his own particular group so that there was no characteristic pattern amongst immigrant pupils. Stoker (1969) has given a most perceptive appreciation of the initial problems of adjustment to school of children of West Indian origin and one paragraph in quotation may serve to indicate the contrasts between home and school with which such children have frequently to cope:

'Problems of stealing and lying by West Indian children were not uncommon, but whereas very often English children who steal take things for their own personal gain such as a toy car or farm animals, West Indian children often found pieces of coloured chalk, counters and bits of colour factor irresistible. In a culture where many material things are held communally, West Indian children were not always aware that they had done wrong. Some teachers allowed the children to take home some of the toys in the evenings in order to give the children more play experience and to avoid the need for the children to steal. Teachers found that children would tell lies because they feared the teacher's rejection if they admitted to doing something wrong, and did not see any point in getting into trouble if it could be avoided by telling a lie. When West Indian parents were told of their children's stealing and lying they were always very upset but usually promised to beat the child as a result. Many parents felt that the teacher should beat the children herself and that she was failing in her duty if she did not do so.' (p.32).

Similar difficulties were frequently referred to by a third of the primary and a quarter of the secondary head teachers who answered a question on discipline by Townsend and Brittan (1972) in their survey of 230 multiracial schools. Approximately three-quarters of the 40 primary head teachers and the 20 secondary head teachers who commented on discipline problems consistently identified West Indian pupils as the immigrant group with which most of the disciplinary problems arose. Many of the comments referred to the different standards of discipline in West Indian homes and English primary schools; discipline in the former being seen by heads as strict, harsh, firm and repressive and often involving corporal punishment, as opposed to discipline in schools which they saw as involving self-discipline, liberal attitudes, understanding, tolerance and informality. One problem appeared to be that West Indian parents saw this difference in attitude as 'soft' (see also Davey and Norburn, 1980b). Many headteachers reported that the attitude of West Indian parents' to lack of learning, motivation or behavioural difficulties was, in each case, to suggest corporal punishment. References were also made to children who attempted to take advantage of the apparently more lenient atmosphere of the school. Secondary head teachers' responses confirmed these points. In general, it seems fair to say that although it is likely that children's behaviour is different in different contexts and may alter between the home and the school, teachers, though appreciating the natural warmth of children of West Indian origin, and often remarking on their greater ebulliance and outgoingness (see, e.g. Louden, 1978), nevertheless also appear to show some lack of understanding of normal socialization patterns in the West Indian family tradition.

In conclusion with respect to ESN it can be seen that the problems associated with the classification of pupils of West Indian origin as mildly educationally sub-normal—namely, difficulties of appropriate assessment materials, language, behaviour and teacher expectation—are the same problems, writ large, as those associated with the schooling of children of West Indian origin as a whole. In the writer's opinion, whilst arguments about special classes or special schools for ESN children are relevant to those who are truly educationally sub-normal (S), such deliberations can only be a hinderance to furthering the provision of appropriate educational arrangements for the many children of West Indian origin who continue to be misplaced. A more general consideration of the placement of pupils of West Indian origin in ESN schools may more properly be undertaken within the larger context of consideration of the schooling of all pupils of West Indian origin in the British school system.

Behavioural deviance and psychiatric disorders
In view of the controversy over the classification of many West Indian pupils as ESN it is appropriate to consider research evidence on the more severe behaviour disorders and deviance among West Indian children. This evidence comes from three main sources: research studies based on individual populations in clinics, teacher questionnaires about school experience, and epidemiological studies of the general population. Findings from reported research in each of these categories will be considered in turn; but first it is worth noting one particular study which attempted to assess the extent and nature of the association between children's behaviour at school and their educational attainment.

The research reported by Varlaam (1974) was not specifically on children of West Indian origin though it included some such children in its sample. This was in fact a sample of 10 per cent of all those children aged 11 who were involved in the ILEA Literacy Survey. Children were assessed on the Rutter Behaviour Questionnaire which is used for preliminary screening purposes in surveys of psychiatric or behavioural disorders in children. A sizeable proportion of the children were assessed by their teachers as displaying abnormal behaviour, either of an anti-social or neurotic kind. This was strongly associated with low performance on verbal reasoning tests and in English and mathematics as assessed by teachers. A detailed analysis was also undertaken of the proportion of children with behavioural abnormalities among children with reading difficulties and among children with no reading difficulties, by holding one of 10 background variables constant in turn. From this it was found that when reading retardation and behavioural disorders are found together there is a better chance that reading retardation preceded behavioural difficulties than the other way round. Moreover, it was particularly likely that educational failure preceded behavioural difficulties in the case of children of West Indian origin. This result also appears to relate to that of McFie and Thompson (1970) who found that white indigenous children who are maladjusted have similar general patterns of IQ and reading test scores to their black counterparts. If such findings are, indeed, generally the case – and there is need of more evidence before it can be definitely said to be so – then educational failure may well lead to maladjustment and possible deviance for such children. Were such a link supported by further research it would, in the writer's view, lend even more positive support in favour of the argument for concentrating not on rectifying behaviour when it deteriorates markedly but on ameliorating handicapping environmental conditions and the effectiveness of teaching during the early years of schooling.

Turning to a consideration of behaviour disturbance, two older studies undertaken in child guidance clinics are of particular interest in that West Indian children and particularly girls were shown to have a predominance of conduct rather than neurotic disorders, quite unlike the usual trend for maladjusted children. Graham and Meadows (1967) studied 55 West Indian children matched for age and sex with 55 white indigenous children who had all been referred to a child guidance clinic in a south London borough over a period of three years. Twenty-nine of the subjects were boys (mean age 9.1) and 26 were girls (mean age 9.6 years) the latter being a disproportionately large group compared with the clinic population as a whole. There was no control group of normal West Indian children. Both West Indian girls and boys, but particularly girls, had experienced more parental separation than the control groups. Although IQ scores are not reported in detail, the IQs of the girls appeared to be lower, but there were no significant differences between the West Indian children or English children on IQ or reading ability. The West Indian children were lower on performance scales of the WISC than on the verbal scales. No differences were found in respect of social class or family size. A comparison suggested that significantly more of both West Indian boys and girls were disobedient in the school setting, and, interestingly, that the West Indian girls were significantly less anxious than the control girls. The authors concluded that '... there is felt to be clear cause for concern in the frequent and sometimes traumatic separations that the current immigration pattern imposes on West Indian family life' (p.114).

The second study, Nicol (1971) investigated 204 West Indian children, 93 of whom were born in Britain and 111 who had migrated from the West Indies who were referred to a child guidance clinic in London during the decade 1960–9. When referrals for 1967 were analysed it was found that there were an unusual number of girls born in the West Indies present in the clinic population but this did not apply for girls of West Indian descent born in England. In a comparison of the two groups, antisocial disorder was found to be much more common in children born in the West Indies than in black children born in England. When the data were analysed further it was clear that among the UK-born black children the antisocial behaviour was associated with separation experiences for boys but not for girls. Social background factors did not differ markedly between the groups and hence could not be advanced as an explanation. It is also of interest to note here that a more recent epidemiologically based study involving a sub-sample of 48 pre-school children of West Indian-born parents matched with a similar number of children of British parents for social class and residence in a London borough found a similar pattern in and prevalence of behaviour problems and their associated social and family characteristics (Earls and Richman, 1980).

However, several investigations using teacher questionnaires have suggested that children of West Indian parents have rates of behavioural deviance above those found in non-immigrant children. As part of the Schools Council project, Teaching English to West Indian Children (1970), the Bristol Social Adjustment Guide was completed by teachers for 220 West Indian children and 102 English children aged five to 13. In the Guide statements under six major headings are underlined by the teacher if considered relevant to the child in question, and a method is provided for detecting and diagnosing types and degrees of maladjustment and emotional disturbance which might contribute to inadequacy with school work or be indicative of delinquent breakdown. In the Schools Council project virtually no differences in rating were found for those West Indian children who were newly arrived here and those who had been born in this country, but the behaviour pattern recorded for 71 per cent of the West Indian population distinguished them from their white contemporaries, particularly by their backwardness and lack of concern for adult approval. At the infant level West Indian children were described as significantly more restless, hostile to adults, and anxious for the approval of other children, whilst at the same time expressing hostility towards them. These characteristics appeared long lasting and also obtained for the children of junior age, who were in addition unconcerned for adult approval, and at the secondary level this was transformed into active hostility towards adults. However, interest, enthusiasm and performance on classroom work was found to be similar for West Indian and white pupils.

Another study (Bagley, 1972) investigated teachers' attitudes to the behaviour of 112 English and 74 West Indian seven-year-old children attending five junior schools with fairly high proportions of West Indian pupils in the London area. Teachers completed the Rutter Behaviour Questionnaire Scale B2 for measuring behaviour disorder in children, by rating 26 statements about child behaviour on a three-point scale. A comparison of scores showed that by teachers' ratings children of West Indian origin were significantly more disturbed than their English classmates (7.4 as opposed to 5.4). Teachers were also asked to provide information on the separation of West Indian children from parents for a period of six months or more. When checked with parents this information proved to be reliable in the grosser cases of separation, but it turned out that teachers knew about less than half the total cases in which separation had occurred. Both black and white children who had experienced separation were found to have a much higher behaviour disorder, and markedly more of the West Indian children (37 per cent) had experienced such separation than the English children (13.5 per cent). The West Indian children from homes undisturbed by separation still had significantly higher behaviour disorders. Teachers' assessments showed that they saw children of West Indian origin as being significantly more squirmy, fidgety, disliked by others, irritable, often miserable, disobedient and attention seeking – all of these symptoms with the exception of being miserable, appearing to fall on the antisocial side of the scale. However, even a detailed analysis did not point to any variable which would account for increased deviance in behaviour.

Taken together these findings indicate that teachers perceive more problems in children of West Indian background. But such questionnaires, valuable though they may be as screening devices, appear to be subject to rating biases especially when teachers know that researchers are investigating behaviour, and their assessments cannot be used alone either for individual diagnoses or as valid indicators of psychiatric disorder.

One particularly thorough study has attempted to take this scaling procedure one stage further by obtaining epidemiological evidence on the general population using personal interview methods in connection with 10-year-old children of West Indian parents (Rutter *et al.*, 1974). By interviewing both parents and teachers of the children it was hoped to provide estimates of the prevalence of psychiatric disorder in children of West Indian immigrants and to throw some light on the causative influences of disorder amongst this group of children. Special attention was paid throughout the study to comparisons between children born in this country to West Indian parents and those who were themselves migrant. There were two stages to the study as with the two other researches which taken as a whole formed a tripartite investigation (Rutter *et al.*, 1974, 1975, and Yule *et al.*, 1975). In the first stage of this study teachers were asked to complete Rutter's Behaviour Questionnaire Scale B2 for 1,613 10-year-olds in one inner London borough in order to assess their behavioural deviance. A social questionnaire was also completed by the teachers and brief interviews undertaken with those teachers of children who were selected for individual study at the second stage. These comprised a randomly selected control group of 106 non-immigrant children and a randomly selected control group of 58 West Indian children; a group of 159 non-immigrant children rated as having behavioural deviance and a group of 116 West Indian children similarly rated; and, finally, 30 West Indian boys and 30 West Indian girls randomly selected for individual study. Parents of these children were interviewed at home by specially trained black interviewers who assessed family interaction, relationships and lifestyle. According to teachers' ratings deviance in children from West Indian families was twice that of non-immigrant families and was slightly more marked for girls than boys. Closer examination showed that the pattern of behavioural deviance was quite different for the West Indian children in that it did not appear for emotional or mixed types of disturbances but was confined to deviance involving conduct; whereas non-immigrant boys scored 14.2 for conduct disorders, West Indian boys scored 40.1, and there was a similar difference for girls (non-immigrant 5.1, West Indian 25.8) both highly significant ($p < 0.001$). Conduct disorders include such categories as restlessness, poor concentration, destructiveness and quarrelsome attitudes. There were far fewer differences on items reflecting emotional disturbance, although some West Indian girls were rated as solitary, miserable and fearful. Hence the pattern of deviance in girls from West Indian families was quite different from that in girls from non-immigrant families who tend to exhibit emotional type deviance. Much the same findings were found for individual ratings, and interviews with teachers and parents confirmed the questionnaire results. However, although between two and three times as many children from West Indian families showed conduct disturbance, it was striking that the West Indian children did not have impaired relationships with their non-immigrant peers. It is also of interest to note that there were no differences in prevalence of deviance or disorder between those children who had been born in this country and those born in the West Indies. As Bagley (1975b) has pointed out, both groups of West Indian children have suffered adverse life experiences of one sort and another which make them at risk, but not necessarily one more than the other. The main finding was that more behavioural deviance was shown at school rather than at home and this appears to confirm the more impressionistic evidence of, for example, Stoker (1969) and Marvell (1974) who reported tensions between home and school. On the other hand, the study undertaken by Pollak (1979) found that teachers made fewer complaints about the behaviour of West Indian children than their mothers who made reports similar to those of the mothers in the study by Rutter *et al.* (1974). In this latter study there were few differences between the West Indian and non-immigrant groups in terms of social background, hence this could not be used to predict behaviour. Indeed interviews with parents revealed no difference between West Indian and non-immigrant children in psychiatric disorder as shown at home. It therefore appears that West Indian children do in fact manifest more behavioural disorders at school than at home, as is also often the case with non-immigrant children.

In conclusion two main features of the behavioural patterns of children of West Indian origin of school age can be highlighted. First there is a difference in the type of behaviour insofar as West Indian children show many more antisocial conduct disorders than do non-immigrant children who tend to manifest more neurotic emotional behaviours. This tends to suggest that the disorders may be more in the nature of immediate responses or reactions to certain specific situations. This finding is particularly striking with respect to West Indian girls who show similar conduct disorders to West Indian boys whereas non-immigrant girls tend to show more emotional disturbances. The reason for this is not clear.

Educationally more significant perhaps is the relatively high rate of behavioural disturbance shown in the school situation. The studies in clinics would appear to suggest that the experience of migration is an important contributory factor to behavioural problems, and, as studies by Bagley (1975b) and Rutter *et al.* (1975) have shown with respect to teachers' estimates of the child's place of birth, where this was not known teachers also appear to associate behaviour disorders with migration. Yet other studies (Rutter *et al.*, 1974 and Schools Council, 1970) suggested that there were no behavioural differences between children born in the West Indies and those born in this country. However, both these studies involved relatively few recent migrants, and it may well be that the stresses of migration are much more significant in the period immediately after arrival and also more critical for adolescents joining their parents in this country. Nevertheless, several educational factors do appear to be significantly associated with behavioural disorders: retardation in general educational attainment and in particular reading has been shown to precede behaviour disorder (Varlaam, 1974); the tendency for children of immigrant families to attend schools with high pupil turnover which are known to be associated with high rates of problem behaviour (Yule *et al.*, 1975); and the evidence of racial discrimination in this country, of which children may well be particularly aware at school. In addition other domestic factors such as a broken home, being admitted into care and disturbed parent-child relationships have also been shown to be related to behavioural difficulties (Rutter *et al.*, 1974). Once again the findings with respect to behavioural disorders of children of West Indian origin seemed to mirror other research findings in their ambiguity and inconsistency. Here, too, there is no obvious or simple explanation.

Part Three

Home and School

**Attitudes, Perceptions, Aspirations and Expectations
of Parents, Pupils and Teachers**
Many of the research investigations reviewed in Part 2, Ability,
Attainment and Achievement (pp.46–141) reported significant
associations between aspects of school performance and home
background variables, usually measured by standard socio-
economic indices. This section is an attempt to assess the more
intangible, less quantifiable evidence on the relationship between
home and school as manifested by the continual interaction of
attitudes, perceptions, values, aspirations and expectations, of
parents, pupils and teachers.

Section 12: West Indian Parents
It is widely acknowledged that West Indian parents express a high
regard for education and are keen to aid their children's schooling.
Yet an earlier section of this report on West Indian family life and in
particular, child rearing practices in the UK (pp.35–45), strongly
suggested many West Indian parents may well have little understanding of the importance of play, toys, conversation and interaction for the development of their child in his early years, as well as
for a basis for later, more formal, learning. It is therefore proposed
to devote this section to an appreciation of West Indian parents'
attitudes towards education in general and the value they place on
it; their expectations and aspirations for their children; and their
perception of and attitudes towards their children's schools,
teachers and the curriculum.
  Whilst it appears to be undoubted that West Indian parents value

education as a good, it seems to be less likely that they value it as good in itself, but rather as an instrumental good through which to achieve increased status. Several studies reviewed earlier in the section on life in the Caribbean (pp.14–23) referred to the class conscious nature of Jamaican society (e.g. Foner, 1977) and the significance of education for blacks as virtually the only means of upward social mobility. In Jamaica, education symbolizes success and is also an avenue to 'the good life' (Foner, 1975). Attention was also drawn earlier to the educational aspirations, acting as one motivation, albeit probably secondary, to migrants who come to this country. However, research by Foner (1975) sheds some light on the change in emphasis placed on the meaning of education by Jamaicans at home and Jamaican migrants in London. Whereas education was the central focus in interviews with Jamaicans studied in a rural village in 1968–9, in an open-ended attitude questionnaire administered by interview to a sample of 110 pre-dominently working class Jamaicans, matched for age, sex and occupational mobility, in London in 1973, education was rarely mentioned, either in general, or more specifically, in terms of aspirations for children. The researcher suggested that this was due to several factors: that education is not the only route to marked material improvement in this country; that secondary education is generally available here; and, thirdly, the respondents' obvious awareness of racial prejudice, though this was rarely explicitly mentioned in connection with education. She concluded that 'among Jamaican migrants in England status distinctions based on occupation and education were superseded by the overwhelming importance of colour' (p.199).

The fact remains that Jamaican parents, though they may not have gained sufficient satisfaction from their own education, are generally thought to have high aspirations for their children. Indeed, many of those who say these aspirations are unrealistically high point to the apparent paradox between parental aspirations and their children's achievement. As Pryce (1979), a West Indian himself, puts it

'The majority of West Indian parents have great academic aspira-tions for their children. They believe that ultimately education is the most reliable means whereby their group, as a whole, through their children, can achieve recognition and status on an equal footing with others in society.' (p.120).

Yet, as a result of his investigations, he feels entitled to say that 'West Indian parents in Bristol want their children to be educationally successful, and expect them to "have brains" despite their own ignorance as parents and the fact that they themselves may not have been anywhere near their children for the greater part of their lives, and can't even now, owing to pressure of circumstances, afford to provide the right environmental conditions and the understanding and patience which are so essential if children are to make progress academically.' (p.121).

The evidence from research on parental aspirations is somewhat scant. This is obviously a particularly sensitive issue and one more than usually subject to interviewer influence. As with investigations of attitudes, both these affective areas must be regarded with some caution and 'findings' seen as tentative only. A CRC investigation (1977) into the perspectives of parents, teachers and educational authorities on the education of ethnic minority children, which covered eight disadvantaged areas across the country found that (195) West Indian parents had greater expectations for their children than the (700) parents of similarly disadvantaged white children (see also Rex and Tomlinson, 1979). Likewise, Richmond (1973) in a study in Bristol noted that West Indian parents were more ambitious for their children than English-born parents in the same working class district. Pollak in her more recent study of nine-year-old children in a London borough (1979) also claimed that the 66 mothers of West Indian children in her sample were likely to have 'higher and unrealistic aspirations for their children' and that the parents were less likely to leave their child's choice of career up to him (p.167).

In contrast to this general impression, the parents in the Jamaican/London study undertaken by Foner (1975) had, she felt, fairly realistic views of *occupational* opportunities for their children. Nearly all those with daughters who were working mentioned the occupation in which their daughter actually worked as the desired occupation, but few sons were in desired occupations; parents generally wanted their sons to enter professional or white collar positions. Many respondents, it is claimed, were aware, however, that their aspirations might be too high: about 25 per cent felt that their children would attain the occupation they listed as desirable if they 'had the brain' and applied themselves; four per cent thought that their children would actually occupy lower status jobs.

Similarly Rex and Tomlinson (1979) felt that the 227 West Indian parents in their Birmingham sample had realistic aspirations for their children's future occupations. Twice as many West Indian parents as white parents (65.5 per cent) did not know what jobs their sons would do and left the decision to them. Sixteen per cent aspired to professional careers for their sons and 65.6 per cent wanted them to stay on at school. There were somewhat different aspirations for daughters: 42.2 per cent made no firm career choice; 71.6 per cent wanted them to stay on at school. Nursing was a popular choice of career (16.7 per cent) for daughters.

A study by Driver (1977) also showed that West Indian parents appeared to have differential aspirations for their sons and daughters – though this time far greater support and emphasis was placed on the daughter. The researcher interviewed the parents of an unstated number of West Indian boys and girls, selected by their teachers as doing particularly well or badly in their third year in a secondary school in the West Midlands. It appeared that regardless of their daughter's performance, parents, and particularly mothers, indicated a strong feeling that the daughter needed to be given 'as much physical and emotional support as possible to establish for herself economic viability and social prestige' (p.354). A system of strong support and control over their daughter's lifestyle was exercised and the parents were seen 'to insist upon their daughter doing well at school and to participate in the effort to find safe and suitable jobs upon leaving school'. By contrast, parents' relations with their sons were often obviously strained, and in the majority of cases communication about school and other matters had completely broken down. Nevertheless, parents, especially fathers, continued to have high aspirations for their sons, placing naive faith in the school's ability to provide their sons with an education, which they themselves had often not enjoyed, and which would lead to a career of modest to ambitious dimensions. This was particularly the case when the parents' own efforts to support and control their sons had failed.

This suggests that the traditional emphasis on girls' self sufficiency has to a large extent been carried over to socialization practices and in parental expectations in this country whilst at the same time being modified by the appreciation of the greater stress placed on aspirations for boys in Western society. However, it is difficult to know how much weight to place on such statements which have an impressionistic ring, subjective on the part of the interviewee and interviewer alike. As views at a point in time they must be credited with authenticity, but no studies have reported on changes or consistency over a period of time–several years would probably be necessary–and so extrapolations to the general West Indian population should not be made, nor trends sought. In addition, it is not always clear from these studies whether those parents whose views have been reported were always thinking exclusively of *educational* aspirations, i.e. attaining examination passes, or of education in terms of the occupational status to which it could lead. On the face of it, the latter seems more likely. However, West Indian parents are generally recognized as frequently giving approval to their children staying on at school, or even to continuing schooling after the age of 18 (Richmond, 1973) and Rex and Tomlinson (1979) found in a sample of 227 West Indian parents that 68.6 per cent wanted their children to stay in education after leaving school and only 15.3 per cent wanted their children to leave school before 16. (see also the section on pupils' aspirations, pp. 178–83).

An issue raised in the study by Driver (1977)–the nature of control in parent-child interactions–is, of course, significant in any relationship and especially during adolescence. It is therefore important that a number of writings have pointed expressly to the authoritarian structure of West Indian family life. For example, Bagley *et al.* (1978) in a most interesting study of the relation of home factors to scholastic success in which 150 West Indian mothers and 84 fathers were interviewed, found that authoritarianism, as measured by the Miller questionnaire, a recognized and reliable scale, correlated, together with several other factors, negatively with achievement in reading, independently of social class. The authors suggested that authoritarianism which is traditional in Jamaican society to depress non-conformity and creativity, may no longer be functional in this country.

Whilst it is extremely difficult to know to what extent disagreements about assertion of parental control occur, to what extent they are usual inter-generational disputes and how much they are part of the normal process of growing up and achieving of independence for youngsters, evidence mainly from studies in the 60s suggests that West Indian parents, possibly vesting their own hopes and fears for their race too directly in their offspring, who are themselves undergoing socialization at school into a different culture, may be particularly prone to conflicts with their children. Evans and Le Page (1967) in a considered review of the adjustment of early West Indian immigrants to English education, have remarked 'home conditions though superficially in favour of educational arrangements and integration often act in fact as a strong brake on progress in that direction. Many West Indian parents are desperately anxious that their children shall do well at school... but at the same time they unconsciously resist the child's moving away from its home background.' (p.23). Among others, both Bushell (1973) and Kitzinger (1978) in particular have noted that West Indian parents seem to retain a traditionally authoritarian outlook on their children's behaviour and in particular appear to show lack of awareness of the adolescent's need to share in his own youth culture and to conform to the new and different norms of his peer group. The often careful and hardworking parent expects his child not to 'waste time' with friends and disapproves even of youth clubs or extra-curricular activities. Rather, work must be geared to helping in the home or to school examinations; it is almost, as Fitzherbert (1967) has observed, that 'parents hold the Victorian attitude that children owe them a debt'. The adolescent, for his part, seeing that his white working class peer is not subject to such treatment, resents his parent's attempts at control, objects vociferously and a real conflict takes place. This may occur in an intense form when the only authority figure for a boy is his mother who may accept responsibility for her son, but resents it and constantly refers to it. Kitzinger (1978) suggests that in such a situation the boy may well turn to the gang for relief and to discover his role as a male through corporate identity. More generally:

'The West Indian adolescent seems to be caught between identifying with the world belonging to his parents and with one which he regards as his own. Most adolescents in their bid to assert their independence, experience a period of poor relationship with their parents, but with the West Indian in England this experience is made more crucial by the clash of the two worlds of which he is part, particularly since he is aware that as a West Indian acceptance by the group with which he identifies is limited to a few rather than the wider more general adolescent world.' (Bushell, 1973, p.91).

A further dimension which should be added is that of parents' attitudes towards schools. It may well be the case as Stoker (1969) has remarked in the context of infant teaching, that the West Indian parent sees herself as responsible for the child's behaviour and the teacher for intellectual development. In relation to the difficulties in adjustment to school, which many, especially first-generation West Indians have been observed to experience, she notes that the child seems to be caught between

'...the accepted attitudes at home and the accepted attitudes at school. Much of the deliberate training in acceptable behaviour that the West Indian parent gives his child is contrary to what is expected and required of the child in an English infant school. Many West Indian parents teach their children to be silent at home, whereas the good infant school encourages the children in free outgoing talk. Where a good infant teacher encourages initiative and self-assertion, some West Indian parents may teach their children to be passive and submissive. Where a teacher wants to train children to have inquiring attitudes, many West Indian parents may train acceptance in their children. Where his two lives conflict to such an extent, the West Indian child cannot but have difficulty in trying to produce two radically different kinds of acceptable behaviour. The enormous pressures put upon the child by this conflict tend to make him react in one or two ways. He either becomes uncontrollable in school and presents great problems within the classroom, or he completely retreats into himself and is unable to communicate or to take part in any school activity.' (p.30).

Such descriptions show how it is that many West Indian pupils have come to be diagnosed as educationally sub-normal by their teachers (see Section 11 on ESN and behaviour p.124–41), and also how lack of knowledge by West Indian parents about the ways in which schools operate and teachers teach may lead them to prepare their children inadequately or inappropriately for schooling. Jackson's (1979) case study in which the West Indian mother's knowledge of the school system seemed, despite having several children already in school, to be wholly influenced by her own experience of schooling in the West Indies and of corporal punishment as an instigation to learning, illustrates this well–though it may be an extreme instance. But Driver's interviews with parents (1977) also reveal lack of understanding of the purposes and limitations of the secondary school and Foner's (1975) Jamaican migrants in London showed no awareness of the differences in quality of comprehensive schooling. On the other hand, the detailed and significant study undertaken by Rutter *et al.* (1975) on the home social life of a group of 10-year-olds in London found that West Indian parents were just as likely as their white counterparts to take their children to the library, to buy books and to help with homework. This finding fits with the general global value placed on education by the West Indian parent and his attested willingness to assist materially in promoting educational goals.

Yet the school itself seems, as for many other white parents, to present a considerable barrier. There appears to be evidence of low involvement of West Indian parents with their children's schools. Mabey (1980, 1981) in the large ILEA investigation noted that only 50 per cent of West Indian parents had discussions with their children's teachers in the year preceeding their literacy survey when the children were eight, compared with over 80 per cent of the white parents. Similarly, in the study of nine-year-old children in a London borough Pollak (1979) found that the West Indian parents were less involved in their children's schooling: they were less likely to take their child to school, had been less often to the school Open Day or concerts and had visited the teacher less frequently. Such findings have tended to substantiate those of Payne (1975) reporting on views of 385 parents in EPAs in London and Birmingham. Among this group the West Indian parents as a whole were less likely to have had any contact with their children's schools, to have seen the head, to have engaged in school activities, or to have gone to school on their own initiative. The West Indian parents in London had slightly more contact with schools than those in Birmingham. On the other hand, Rex and Tomlinson (1979) discovered in Birmingham that 79 per cent of the 227 West Indian parents in their sample had visited school recently which, they suggested, does tend to show parental interest. Indeed the Haringey Reading Project which involved close teacher–parent co-operation in encouraging children's reading demonstrates the effect that all parents can have on increasing their child's skills (Tizard *et al.*, 1980).

Thirty heads interviewed by Tomlinson (1979) in connection with ESN(M) assessment were unanimous that West Indian parents wanted their children to benefit from school. However, teachers may not necessarily think that parents show an interest, as Brittan (1976b) found that a national sample of 510 primary and secondary teachers were almost equally divided on the question as to whether 'West Indian parents usually show considerable interest in the education of their children', and teachers in 70 per cent of the 525 secondary schools in the recent Schools Council project Studies in the Multi-ethnic Curriculum said that ethnic minority parents were less active in PTA groups and other forms of parental involvement (Little and Willey, 1981).

Whether West Indian parents have close associations with schools or not does not mean that they do not have views about teachers and schools. Although 74 per cent of Rex and Tomlinson's parents were satisfied with their children's schooling 50 parents were not. They gave low standards, teaching methods, teachers themselves, and lack of encouragement to slow learners as reasons for their dissatisfaction. The researchers remarked that schools and teachers did not seem to fulfil the expectations of the West Indian parents which had been shaped in the West Indies; they found British schooling too liberal thus confirming similar early findings of Payne (1975). Moreover the CRC investigation in eight disadvantaged areas of the country (1977) discovered that West Indian parents were least likely to like their children's schools, although 44 per cent claimed to be satisfied with discipline. Fourteen per cent of their children's schools had West Indian teachers, but the remaining parents for whom this was not the case were almost equally divided on whether they would or would not like West Indians to teach their children, although 50 per cent mentioned that their children were either taught nothing or not enough of their own culture. More controversially, and without supplying evidence, Mack (1977) confirmed the views of such parents about the lack of appreciation of black culture in schools, and also alleged that most West Indian parents' complaints concerned discrimination and discipline as well as teacher expectation, which, she claimed, they believed to adversely affect their child's performance (see two later sub-sections pp. 183–9 and p. 193ff on institutional racism and teacher expectation). A somewhat cynical, but none the less telling, statement from a West Indian parent mentioned by Mack in that same article, is worth quoting, since it pointedly highlights the main issues involved here and reveals the ambivalence towards education which many West Indian parents seem to feel:

'If our children manage to get a CSE, as far as the teacher is concerned that's a great achievement. If they get a Grade 1, they're a genius. If the child manages to pass an 'O' Level he is different, distinct. I tell you: if that child is achieving, no more is he black.' (Mack, 1977).

Lately, some more positive evidence concerning ethnic minority parents' values and views about their children's education and their influence on their children's perceptions of other ethnic groups has been reported (Davey and Norburn, 1980b). As part of a larger study 491 parents of 512 children of primary age of whom 256 were white, 128 West Indian and 128 Asian, and who lived in London or industrial Yorkshire, were interviewed in their homes by interviewers of their own race. Forty-five per cent of the West Indian fathers were in semi-skilled or unskilled occupations and 87 per cent of the West Indian mothers were at work, some, especially in London, in non-manual occupations, and more than half in full-time posts. Most parents claimed their contact with their child's school was frequent, though only five per cent of the West Indian parents had helped to organize an event recently. The West Indian parents were overwhelmingly (90 per cent) in favour of children of different ethnic groups being educated in the same schools. Most of the parents could identify their children's friends, and, like the white parents, the West Indians were concerned to show that their children had other-race friends and, in contrast to the Asian parents, few wished to interfere with their children's choice of friends. In the context of considering three hypothetical racial incidents devised by the researchers it transpired that 75 per cent of the West Indian parents expected the teacher to be firm in dealing with classroom behaviour and a third would support their child's retaliation in a racial incident. Parents reported little curiosity on the part of their children about differences in colour, religion, customs or countries of origin and although one-third said they would help to explain these matters to their children, in the researchers' view they obviously relied a good deal on the school to perform this function. Indeed 70 per cent of the parents believed that schools should have a multicultural curriculum. More generally, most liked their neighbours and neighbourhoods and thought they were good places for bringing up children. Indeed, there was a strong association between this view and approval of their child's school, which appeared to be more important to them. Nevertheless all parents in the different ethnic groups were pessimistic about the racial climate in general, especially those in London, and the West Indian parents blamed the host society.

This research is also of especial interest in the context of the education of pupils of West Indian origin since there appears to be very little other empirical data on links between West Indian parents' views and those of their children. Although an association was found between children's attitudes (as reported in Davey and Mullin, 1980 and Davey and Norburn, 1980a) and the beliefs and values manifested in their parents' responses, this was not strong. As Davey and Norburn (1980b) point out, this was partly because racial matters were not a preoccupation of the parents, but also children are obviously subject to other influences, peers and the mass media for instance. One or two links between parents' and children's attitudes shown by statistical analysis were of particular interest. For instance, parents who approved of multicultural education tended to have more tolerant children. Curiously West Indian parents who advocated on-the-spot justice from teachers in response to discriminatory behaviour by pupils in the classroom had fewer highly ethnocentric children. Only in the West Indian group did the extent to which parents felt responsible for their children's attitudes and the strategies which they employed to deal with their child's questioning on racial matters have an association with their children's ethnocentricity. Eighty-two per cent of those West Indian pupils who expressed favourable attitudes to other ethnic groups had parents who acknowledged a responsibility for inter-racial education. This, as the researchers note, is especially interesting when considered in relation to the attitudes of the remaining West Indian parents, who, more firmly than either the white or Asian parents, placed the main responsibility for multi-ethnic education with the schools. It is perhaps encouraging to close this section with a review of a well designed and complex research study which has the especial merits of taking into account community influences on parents' values and beliefs and attempting, in turn, to examine the differential impact of these parents' views on the attitudes of their children to other ethnic groups. This genre of research would seem to be particularly helpful to those attempting to assess the current educational position of ethnic minority pupils. It is to the attitudes of those pupils of West Indian origin to which the following section is devoted.

Section 13: Pupils of West Indian Origin

This section will review what research has discovered about pupils' attitudes, expectations, aspirations, values, and perceptions in relation to race, others, especially peers, the pupils' own self-image, their schools and future careers. Of these, the issue of self-image or esteem is of particular importance and has of late been the focus of several researches and received extensive treatment in the literature.

It is now generally recognized that attitudes have a three-dimensional nature with cognitive, affective and behavioural components. However, the behavioural dimension, despite the often noted differences between pupils' behaviour at home and at school, will not be examined here since most studies in this area have, initially at any rate, been clinical, and only later has research on behaviour been undertaken in schools. Hence, it seemed more appropriate to review behaviour in terms of performance in connection with schooling for the educationally sub-normal (p. 135ff) where it is, of course, a major feature of diagnosis.

Finally, it is necessary to point out that many of the attitude scales and measurements which are mentioned in what follows, especially those used in the earlier studies, may be particularly subject to ethnic bias, since like intelligence tests, they were largely constructed for use with a white mainstream population. Moreover, attitude testing is also subject to possible effects of colour of tester, context of testing and perhaps, especially, expectation of tester, as the respondent may well be particularly influenced by what he supposes the expectation of the tester to be and hence how he should respond.

Attitudes to race

Any attempt to evaluate racial awareness may well depend to a large extent on both the racial composition of the area in which the pupils under investigation live and study, and also the racial climate obtaining whilst the research is in progress. As Verma and Bagley (1979) point out, the consensus of evidence indicates that children usually acquire the racial stereotypes and prejudices of their parents at an early age, although they may not necessarily be negative. It seems that it is possible to modify negative views, but as children grow older their attitudes become more complex and entrenched and less amenable to change. Indeed there is considerable evidence (as mentioned and listed on pp.352–5 of Verma and Bagley's

(1975) collection) that children acquire the concept of ethnic differences at an early age. Most of this research, with the notable exceptions of that of Milner (1975) and Davey and Mullin (1980) which investigated tri-dimensional ethnic attitudes and which will be mentioned in detail in the sub-section concerned with self-esteem, has been undertaken in the United States. However, Jahoda *et al.* (1966), working in London, reported that well-marked ethnic preferences revealed themselves among nursery children and a sharp increase in hostility was noticed in their second year. Although 172 white children were involved in this study, only 10 black children were similarly observed and hence this cannot be seen as saying much about the attitudes of black children to race. On the other hand, Laishley (1971) who studied children from three nursery schools, two in areas which had few immigrants and one which had a high proportion of immigrants, found that awareness of colour was not a significant feature in these children's interactions, nor was it negatively valued. There were, however, very small minorities of coloured children in these nursery schools.

Findings from a recent large-scale study of racial awareness in children (Davey and Norburn, 1980a) also demonstrate that ethnocentric attitudes are acquired at an early age. In one set of cue saliency tests, a sorting task and a jig-saw puzzle technique, the importance of pigmentation as against dress, sex and age was evaluated. Equal numbers of children aged seven, eight, nine and 10 from 16 primary schools in London and industrial Yorkshire took the tests. There were 256 white children, 128 each of West Indians and Asians and in each school a white child was paired with a West Indian or an Asian. In each region half the schools had 50 per cent or more Asian or West Indian children and half had 15 per cent or less. In the sorting task all the children regardless of ethnic group, sex, locale or concentration accorded overwhelming importance to the race cue. The sex and age cue alternated in second or third place and dress was always last. However, on the puzzle test the sex cue was first, then race and dress. This was consistent for boys and girls, in both regions and irrespective of concentration of ethnic minority pupils in the schools. The researchers considered that although children obviously attach importance to ethnic characteristics as grouping criteria they also take context and purpose into account and these are modifying factors (see also Richardson and Green, 1971; Madge, 1976).

Moreover, in a second set of tests the children's feelings towards other groups relative to their own were examined. Two tests, of paired comparisons and limited choice, were based on picture ratings and choices concerning sharing of sweets and provided an assessment of attitudes towards persons of different ethnic minority groups. The third test of stereotypes involving posting photographs to the different groups and 'nobody' gave a measure of the emotional value of the various statements. On each of the measures the children showed a considerable degree of bias toward their own groups, especially the white children. On the paired comparison test the West Indians and Asians included a white child in their first four photographs and they were also markedly more out-group orientated and at the expense of each other on the limited choice test. Girls were especially fair-minded. These results were complemented by those on the stereotypes test in which the whites showed a greater readiness to assign favourable attributes exclusively to themselves, whereas the West Indian and Asian children described their own group and the whites favourably, reserving the derogatory statements for each other. However, neither of the minority groups thought the whites more attractive than themselves, although they both thought the whites were to be preferred to each other. Thus the findings, which were very consistent within each group regardless of geographical location or proportion of ethnic minority children in schools, may be taken as evidence against the phenomenon of rejection of own race by ethnic minority pupils. Rather, it would seem that their feelings of dislike were directed not towards the host community but each other's groups.

At the other end of the age range as part of a concern to establish whether curriculum innovation and teaching about race can change the perception which different ethnic groups have of one another Bagley and Verma (1975) attempted to assess the extent of racial antipathy in a sample of British teenagers. One hundred and eighteen white, 58 West Indian and 44 Asian teenagers aged 14 to 16 in 12 schools in multiracial areas of London and the Midlands completed a modified and extended version of the Wilson-Patterson Conservatism Scale which appears to be a valid and reliable scale, free of some of the biases which bedevil attitude measurement. The five scales were concerned with: general racism, anti-West Indian, anti-Asian, and anti-white attitudes and black power ideology. Items in each scale consisted of words or phrases, such as 'employing West Indians', to which the subject had to respond with 'yes' and/or 'no' to the question 'Which do you favour, approve of or believe in?' On the general racism scale West Indians were found to obtain significantly lower scores than whites, though they had much higher scores than Asians on the anti-white scale and the highest score on the black power ideology scale. As the authors remark in a later study (Bagley *et al.*, 1979) it is not clear whether the expression of anti-white attitudes represents lack of adaptation of an individual or his realization that the sources of racism and discrimination in British society are the attitudes and behaviours of white people. It is also of interest to note that the commitment to black power ideology appeared to be unconnected with hostile perceptions towards whites, though hostility in the classroom is not always particularly noticeable since it may take the form of ignoring the other group. This aspect of racial perception will be looked at again later in connection with white pupils' views of black pupils considered in the context of the school (pp.189–93), and also when reviewing the research evidence on friendship and peer groups (pp.157–61).

Another study in this field attempted to construct a new scale which can be used with different ethnic groups as a valid comparative measure of their attitudes to race (D'Souza, 1978). This scale, the tri-dimensional intergroup attitudes scale (TIA), attempts to measure three attitudinal components: cognitive, affective and behavioural. Subjects respond to six positive and six negative items for each component on a five-point scale, for example, 'Do Asians have the following qualities?'; 'Do you feel the following towards Asians?'; 'Would you like to do the following to Asians?'. Parallel schedules require responses to attitudes to West Indians and white British. The scale was administered to 113 South Asians, 105 West Indians and 113 white British with a mean age of 14.8 in nine multi-ethnic schools in five boroughs of London. Although several earlier studies, notably that of Milner (1975) and Bagley and Coard (1975) have shown that minority group children prefer characteristics of the majority or 'superior' group (see pp.162–5), these findings have been contradicted by more recent research, in particular that by Davey and Mullin (1980), Coopersmith (1975) and again in D'Souza's study. Thus, all the individuals had more favourable stereotypes, feelings and behavioural inclinations towards the in-group than towards the out-groups. Seventy-two per cent of the West Indians held positive attitudes towards the white British; none held extremely negative attitudes. The West Indian girls had more favourable, but not significantly favourable, attitudes towards the out-groups than their boy peers. When social class background was taken into account West Indians from lower social classes had the lowest out-group scores. Of particular interest is the finding that the 68 per cent of the West Indian sample who were born in this country were least disposed towards the white British. Christians who attended church regularly tended to have more favourable out-group attitudes than those who did not. No clear pattern emerged in the relationship between school contact and inter-group attitudes. These studies have largely concentrated on attitudes to race. Although attitudes and behaviour are not the same or only in the narrow sense in which verbal attitudes may constitute behaviour, they do function as instigators to behaviour. For instance, Bagley and Verma (1975) in the study reported earlier in this sub-section noted a significant concordance between attitudes and actual inter-ethnic behaviour on the part of the pupils whom they observed in the classroom situation. It is to this aspect of West Indian pupils' lives, their attitudes to their peers and the influence of these on racial awareness, to which attention will now be given.

Attitudes to peers

Most studies which have attempted to measure black pupils' attitudes to their peers have concentrated on friendship patterns and friendship groups. However, it is strange that though friends might be considered to be of particular importance in adolescence, the majority of reseach investigations have concentrated on children of primary age. This may well be because of the difficulty of obtaining suitable materials and in particular devising appropriately discriminating questions which could be used to effect with pupils of greater age. In addition, it should also be noted that, though the researchers rarely make the connection explicit, their investigations are really concerned with the influence of skin colour on the choice of friends.

Although research into inter-ethnic friendship patterns began in America in the 1950s, it does not seem to have taken hold in this country until the late 1960s when a spate of research was reported indicating that most children choose the majority of their friends from their own ethnic group. Rowley (1968) questioned 1,747 children of whom 63.5 per cent were white, 20.5 per cent Asian and 14 per cent West Indian, on personal characteristics and choices of friends for 'play', 'sitting in class', and 'tea at home'. The majority of these children in 60 classes in the primary and secondary modern schools of a county borough in the West Midlands chose their friends from their own ethnic group. However, the proportion differed insofar as 90 per cent of the white children chose white friends, whereas the West Indian children also showed a marked preference for white friends, only 60 per cent of them choosing friends of their own colour.

These findings were largely confirmed in a study by Kawwa (1968a) which investigated the friendship patterns of pupils in a junior, a boys' secondary modern and a comprehensive school in London. Although the numbers of pupils involved were quite large, being the populations of the schools, unfortunately only a small percentage of pupils in each case were black. The junior school pupils named their two best friends, and the boys in the secondary school also chose two best friends, one from their own class, the other from the school as a whole, and named one boy least liked or disliked. In the comprehensive school pupils were asked to list in order of preference their five best friends of the same sex in the school. It was found that black pupils, particularly those in the junior and secondary modern schools, appeared to be more ethnocentric than others and they showed a greater expectation than any other immigrant group of being ignored by white British pupils.

One of the most important investigations in this field, since it drew on a large national sample, was that of Jelinek and Brittan (1975) who studied the patterns of friendship among pupils from a number of ethnic groups when aged eight, 10, 12 and 14 in 1972. Thirteen primary and 12 secondary schools with 18 to 84 per cent of pupils of ethnic minority origin were involved. West Indians numbered 188 out of 677 pupils at eight, 152 out of 611 at 10, 244 out of 1,507 at 12 and 234 out of 1,505 at 14. All these pupils were asked three questions, two on actual friendship and the third on desired friendship. Pupils were asked to name up to three friends they would like to 'play with at school', 'to have as friends' and 'to go about with at school'. The researchers found that by the age of eight ethnicity was already a strong factor in the choice of friends with the majority choosing friends from their own ethnic group. In particular the West Indian primary children showed greater own-group preferences in 'desired' friendship than did the Asian children and in secondary schools West Indians showed a greater own-group preference than indigenous pupils. Moreover, it is of interest to note that the West Indian secondary school pupils were much more likely than the white indigenous children to actually choose friends of their own colour. This trend towards in-group preference with age has also been recognized by Rowley (1968) and Robertson and Kawwa (1971). In addition the preference of West Indian adolescent girls for boyfriends of their own colour was also discovered by Hill (1968).

At the other end of the age range a well planned but very small-scale study (Madge, 1976), found that children in the top class of a multiracial infant school in London were aware of ethnic differences, but the extent and direction of their expressed preferences was strongly influenced by the situational context and by the range of choice which was presented to them. Black children tended to prefer 'approved' figures who appeared in stories, irrespective of their skin colour or age, but chose more 'friends' of their own skin colour. Despite the limitations of this study it is important in again pointing to the influence of the context and extent of choice presented in these researches – factors which have not been adequately considered in many of the studies reported (but see Davey and Norburn, 1980a). In addition, there may well be geographical differences according to whether there are large proportions of minority ethnic groups in the community from which the children studied are drawn; for example, Kawwa (1968b) found that whilst the majority of the London secondary school children in his study expressed negative attitudes to immigrants only a small minority of adolescents in Lowestoft did so.

In contrast to the general trend discovered in all these studies for West Indian pupils to prefer friends of their own race, three investigations (Milner, 1975; Pollak, 1979; Davey and Mullin, 1980) have found that black pupils would at least prefer to have, even if they do not in fact have, more white friends. Milner's careful study carried out in 1970 in two large English cities sampled a group of 300 well-matched West Indian, Asian and English children aged five to eight. Among other questions (see pp.162–4) the children were asked to indicate their straightforward preferences for one racial group over another by means of selection of white and black dolls. The children were asked which of the two dolls 'do you like best', 'would you like to play with in the playground', 'sit next to in class', or 'share your sweets with'? and 'Which figure looks like your best friend?'. Milner found that on this preference section 72 per cent of the West Indians 'made a majority of choices which favoured the white figures over the figures representing their own group' (p.122) though separate percentage responses for the two questions are not given. Yet interestingly, he later (p.127) acknowledges that the children's answers to the second question had a greater basis in reality in that they corresponded to children's actual friendships than did their replies to the straightforward attitude questions. It was significant that there was a much lower level of out-group choices on this question than on any others on that section even though West Indian children chose white figures more often than English children chose black figures. Obviously, to indicate someone as 'a best friend' involves an element of reciprocity which it would be difficult to claim if it did not in fact exist and only 17 per cent of the white sample indicated a black best friend so it looks as if in this study, too, black children actually tended to have black best friends.

Similar findings on a sociometric test have also recently been reported by Davey and Mullin (1980) with 238 seven- to 10-year old children in schools where the ethnic ratio was 50:50. Pupils were asked to say 'who are the two children you would most like to sit next to in this class?'; 'who are the two children in the school you would most like to play with in the playground?'; and 'who are the two children in the school you would most like to invite home?' Overall 66.5 per cent of the children wished to have some other-group friends and 78.5 per cent of the West Indians did so. However, West Indian children who named no other-race friends were also more likely to have chosen their own race on another test of group preference for own identification ($p < 0.025$). The authors suggest, however, that since this relationship comparing choice between an imaginary photographically illustrated situation and what is desired in a known real-life group context is fairly weak it implies that the attitudes of primary age children are not yet so rigid as to reject characteristics which conflict with their ethnic expectations.

It is tempting to conclude that what is in fact being measured in these studies is a degree of wishful thinking, preferences for some ideal state of friendship rather than indications of actual friendship patterns. Even evidence from Pollak's study of nine-year-olds in a London borough is ambivalent, for although it appears to suggest that a majority of West Indian children (68 per cent) did in fact have white friends, oddly enough this researcher, too, is inclined to play down this finding, talking in terms of children's 'aspirations' to have white friends rather than their actually having them. Incidentally from Table 16 (p.43) in her report (Pollak, 1979) it can be seen that many more of the West Indian children claimed to have 'lots' of friends although they were significantly less likely to have visited friends in their homes or to have had these friends visit them at home.

Although most of the studies reviewed in this sub-section have paid attention to such variables as age, sex, ethnicity, concentration of ethnic minority children in school, variations in methods and assessment techniques used, locations and chronology all combine to make cross-study generalizations highly speculative. However, it seems fair to say that the balance of earlier research evidence indicates that West Indians, as with other ethnic groups, do seem to have preferred friends of their own colour, and that this preference is likely to be more marked as the children grow older. Against this however, has to be set the findings of studies undertaken in the later 70s which appear to show that where there is a more even distribution of white and black pupils the majority of pupils of West Indian origin wish to have and may well in fact have white friends.

Attitudes to self: identity and self-esteem

The preceding section has already indicated that choice of friends is very likely to be influenced by a person's perception of his race. It is also likely to be influenced by that person's perception of himself and this, by turn completing the circle, is influenced by how he is seen by others. Thus, the material presented in this sub-section on self-esteem and identity must be seen in the wider context of life in Britain, the background factors of discrimination in housing and unemployment and the prejudice of the host population, as well as the specific factors of the immediate school neighbourhood, the hidden curriculum of the school itself and the prejudices of teachers and pupils working within it – all of which may serve to alienate the black pupil from himself and his true potential. (The attitude of the pupil of West Indian origin to school will be dealt with in the following section, pp.175–83).

An obvious feature of the affective dimension which may loosely be described as 'attitudes to the self' is its characteristic terminological and conceptual confusion. Attitudes to the self have been variously represented as self-image, self-concept, identity, preference etc. The time available for this research review did not permit an analysis of the different functions of these concepts in the research literature, nor did it allow for the underlying empirical or theoretical dimensions of the many different methods and techniques used for measuring these concepts to be evaluated, even supposing sufficient information on these matters enabling one to do so were provided in the reports themselves. However, a most useful summary of the major research literature related to this area is given in a collection of articles devoted entirely to the issue of identity (Verma and Bagley, 1979) and Bagley, *et al.* (1979) discuss definitions of self-contempt etc. in Chapter 11 in that book. As those authors put it

'Self-concept in its purest sense is a cognitive variable, and concerns what it is about himself that an individual recognizes as salient or relevant. But this self-conception almost always involves an evaluation of oneself, and is thus related, in a logical way to self-esteem. Self-esteem is largely an affective or evaluative dimension, measuring how the individual feels about himself, and evaluates himself relative to others.' (p.177).

A useful definition which has guided most of the work undertaken by the research reported in the book edited by Verma and Bagley is that given by the American researcher, Coopersmith (1975) who has devised a scale to measure self-esteem which has been widely validated in the USA.

'The concept represented by the person's picture of himself to himself has been variously called the self-image, self, or *self-concept*. Persons not only form pictures of themselves, they also develop feelings and attitudes about the content and quality of that image. They may like and admire the image they see in their mind's eye or they may feel varying amounts of dislike and even hostility about the self they have formed. These positive or negative attitudes and feelings about the self are the evaluative sentiments known as *self-esteem*. Thus the self-concept is the symbol or the image which the person has formed out of his personal experiences while self-esteem is the person's evaluation of that image.' (p.148).

It will be useful to bear this distinction in mind when attempting to evaluate the research reviewed in this section. Much has been written, especially during the mid- to late 70s, about the low self-esteem which West Indians are said to have, lower in fact than that of any other racial group. In what follows an attempt will be made to discover whether this claim is accurate.

Undoubtedly the best known investigation which appears to have shown the markedly disparaging view which West Indian children have of themselves is that of Milner (1975). In the first part of a two-pronged investigation undertaken in 1970 he studied four aspects of 300 children's attitudes towards racial groups, via a separate set of questions on identity, preferences, stereotypes and aspirations. The questions on identity and stereotypes, which are particularly relevant here, required each child to make a choice between two dolls, one representing the child's own racial group, the other the principal racial group in the child's immediate environment. On the identity question the child was asked 'Which doll looks most like you?' and 'If you could be one of these two dolls, which one would you rather be?' On the stereotype question the child was asked to point out the 'bad', 'nicest', and 'ugliest' doll. Whereas 100 per cent of the English children correctly identified themselves, only 52 per cent of the West Indians did so, 48 per cent choosing the white doll. The difference was, however, much more marked when the child chose an ideal identity, as no fewer than 82 per cent of the West Indians chose to be like the white doll apparently suggesting that they would prefer to be white than a member of their own group. Milner argued that these findings showed that a majority of black children are in conflict with their own identity. He claimed that the findings of the stereotype question also underlined these results, as 58 per cent of the West Indian children maintained that the black doll was 'bad', 82 per cent said it was 'ugly' and 78 per cent stated that the white doll was the 'nicest'. Another correlation was discovered in that all the West Indians who identified with whites also stated on the preference question that they would rather be the white doll. After a year Milner gave a series of identification tests to some of the same West Indian children (numbers not supplied). Half the sample maintained the same choice of figure from the first test to the second whereas the other half changed their choices.

Identified with Black on Both Occasions	Black to White	White to Black	Identified with Whites on Both Occasions
31.25%	6.25%	43.75%	18.75%

No differences were found to be associated with intensity of skin colour, age or sex although there was a trend for the tendency for out-group identification to decline with age.

In Chapter Four of his book *Children and Race* Milner gives an illuminating and fair discussion of the meaning of these findings for black children. He maintains that there are two extreme groups in his study both sure of their identity, but between these groups are the majority of children who have varying degrees of conflict about their identity. Put simply, they are black, which is a realistic but undesirable identity in our society, he claims, while subjectively, many would like to be white, which is an unrealistic but desirable identity. This attitudinal continuum must be expressed by a choice between the black or the white doll in the experimental situation. He acknowledges that this choice may be influenced by the race of the interviewer, although there is inconclusive evidence in general as to whether greater out-group orientation is shown as a consequence of using a white experimenter with black pupils (see Thomas, 1978 and Anderson and Thomas, 1979). Madge's study (1976) also shows that other aspects of the experimental situation may influence choices. In spite of these variables Milner claims that a higher proportion over and above the children who simply identified with the white doll have a positive orientation towards whites and desire to be like them but may be inhibited from expressing this by the phrase used in the test itself saying that they '*are* like' them. Milner concludes that his experiments display 'the conflicts the black child experiences with his social reality. That reality focuses on the racial aspects of his identity, and renders his blackness a highly negative attribute, while at the same time idealizing the white majority group and conferring on whiteness a highly positive value.' (p.135). This, he maintains is what makes a substantial number of the children of West Indian origin in his experiment opt to deny their true identity. Recently a further refinement in this field (Bagley and Young, 1979) has interestingly shown that mixed race children who have been adopted by whites, tend, like Milner's black West Indians, to identify with and prefer whites, but this is less likely for those who have not been adopted.

Whilst the tendency for black children to deny their identity. has also been noticed in their reluctance to colour their self portraits black or brown, preferring instead to leave them white (by e.g. NFER/Schools Council Education for a Multiracial Society Project, 1973–6, Schools Council, 1981, only one other research study appears to support that of Milner and again somewhat indirectly. Part of an investigation into ethnic identity and cultural knowledge of children in three multiracial schools in London (Bagley and Coard, 1975) found that in a one in seven random sample of white and West Indian children aged five to six, seven to 10 and 11 to 14 (numbers not given, but less than a hundred), a substantial number of West Indian children rejected their ethnic identity when questioned about eye, hair and skin colour. Of the 42 black subjects 40 per cent did not wish to change themselves in any way, whereas 60 per cent wished to change one or more of these three aspects and 19 per cent wished to change themselves in respect of their eye, hair or skin colour. Interestingly children did not vary in their responses whether they were interviewed by a black or a white researcher.

Some findings which refine and contrast with the results of Milner's work in 1970 have recently been reported by Davey and Mullin (1980). This work, part of a large-scale and carefully designed investigation into racial awareness in young children, tends to diminish the importance attached to the phenomenon of self-rejection amongst minority group children and to confirm findings of greater acceptance of ethnic identity by blacks as found in America during the 1970s. A total of 512 children – 256 white, 128 West Indian and 128 Asian – aged seven, eight, nine and 10 from 16 primary schools, eight in London and eight in industrial Yorkshire were involved in the research. Two schools in each region had more than 50 per cent of Asians or West Indian pupils and two had 20 per cent or less Asian or West Indian children. In each school a white child was paired by age and sex with an Asian or West Indian child. On both the identification and preference tests described here black and white photos of identically dressed children in the middle of the age-range were used. Children were interviewed individually by white testers on two occasions four to six weeks apart. On the first visit children were shown three photos of same sex children, one for each ethnic group, and were asked 'Which one looks like you?' On the second occasion they were shown the same photos but asked 'If you could choose which one would you most like to be?' The researchers discovered that a black child was no more likely to say that he looked like a white child than a white child was to say that he looked like a black child. No consistent trend for out-group orientation was found for West Indian pupils in schools where they were in a minority, nor was region a significant variable.

However, on the preference test there was a marked difference in the responses between black and white children. Eighty-six per cent of the white children preferred their own group but less than half the West Indians and Asians made own-race choices (p < 0.001). Yet these two ethnic minority groups did not desire to be like each other, rather they had an overwhelming preference for the white child. This was not affected by size or concentration of group or region although more West Indian girls in high density West Indian schools would prefer to be white. As the children got older they appeared to be more accepting of their ethnicity. Another detail is of interest: when an analysis was made of West Indian children's preferences according to skin shade, those with lighter skins made fewer own-race choices. When a comparison was made between identity and preference choices it was found that in all groups more than half of the children expressed own-group choice on both tests yet 40 per cent of the minority group children identified with their own race but preferred another. Davey and Mullin eschew the explanation that has often been advanced that pupils' ethnic attitudes are significantly determined by the proportion of an ethnic group represented in a school or neighbourhood. Rather, they claim, it is the experience of 'being black in Britain' which is the critical factor behind the choices. They further explain the relatively high frequency of discrepancy between own-group identification and other-group preference which occurred for 42 per cent of West Indians in terms of differences in heightened sense of personal worth and pride in their own culture and perceptions of the generally more favourable status of the white majority. The researchers argue that collectively these findings show evidence of the sensitivity of ethnic minority children's self-images to changes in intergroup situations in the last decade. In the author's view, however, their results do not necessarily show greater self-esteem on the part of ethnic minority junior pupils, but, in contrast with Milner's findings, they indicate that such pupils do have a clear idea of who they are and a more realistic appraisal of their position in British society such that they perceive the advantage of being white.

Most of the spate of studies which followed in the wake of the wide attention given to Milner's work concentrated on assessing self-esteem and especially in terms of providing an explanation linked to one other variable. For instance a very small-scale but intensive study, reported in a BEd thesis by Aisthorpe (1976), which was designed to test out the view expressed by Milner with children in the author's own school in a Manchester EPA, found that there was no firm evidence to support the hypothesis that 'under-achievement in West Indian children stemmed from low self-esteem acquired as a result of identification with the values of the host culture leading to an awareness of membership of a low status group and internalization of negative attitudes towards that group'. A group of 29 West Indian children of high and low achievement, as measured by a reading quotient and IQ test, were assessed on perception of social roles of blacks and whites, racial preference and perception of racial characteristics, self-concept, and perception of teachers' attitudes to self. The results were then related to a teacher's evaluation of the child and the teacher's attitude towards West Indian children in general, and it was found that the high achievers with better self-concepts showed less of a preference for their own group whereas the low achievers had poor self-concepts and a preference for their own racial group. Although this study is of very small scale and the tests are not standardized, the items used were specially constructed and appear to have been very sensitively adjusted to the needs of the particular children assessed. In this connection it is also relevant to note that D'Souza (1978) found that there was a higher out-group preference amongst those children who came from a higher social class.

Moreover, sports activities are often claimed as a means of increasing black self-esteem (Driver, 1977). In one school in the West Midlands which included 66 West Indians in its fourth year Driver found that there was a considerable variation between peer-group activities in curricular, extra-curricular and leisure time. Whereas soccer tended to be a means whereby the top- and middle-stream boys could transcend their ethnicity in a way legitimized by the school and acknowledged and respected by the teachers, Reggae was used by both boys and girls in order to gain special recognition of themselves and this particular activity within the life of the school. Thus their ethnicity was maximized and a distinctive sub-culture formed. A third group of West Indians formed a gambling group based on dominoes and cards which exclusively employed a dialect form of Jamaican Creole and West Indian rules.

In a more psychometric study, Jones (1977) examined the hypothesis that success in sport would be associated with high levels of self-esteem in black pupils. He used a 23-item measure of general self-esteem, derived from the Coopersmith scale, on 1,612 English and West Indian adolescents attending London secondary schools. He discovered that both West Indian males and females had significantly poorer levels of self-esteem than their white peers. Secondly, West Indian pupils were much more likely than whites to use the sporting and social facilities of the schools in the evenings, making the school rather than the home the focus of activity. West Indians were more likely than whites to be included in school sports teams and excelled in sport generally, but this success was not found to have a correlation with levels of self-esteem. Even those black pupils who excelled in sport were likely to be found in lower streams and the researcher suggested that this would have been the most powerful influence on self-esteem. Those West Indians who were in higher streams tended to have levels of self-esteem which were equal to those of their white peers. The author suggested that these West Indian high achievers came from rather different family situations than the somewhat authoritarian setting of the average pupil of West Indian origin, as was described in Section 12 on parents (pp.146–7). This speculation was subsequently supported in a study by Bagley *et al.* (1978).

Another hypothesis which has been put forward occasionally during the 1970s is that confusion over identity experienced by West Indians should diminish over time, especially for those born in Britain. Although the recent research with primary children (Davey and Mullin, 1980) seems to indicate that this is the case, yet the findings of three earlier studies with adolescents do not seem to support this view, or at least suggest that changes may occur with increasing age. Dove (1974) in a study of 545 teenagers of various ethnic groups in three London comprehensive schools found a much greater confusion over their ethnic identity amongst West Indian adolescents, but proposed that as racism should diminish over time in England a parallel reduction in confusion of identity should also occur. However, Hill (1975) found that those West Indian adolescents in Birmingham who had been resident longer in Britain had higher levels of neuroticism compared with their English peers, suggesting that prolonged exposure to racism had negative rather than positive effects on the adaptation of identity. Moreover, Lomax (1977), who examined girls' self-esteem in a large secondary school in London by means of a sentence completion test, discovered that although black girls were disproportionately allocated to lower streams, they had significantly higher levels of self-esteem than their white peers. Nevertheless, West Indian girls born in Britain had poorer self-concepts than West Indian girls born in the Caribbean.

The study by Lomax is of particular interest since the girls belonged to a secondary school in which over two-thirds of the pupils were West Indian and yet the researcher noted that the supportive context of the school was not sufficient to overcome the depressing effect on self-esteem of a longer exposure to English culture. Several researches have tended to indicate that the proportion of pupils from ethnic minorities in schools might well influence measures of self-esteem, though again the evidence is variable on this. For example, Verma (1975) having administered the Coopersmith Self-esteem Inventory to assess the perceptions of 366 pupils, aged 14 to 16, from four multiracial schools, of their peers, parents, schools and themselves, found that the self-esteem of black pupils did not vary according to the percentage of West Indians in the school. It is, of course, difficult to know in this kind of study to what extent the atmosphere and quality of the school was distinct, and in the Verma study, where there were only four particular schools being investigated, it is possible that they were atypical. A contra-indication is, for example, given by Aisthorpe's finding (1976) in his primary school in which 75 per cent of the pupils were of West Indian origin in that the West Indian pupils generally had lower self-esteem. A third variant of the assessment of influence of percentage of black pupils is indicated in a recently reported study (Young and Bagley, 1979) in which 400 children in nursery and infant schools in Jamaica and London, were examined by a black tester on a newly devised test of colour meaning and racial attitudes, as well as a self-esteem measure. It was found that the West Indian children in the London schools, in which over half of the pupils were from an ethnic minority group, had significantly better levels of self-esteem. However, the proportion of ethnic minority pupils does not seem to have been relevant in the investigation by Davey and Mullin (1980) with primary pupils.

In this connection two other carefully carried out studies are well deserving of mention since they help in refining more precisely the influence of percentage of ethnic minority pupils on self-esteem of black pupils. First, Louden (1978) investigated self-esteem and locus of control in Asian, West Indian and English adolescents using two well known American scales (Rosenberg's on self-satisfaction and the 12-item Nowicki and Strickland scale), both adapted to a British context. The main study was carried out with pupils in the fifth forms in four secondary schools in the Midlands, one all girls school, one all boys school and two mixed schools. Reading ability and social class were controlled. There were 74 West Indian boys, 66 West Indian girls, 59 Asian boys, 68 Asian girls, 53 English boys and 53 English girls in the sample. No significant differences in self-esteem were found between the groups, but the boys in all groups had higher self-esteem than the girls. The black adolescents had a tendency to disparage other minority groups which Louden interpreted as a self-protective device. West Indian adolescents were also found to have the most external locus of control of the three groups. In general, Louden associated the higher level of self-esteem in the black pupils with the higher concentration of blacks in the school. The relationship, however, was curvilinear and it was the group of West Indians in schools with medium concentrations (between 30 and 50 per cent of blacks) who had the highest levels of self-esteem. It is of interest to note here that Dawson (1978) found that 14 year-olds in schools with roughly equal numbers of black and white pupils held more favourable attitudes to schools and parents.

A similar curvilinear relationship, but only for boys, was discovered in an investigation which involved 1900 pupils of various ethnic affiliations aged 14 to 16 in 39 schools in London, the Midlands and the North of England (Bagley *et al.*, 1979). All the subjects completed a large test battery and some interesting findings on self-esteem emerged. Twenty-nine of the schools were multiracial and contained a total of 141 West Indians, 77 girls and 64 boys. As in Louden's study, the relationship between the self-esteem of West Indian boys and their proportion in the school classes was curvilinear, with those in the classes of between 10 and 29 per cent blacks having the highest levels of self-esteem. However, the relationship for girls was linear, with girls in the classrooms of the highest concentration of more than 30 per cent blacks having the highest self-esteem and those with the lowest percentage of black pupils having poorer self-esteem. Overall in this study a significant trend for the self-esteem of black pupils to be enhanced at greater levels of ethnic concentration was established, but the balance of evidence would indicate that a more even distribution of black and white pupils might be more conducive to increased black self-esteem.

Another hypothesis which is often advanced is that girls have higher self-esteem than boys. As has already been seen, however, this did not apply in the study with adolescents conducted by Louden (1978), nor did it appear to be the case for West Indian girls of primary age in Davey and Mullins' work (1980). Yet Bagley *et al.* (1979), whose findings were to some extent comparable with those of Louden, reported that not only did West Indian boys have significantly poorer self-esteem than the English boys in the control group, whereas West Indian girls and English girls in the control group did not differ significantly in self-esteem, but the West Indian boys had, in addition, significantly lower self-esteem than their girl counterparts. An earlier study, reported in an MEd thesis (Hill, 1968) which appears to have been thoroughly executed, also discovered that the West Indian girls' self assessments were higher than those of the English groups. The researcher aimed to measure and compare attitudes of 400 English and West Indian girls and boys, aged 14 to 15 years, drawn from six secondary modern schools in the West Midlands three of which were all boys, two all girls, and one mixed school, by using a semantic differential technique. Pupils, who were carefully matched for reading ability and social class, expressed their attitudes towards home, school and community. All the West Indian pupils had lived in the UK for at least three years. The West Indian group as a whole enjoyed higher self-assessments and in particular the girls scored more on 'industrious, valuable, friendly, wise and serious'. The West Indian boys' assessments by contrast, tended to associate more with racial stereotypes.

Enough has been said in the foregoing paragraphs to indicate that the question of black pupils' self-esteem has received serious consideration in research. That it is of crucial importance cannot be denied (see, for example, Bagley, 1979). In addition, two further questions, implicitly dealt with by much of the discussion in the research studies already reviewed need to be brought out here. First, how is self-esteem acquired and, second, what are the ways in which a black pupil's self-esteem is likely to be affected and how can it be increased?

A number of explanations giving different weights to different contributory factors have been proposed in the literature. For example, Aisthorpe (1976) in relating the findings of his study to previous research suggested that under-achievement results from a poor self-concept acquired during early socialization within the family and maintained by exposure to racial prejudice in the community, language handicaps and alienation from mainstream values as expressed by the school. The section on the school which follows (p.183ff) will consider this latter point, but it may be observed in passing that as the earlier section on language (pp.68–82) indicated, language difficulties are in many cases underestimated. As a result of a modest study Edwards (1978) suggested that there were strong links between attitudes towards a language and attitudes towards the speakers of that language and in a short article Edwards and Sutcliffe (1978) pointed out that the links between language and identity are so strong that attempts to correct non-standard speech may well be interpreted by children as criticism or rejection of themselves, their family and friends. In connection with socialization even black community groups themselves (for example BPPA, 1978) have recognized that the West Indian child has a home life whose Caribbean culture has a strong British influence and cannot provide a distinct alternative identity which appears to be necessary to combat what has often been supposed to be a racist society.

Yet other ethnic minority groups, particularly Asians who are also subject to prejudice due to colour, do not seem to suffer in the same way. By contrast with the Asian pupils the West Indian pupil seems to have fewer positive resources of identity which counter-balance the pressure towards a derogatory self-image. For instance, his parents may have internalized a sense of inferiority conveyed by the host society and an awareness of cultural disadvantage compared with Asians (see, Rex and Tomlinson, 1979) and may have transmitted this negative image unwittingly to their child. In addition, in comparison with the Asian child, the West Indian boy or girl is likely to have a less close-knit family structure, more authoritarian upbringing, possibly overarching parental aspirations, less strong religious beliefs and adherence to them in daily life, and a weaker cultural heritage. As a consequence he has less to support him, not only in what to do but in suggesting to him what he is. He may well therefore not have such a positive image of himself.

However, to counter-balance this it must be acknowledged that, as has been seen from the review of research studies, by no means do all pupils of West Indian origin in fact have a poor self-image or low self-esteem. What may distinguish West Indian pupils might be the extent to which they have internalized the conflict between their desired image, what that image actually is and the impressions which they receive about themselves from society in general. Indeed, it is quite possible for a West Indian to accept the view of his own group which is transmitted to him by society but still to maintain his own self-esteem by distinguishing himself from the group in general. An example of such adaptation apppears to be Ron Hope, a Guyanese Inspector in the London Metropolitan Police, who, in the March issue of *The Caribbean and West Indies Chronicle* for 1980 is reported as saying 'it is true my colour may have encouraged me a little bit to try to get on to prove a point.' This particular case lends force to Louden's (1978) argument that the assumption that the low social status of a group will generate low self-esteem seems superficially attractive, but it fails to take account of the specific environment in which the adolescent exists. The West Indian child or adolescent is not just a mere processor of information, observing and meekly internalizing the reactions and views of the host society, but he also responds to these communications by selecting and interpreting the information which he receives about himself and the group of which he is a member. He may do so in such a way as to fend off threats to his self-esteem. On the other hand, many West Indian youngsters may lack full and explicit awareness of the position of their own group in society. Even if he is aware of the position, a West Indian adolescent may still not believe that he personally is unworthy. Another way in which the young black youth can inflate their self-importance is by pride in their group and by stressing a black cultural orientation which would include greater knowledge about black heroes and which, as several research studies have tended to show, may be enhanced by living primarily in a black environment where these role models will more often be found.

The importance of role models, especially for boys, has often been pointed to as a significant factor in increasing self-esteem. In an article which explores West Indian under-achievement and ways in which the self-image of blacks can be improved, Holberton (1977) claims that a major contributory factor to an improved self-image is identifying with achieving models fulfilling responsible roles in society. Yet qualifications are required to achieve these responsible roles and, in turn, to achieve qualifications a good academic career and an ability to pass exams is required. A major pre-requisite of a good academic career is a stable self-image. Yet, as many of the studies have shown, the self-image of black children is low. Is this, then, a completely vicious circle? As Holberton suggests, in many ways pupils of West Indian origin resemble lower working class white pupils (see Durojaiye, 1971). And yet there is an additional factor – that of colour – which can in no way be minimized. But the interactive effects of colour and class are extremely difficult to disentangle. One possible explanation in terms of social class (cited by Aisthorpe, 1976) runs as follows: middle-class blacks tend to have a more positive self-concept and to be more rejecting of their own racial group. Their higher aspirations mean that they identify with mainstream values but suffer greater frustration which is caused by marginal status and consequent rejection of that marginal status in minority group membership. On the other hand, lower class blacks have less identification with middle-class values and aspirations and are limited by their sub-cultural norms, are less likely to encounter frustration and therefore do not reject their own group. However, unsatisfactory living conditions and perceived life chances common to any lower class group may have a negative effect on personal self-concept.

Alternatively, an explanation of self-esteem may be advanced in terms of achievement. Those blacks who are high achievers may well find themselves at odds both with their own racial group and with the host society. Somehow, although they have managed to maintain high self-esteem and have adjusted to the middle-class orientation nor to the middle-class white group to which they aspire, but in which they are not necessarily accepted by whites. An interesting case study of one boy in this position (Weinreich, 1979) shows that in such cases of cross-identification, even though new reference groups may be sought, problems in the formation of identity for achievers still remain. In comparison with this group is a much larger group of non-achievers with a working-class orientation who have aspirations but who on account of their lack of achievement can only have their black identity confirmed. This alienation may be increased by the knowledge that their culture is not particularly respected by society at large. As a result, their experiences may well give rise to a kind of existential pain or anger which has occasionally been noted amongst the black community and is, for example, perhaps expressed on their behalf by an articulate young student (Scipio, 1973). It seems likely from the evidence supplied by research that those who achieve less are more likely to be black males and in schools where there are a low percentage of ethnic minority pupils. As Kitzinger (1978) has suggested, these boys may well find identity in black consciousness groups where they can also discover models for masculine behaviour. And yet they are not in this way removing themselves from the patterns of authority and authoritarianism of their schools and homes. Rather they are substituting new rules for old and probably repeating a structure of dominance and submission. Yet, it would be wrong to suggest that there were general patterns in such a movement. For, as has been pointed out already the West Indian communities are not homogeneous; there are differences on account of island of origin, sex, location in the United Kingdom and as between generations. As 'the first generation of a new experience' (Holberton, 1977) young blacks born in this country are obviously carving out a new identity both for themselves as individuals and their group as a whole. One way in which they can realize this is through their achievement in education. Indeed, enough has been said to show that self-esteem and identity and educational achievement are inextricably linked. Yet as several authors have pointed out (BPPA, 1978; Louden, 1978, and Bagley, 1979) the tendency to see self-esteem as the key to achievement, thus acting as a substitute scapegoat for earlier criticism of IQ testing, must not be allowed to obscure the complex and multidimensional nature of the problem. Whilst undoubtedly the school can modify or enhance particular levels of self-esteem it is not the only factor in this process. Before pausing to reflect what might be achieved by the school in this connection (pp.232–40) there remains in the following sub-section to take account of black pupils' attitudes to the school. Finally, Section 14 will consider the school as a social institution, the attitudes and expectations of teachers who work within it, and the attitudes of the black pupils' white peers.

Attitudes to school and career aspirations
Somewhat surprisingly, there appears to have been rather little research undertaken explicitly on West Indian pupils' attitudes to school. One of the few studies undertaken (Hill, 1968) with a sample of 400 pupils aged 14–15 years in six secondary modern schools reported that West Indians in general had a favourable attitude towards education, but although the girls had favourable

attitudes towards school they did not feel similarly towards their teachers. West Indian boys, in contrast, regarded their teachers as figures to emulate.

Another study (Evans, 1972) in which 150 West Indians aged 16–24 in Birmingham were interviewed also found them to express generally favourable retrospective attitudes towards their schools, but on the whole they thought they had done less well at school than they expected. Yet John (1971) who interviewed 200 16-year-old West Indians found only 40 per cent who had a positive attitude towards school and the majority were disillusioned with what they had learnt at school and the type of jobs they were likely to find available to them. It may also be noted that Marvell (1974) in an investigation into the influence of the community, school, home and playgroup on young people from various ethnic minority back- grounds found that the small number of West Indian youngsters in his participant observation study tended to see the head teacher as a remote figure. Moreover, Rex and Tomlinson (1979) found that two-thirds of the 25 West Indian 16–21-year-olds whom they interviewed said retrospectively that they did not believe their teachers were interested in their progress.

The major study of West Indian pupils' attitudes to school is undoubtedly that of Jelinek (1977) which formed the third part of a series of NFER researches on immigrant children which began in the early 70s. The research drew on a sample of 3,551 pupils from 13 primary and 12 secondary schools throughout England. Six hundred and four pupils were tested at 10-plus, 1,488 at 12-plus and 1,459 at 14-plus and they included 148 West Indian pupils at 10-plus, 240 at 12-plus and 219 at 14-plus. The views of pupils from seven ethnic groups towards the 'atmosphere' of the multiracial school, schoolwork and school in general were assessed on the basis of responses on a five-point scale to a specially constructed 33-item attitude questionnaire. It was found that West Indian pupils held attitudes close to the overall levels about attitudes to schoolwork and general attitude to school, but they held distinctive views about the multiracial school. Of the ethnic minority group pupils they held the least favourable attitudes towards the atmosphere of the multi- racial school, especially at 10-plus. They were not very concerned with school work, particularly at 12-plus, but they had favourable attitudes towards school in general, and this was especially significant for the West Indian girls at 10- and 12-plus. Obviously, most of these studies were concerned with many pupils who had actually been born in the Caribbean and may have undergone some of their schooling there. Moreover, the adolescent pupils' attitudes are an expression of feeling towards secondary schools and may not be applicable to the pattern of comprehensive schooling into which most leas have since reorganized.

Yet more recently similar results to those of Jelinek have been found by Dawson (1978) in an investigation of attitudes held by 480 14-year-olds to schools and parents. Particular attention was paid to sex, ethnic background and socio-economic status of the pupils and school composition. The pupils came from four schools with a range of less than 10 per cent to greater than 60 per cent black pupils and serving predominantly working-class populations. Eighty-two black boys, 74 black girls, 183 white boys and 141 white girls answered a 45-item questionnaire ranking their responses on a five-point scale. A set of detailed statistical analyses was undertaken from which it was found that both black and white pupils had positive attitudes to school, especially as a means of vocational preparation (80 per cent), and thought it worth working harder at school to get a good job. Yet most of those same pupils, except those in the higher ability band, felt that schools had too many rules and were too strict. Those who were positive towards school were also likely to be positive towards their parents. There were no significant differences between girls and boys. However, black pupils scored significantly more highly than white on all attitudinal scales and especially on attitudes towards school in general and the usefulness of further education. They also obtained higher scores for parental respect. This was despite the fact that they tended to be over-represented in lower ability bands. It happened that the lea in which the research took place had taken positive steps to promote multicultural education and two of the schools with the highest proportions of black pupils were judged by the researcher to be especially caring communities. Further analyses also indicated that pupils had a more favourable attitude towards school and parents when they attended schools with approximately equal proportions of black and white pupils and that for black pupils the commitment to further education is highest in the school with the greater proportion of white middle-class pupils. The author also draws attention to the contrasting finding of Louden (1978) whose black 16-year-olds were much less positive in their attitudes to school possibly because they were becoming more work-oriented in their outlook. The evidence suggests that there may be some change in attitude during the last two years of schooling.

There is relatively little direct evidence about black pupils' aspirations. At age nine only five of the sample of West Indian children in Pollak's study (1979) made any reference to school when giving a generally amusing and varied catalogue of their wishes and hopes. Whitehouse (1973) referring to an unpublished thesis of 1971, but without giving many background details, stated that when the 104 West Indian pupils in his sample were matched for socio-economic status and intelligence with 91 indigenous children the West Indian boys aspired 11 times more highly than their indigenous counterparts in relation to education and twice as highly in relation to their career plans. He also found that girls tended to over-aspire in relation to their IQ in comparison with white girls.

Townsend and Brittan (1972) in a national survey of 98 multi-racial secondary schools, found that twice as many West Indians and other immigrants as non-immigrants stayed on at school for fifth-year courses and also that proportionately more members of each immigrant group remained at school for sixth-year courses. The determination of many of the immigrants to achieve some examination success was shown by the fact that many were still pursuing CSE and O-level courses into the sixth form. This trend was also confirmed by Rex and Tomlinson (1979) and the OPCS Surveys (1973, 1974) which showed that compared with a similarly educated group of white youngsters school leavers of West Indian origin were more likely to attend a course of further education and to study for higher qualifications, even though they were less likely to be allowed time off work to study. Although 55 per cent of the whites and approximately 80 per cent of both groups of West Indians had attended a course at some time over a five-year period (OPCS, 1980), only 30–40 per cent had obtained any kind of qualification. Thus only 54 per cent of whites and 49–51 per cent of West Indians had succeeded in completing courses. Nevertheless West Indians continued, albeit in smaller numbers, to embark on courses of further education for a period of up to five years after leaving school (OPCS, 1980). Indeed, when asked to consider what advice to give to a person about to leave school 48–53 per cent, three times as many West Indians as whites, thought it best to get as many qualifications as possible, either by staying on at school or by taking up full-time further education.

Recent evidence on trends in participation in further and higher education by West Indians is supplied by the findings of a pilot study which sampled 2,874 fifth and sixth formers of whom 257 (nine per cent) were West Indians, in all the secondary schools in one outer London borough in 1979 (Craft and Craft, 1981). In the first year a questionnaire was administered to the pupils about the examinations they would take, their social class, ethnic identity and educational and occupation aspirations, and in the following year teachers completed questionnaires about outcomes. It was found that fifth-year West Indians performed less well than their peers in public examinations, even when they were matched for social class. This by definition tended to reduce the likelihood of their access to the sixth form and beyond. Nevertheless they were more likely to take up a course in further education even when compared with middle-class or high performers. Yet almost half the medium performers (i.e. with at least five CSE passes and possibly some GCEs) left full-time education altogether.

An earlier study (Beetham, 1967) which involved a sample of fourth-year pupils in a selection of Birmingham secondary modern schools found that West Indian pupils had higher educational and job aspirations than their English counterparts. Eighty-one per cent of immigrant pupils in the fourth year as compared with 36 per cent of the white children intended to stay on. Moreover, 10 per cent of the immigrants compared with one per cent of the English children expected to attend further full-time education. The researcher found that the main influence on immigrant children's career aspirations was their parents, who were prepared to enable them to stay on for further education. Thirty-five per cent of the West Indians said their career choice was the same as that of their parents. These findings tend to confirm the influence of parents, which was pointed out earlier (pp.144–6) but may be seen as somewhat alarming in view of the general lack of accurate information which West Indian parents appear to have about school and education, and hence, it is to be imagined, about appropriate career choices. Perhaps there is an indication of a change of influence over time as the OPCS Survey (1980) found that although in retrospect West Indians esteemed their parents' guidance on jobs more highly five years after entering employment, possibly because of more continuous contact than with teachers or careers officers, they nevertheless attached less value to it than did the whites. Indeed they appeared to feel that their parents should have given them better advice but were unable to do so.

Moreover, although a CRC survey in 1974 indicated that half the unemployed blacks in the survey were not registered at careers offices or employment agencies there would appear to be more evidence that such agencies are now more frequently used by West Indians. The OPCS Survey (1980) found that there was no evidence that unemployed West Indians were less likely than whites to register at employment agencies and indeed an increasing percentage of West Indians' jobs had been obtained through this channel. This is in line with what would appear to be an increasing trend for West Indian pupils to consult a careers officer. Allen and Smith (1975) in their study of school leavers in Sheffield and Bradford found that West Indian pupils had seen careers officers on average three times. Although the attitudes of pupils were generally more favourable towards the Youth Employment Services (YES) than towards school careers advisers, a few West Indian pupils in particular associated the YES with school and saw it as irrelevant to the working situation. Similarly, another study (Rex and Tomlinson, 1979) showed that West Indian school leavers do not necessarily regard such agencies as helpful. In a sub-sample of 50 out of 256 persons aged 16–21 who were children of the 1,100 householders in their main sample in Handsworth, Birmingham, 21 out of 25 West Indians interviewed reported having discussions with a Youth Employment Officer (YEO) but only six said it was of value. They saw the YEO as trying to talk them out of better jobs and seven out of the 15 employed had found their jobs without the aid of the YEO. Although it seemed that the West Indians were persistent in obtaining jobs 12 out of 15 said that the employment they were engaged in was not the job they wanted when they first left school, yet eight were satisfied.

Perhaps it is rather a question of establishing a continuing relationship with such agencies and hence greater familiarity with the kind of assistance they are able to offer. For example, in a study of 924 school leavers of various ethnic groups from three Slough comprehensive schools in 1974–5, concerned with the implementation of a youth advisory service to assist the transition from school to work, it was found that more than one in four boys and one in three girls in the small West Indian sample either stayed on at school or went to college. West Indians in work were among those least satisfied. Pupils of West Indian origin used the referral agency more than any other ethnic group possibly, the researchers suggest, because of determination to make full use of 'the system', a lack of relevant knowledge by parents, or because the school leavers knew the referral agent better than the careers officer, but no breakdown by ethnic group is given as to the particular kinds of problems discussed (Seckington and Reid, 1980). This suggests that more careers officers specializing in placement of West Indian school leavers in areas of West Indian population could be particularly beneficial.

Otherwise doubtless West Indian pupils' aspirations will continue to be influenced by those of their peers and the satisfaction of them will depend greatly (as seen in the sub-section on employment pp.27–35) on the prevalent racial climate in society at large. For instance another small study (Hilton, 1972) which reported on the ambitions of fourth-form school children in Manchester found that West Indian boys tended to have a narrow field of occupational aspiration which appeared to be more influenced by peer-group expectations than by their fathers' occupations. This tends to agree with Figueroa's (1974, 1976) study of West Indian school leavers in ten London secondary modern schools with 11–47 per cent of immigrants on the school roll, in 1966–7. The West Indians were matched with white British pupils of similar attainment. A questionnaire was administered in the last school year to 261 British and 88 West Indian pupils and a follow-up interview of 43 British and 43 West Indian respondents who had actually started working was carried out a year later. The results suggested that the prospects for West Indians were worse than for their British peers from similarly deprived backgrounds and they were much less likely to have had jobs to go to on leaving school. In fact they were found to have been less successful in attaining the jobs to which they aspired and also to have had a narrower range of choice. West Indian boys were more likely to enter lower level occupations than British boys, and, as with the West Indian girls, were less well paid. The majority of respondents, and especially the British, thought that 'immigrants' were discriminated against, but they were also more likely to have negative than positive attitudes towards the West Indians, and there was evidence of social segregation. It is not clear, however, whether the findings with respect to West Indian job prospects were associated more with a disadvantaged background, cultural differences or colour discrimination, though the author cites British racism as one of the important factors accounting for the depressed prospects of West Indian school leavers. Similar, later findings of the OPCS surveys, as have been seen, tend to indicate the latter factor is still very much in evidence (OPCS, 1980).

On the other hand, a preliminary report of evidence from a study carried out in the winter of 1979–80 when 240 young men aged 16–25 were interviewed in London (Gaskell and Smith, 1981) suggests that the young West Indians involved did not see their 'alienation' from British society, (i.e. the economic system or discrimination) as being the main factor in their inability to achieve their career aspirations or even to remain in employment. Those interviewed were drawn from the register of unemployment benefit offices, black self-help groups or from various London employers and were asked about jobs and lifestyle aspirations, perceived obstacles to their fulfilment, levels of felt deprivation, and attitudes towards using Jobcentres, careers offices, benefit offices and further education colleges. The unemployed blacks and users of self-help groups were extremely deprived, both having spent 20 per cent of their time since leaving school unemployed, and 51 per cent were without any qualifications. The researchers argue that the failure of the blacks in their study to achieve their job aspirations was not because they were unrealistically high: the largest proportion among the unemployed blacks and the self-help group users most wanted to do skilled manual work, though there was more mention of semi-skilled work when respondents were asked about the actual jobs people would probably be doing. The most frequently mentioned obstacles to getting desired jobs were a mixture of internal and external factors: lack of willpower or qualifications, being black, lack of jobs and not being clever enough. Moreover the unemployed blacks were found to be more positive than unemployed whites on 11 out of 12 attitudinal items. They held positive attitudes towards going to college, Jobcentres, career and benefit offices, the school system and further education, TV, newspapers and the average British person. They were, however, negative about the current job situation and British politics and neutral in their feeling about the average employer. Although some of these

institutions were criticized for their modes of operatio
of the young blacks had used Jobcentres and careers (
per cent of the unemployed were registered and had be
cent of the total time unemployed since leaving sch ., ..gures
which are comparable to other national statistics for West Indians
(OPCS, 1980). The authors point out that almost 25 per cent of the
black unemployed men spontaneously mentioned problems with
the law as the main obstacle to achieving their idea of a best life for
themselves. A higher score for this group on a psychological test of
anomie was also taken by the researchers to indicate feelings of
hopelessness and despair. They suggest that such young blacks view
society positively and wish to succeed in it but have little chance of
realizing their aspirations (Gaskell and Smith, 1981).

In conclusion and in general it appears that West Indian pupils
are very concerned about their future social and personal relationships in the community at large (Hill, 1968). Milner (1975), from
answers to a question on the young child's social aspirations, also
discovered that West Indians aspired to have white neighbours, to
go to work with whites and to have white companions. Whether the
school can be seen as representative of society at large, whether it is
conducive to the promotion of harmonious and reciprocal multi-
ethnic relationships, and to what extent it prepares pupils of West
Indian origin for work and life in the wider social context will be
examined in the following section.

Section 14: Teachers and Schools
Institutionalized racism?
Having considered some of the research evidence on parents'
attitudes and aspirations for their children and pupils' attitudes
towards themselves and others, attention must now be directed
towards the third main influence on the education of children of
West Indian origin, namely the school, and the teachers and other
pupils who work within it. Earlier sections of this review
(pp.24–35) have indicated that black people in this country suffer
from serious disadvantages with respect to housing and employment and that these result to a large extent from discriminatory
practices by the white majority or host population (Daniel, 1974).
That prejudice towards minority groups is fairly widespread, and
especially towards black people, has been well established by a

number of surveys (see Hill, 1967; Rose *et al.*, 1969) including more recently those by the Political and Economic Planning Group (PEP) (McIntosh and Smith, 1974). It remains to consider therefore whether discriminatory practices exist also in education and in particular whether the charge of institutionalized racism is true in the case of schools. Rutter and Madge (1976) conclude their section on race relations in Chapter 10 on ethnic minorities in Britain with a general description of racism as follows:

'Prejudice against immigrants and especially against black people, is fairly widespread among the white population in Britain, although it is by no means universal. Prejudicial attitudes develop early in childhood, but can be modified in adolescence or adult life, given the right circumstances. Whether a person exhibits racial prejudice is to some extent influenced by the attitudes of his parents and by his pattern of upbringing, but to a considerable extent it is shaped by the attitudes he meets at school and in the community in which he lives. The extent and nature of his contact with people from ethnic minority groups, the attitudes and teaching at school, the mass media and legally enforced patterns of behaviour are also likely to have a major impact on how he feels about black people and how he behaves towards them.' (pp.300–1).

And Spears (1978) provides a more sharply focused interpretation of institutionalized racism:

'Many people have the view that racism is an overt phenomenon which attaches to the individual. Racism has to do with personal attitudes and willful behavior. This view can be contrasted to that which holds that racism does not reside only in the individual. More importantly, racism is a basic feature of the entire society, being structured into its political, social, and economic institutions. Since it is institutionalized, all cases of racism do not result from the willful acts of ill-intentioned individuals. It is in its most profound instances, covert, resulting from acts of indifference, omission, and refusal to challenge the status quo. Thus, an individual need never have willfully done anything that directly and clearly oppresses minorities, she/he need only have gone about business as usual without attempting to change procedures and structures in order to be an accomplice in racism, since business as usual has been systematized to maintain blacks and other minorities in an oppressed state. The institutionalized view of racism does not see it as a function of individual attitudes and preferences, then, but as a clash of group values and interests, namely, the maintenance of privilege'. (pp.129–30).

Many studies (see most recently Spears, 1978, and Glatt and King, 1979) have considered whether and to what extent racism exists in schools in America, and in the case of the latter authors have made a spirited attack on religion, the media and historical documents which seem to be the main sources for the expression of racist attitudes and interpretations. However, as has been argued (pp.5–6) there are considerable differences between the position of blacks in America and in this country and it would be wrong to draw heavily on these arguments in an appraisal of racism in British schools. In contrast to the marked awareness of racism in American schools, few studies have been directly and explicitly concerned with the school as an agent of socialization and acculturalization in relation to blacks in this country. Whilst it is recognized that the school is not the primary socializing institution for class or ethnic cultures, it is of interest and pertinent to examine to what extent the school can both insulate young black people from racism in society as a whole and also how it can act to change racialist attitudes by educational means. Yet it has to be admitted at the outset that the school can only be seen as one factor in this process, and possibly the most limited direct agent of change at that. One hypothesis which has recently been advanced, but not tested, is that the influence of the neighbourhood of the school, in particular the concentration of ethnic minority groups within that environment and the degree to which they are accepted by the host population, may be more significant than that of the school itself, but Davey and Norburn's research (1980b) indicates that parents at least see the school as more important than the state of race relations in the immediate locality for their children's education.

Institutionalized racism in schools is assumed by some researchers as a background to their research, especially by researchers who are themselves black (see for example Coard, 1971 and Giles, 1977) but not necessarily so, as Driver's (1977) work indicates, and other writers e.g. Jeffcoate (1977) have spoken of the 'hidden curriculum of overt and covert racism' which may not always be intentional or deliberate but is equally expressed, it is claimed, by acts of indifference or omission (see also Jeffcoate, 1979, Ch.6). Those who allege that the school is a racist institution have also argued that the poor attainment of many children of West Indian origin is due to the administrative apparatus of the school, low teacher expectation, tests and the colour of the tester and a general depreciation of black identity in the classroom. Whilst it is proposed to concentrate in this Section on the attitudes of white and other ethnic minority pupils towards their West Indian peers and teachers' expectations for and attitudes to pupils of West Indian origin, it is relevant to consider briefly a number of more obvious features of educational organization and teaching materials which have been alleged to demonstrate bias towards the white majority population.

It has often been claimed, both by black organizations (e.g. BPPA) and research workers who are in favour of multicultural education (e.g. Rogers, 1973; Jeffcoate, 1979), that there has been considerable official reluctance to recognize the difficulties involved in education for a multiracial society although there is much that the individual school and teacher can and have done. Whilst it may be fairer to say that difficulties in implementation of such policies at a national level have possibly been allowed to outweigh recommendations for implementation in certain localities of obvious applicability, it may indeed also be true to claim that there has been a certain lack of sympathy for such approaches. At the level of local authority organization there may again be differences of interests not only between localities where there are high, medium or low concentrations of ethnic minority groups, or where they are even virtually non-existent, but also in respect of different schools within each local authority where these same variations may apply. Whilst some consideration has been given to the influence of proportion of ethnic minority pupils both from an administrative viewpoint (see Townsend, 1971) and with respect to educational attainment (e.g. Mabey, 1974) and incidentally to many other studies reviewed in this book, rather less attention has been paid to the overall quality of schooling which pupils of West Indian origin are likely to receive, given that as Yule *et al.* (1975) discovered, immigrant children are more likely than indigenous children to attend schools associated with high rates of reading difficulties and behavioural problems, high pupil turnover, high absentee rates and high proportions of children receiving free school meals – all variables which are known to be associated with poor scholastic attainment.

It is not surprising moreover to find a wide variation in school facilities depending on the response of individual schools to the challenge of educating in a multiracial society. As well as the diversity of provision for special language teaching (noted by Townsend, 1971; Townsend and Brittan, 1972; and Great Britain, DES, 1972a) it was discovered that few teachers had undergone any preparation for teaching English as a second language or for any kind of work in a multiracial school. This situation obtained despite the recommendation by the Select Committee on Race Relations and Immigration (Great Britain, Parliament, House of Commons, Select Committee on Race Relations and Immigration, 1969) that such preparation should be provided not only in colleges and institutes, but also as part of in-service training. The courses should include race relations and problems facing immigrant children. The same report also proposed that multiracial schools should employ more teachers from the same ethnic background as the children so that they might facilitate both understanding of the children and the children's identification by their teachers.

Although a number of courses in multicultural education have been established in teacher training colleges and as in-service courses in recent years it would appear that there are still relatively few specialist advisors or teachers. Recent minutes of evidence from the DES (Great Britain, Parliament, House of Commons, Home Affairs Committee, 1980) suggested that about half of all initial training institutions appear to be offering relevant compulsory or optional studies of some kind in the field of mulicultural education. Paragraphs 32 and 33 of the same document also refer to a variety of in-service provision ranging from long degree or diploma courses in universities, colleges, or polytechnics to locally organized short courses and workshops aimed at raising the general awareness of teachers to the implications of teaching for life in a culturally diverse society. A DES funded project on In-service Teacher Education in a Multiracial Society, undertaken at Keele University, which has recently been completed should provide further information on this matter, but in 1980–1 it was anticipated that there would be at least 10 long courses, four short courses run by the DES itself, as well as all the lea-based initiatives.

Similarly, although the 1977 Select Committee report (Great Britain, Parliament, House of Commons, Select Committee on Race Relations and Immigration, 1977) recommended that statistics should be collected on the numbers of black teachers in schools and training, it is only possible in the absence of complete numerical information to rely on the impression that their numbers are disproportionately few, and though schools may wish to recruit more (Little and Willey, 1981) it is common for a black child to complete his schooling without ever having been taught by a black teacher. Recently it was estimated that there are probably 800–900 black teachers, mostly in London and the south-east (*New Society*, 27.11.80) whereas another estimate, in 1977, suggested that there were 125,000–150,000 pupils of West Indian origin in British schools. A small-scale case study of 27 West Indian teachers in London schools (Gibbes, 1980) indicated that half were on relatively low scales of pay in spite of years of classroom experience and that many had made more than 200 attempts to gain promotion. Many had had difficulty in obtaining and keeping jobs. Yet the significance of the presence of black teachers as motivating forces for black pupils has frequently been noted in the research literature. In an attempt to improve employment prospects of black teachers a new 'umbrella' organization, The National Convention of Black Teachers, has been set up in 1981. Moreover, a recent advance report on one-year foundation courses which, according to DES evidence (Great Britain, Parliament, House of Commons, Home Affairs Committee, 1980, p.241) were 'aimed particularly at students from ethnic minorities to enable them to reach the standard necessary for entry to training courses for teaching, social work or general higher education,' reveals that 47 per cent of the students on the 11 courses in 1979–80 were West Indians. Women outnumbered West Indian men by four to one and their performance was more than twice as good. Eighty-two per cent of the West Indian students were subsequently offered places in higher education (Lodge, 1981). This would appear to suggest that, for West Indians at least, recently introduced schemes may be having some success in increasing recruitment to the teaching profession.

Of late many writers have been at pains to point out that not only do teaching style and subject teaching often involve biases towards the white majority, but so do the very textbooks and materials used in connection with the teaching of subject content (Hatch, 1962; Dummett, 1973). Some books teaching reading, for example, have been found to include crude racial stereotypes and often to be illustrated by white middle-class children or with the non-white and foreign children appearing to be subordinate or objects of sympathy (Hill, 1971; Council on Interracial Books for Children, 1975). Textbooks in history (Glendenning, 1971) and geography have perhaps been particularly prone in the past to present biased accounts and interpretations of events and outdated facts. But English literature and religious education have also fostered ethnic biases. Despite this publicity research carried out in 1972 (Brittan, 1976a) with a national sample of 510 primary and secondary teachers revealed that only 45 per cent of teachers agreed and as many as 27 per cent disagreed that there was racial bias in books. The researcher argued that this finding tended to support the view that there was a sizeable proportion of teachers who were not particularly sensitive to the way in which books could foster racial bias (see, e.g. Bolton and Laishley, 1972). However, it is probably fair to say that since attention has been drawn to such features a number of children's books presenting a more balanced view of a multiracial society are now widely available and being used in many schools, especially as stocks of readers are gradually replaced. As awareness of such tendencies increases, it is to be hoped that ethnic minority groups will be seen in a less inferior light through the materials which are used in teaching. However the purging of stereotypes will not in itself alone assist in constructing a multi-cultural curriculum for there is still the influence of society at large to take into account, as it appears that prejudice against black people continues to be transmitted through the mass media (Hartmann and Husband, 1974)—an institution of far more power and omnipresence in the 1970s and 80s.

Such sketchy attention is insufficient to do more than indicate that school facilities, materials, ethnic mix, and quality of schooling are all important factors, but it seems likely that of ever greater influence on the life in school of a black child will be the attitudes of his white peers and those from other ethnic minority groups and, perhaps even more so, the expectations and attitudes of his teachers. It is to a consideration of these more personal influences that the remainder of this section is addressed.

Attitudes of peers
Mention has already been made in the section on West Indian pupils' attitudes to a number of researches which also provide reciprocal information on attitudes of white pupils to blacks (see

pp.152–61). Attitudes to race are indicated by a study by Bagley and Verma (1975) in which 118 white, 58 West Indian and 44 Asian teenagers in 12 multiracial schools in London and the Midlands were asked to indicate their general attitudes towards other ethnic groups (pp.155–6). It was found that whites and Asians both had unfavourable attitudes towards West Indians and that the whites also had the most unfavourable attitudes towards other ethnic minority groups. However, the hostility of white students tended to be general in nature, extending to diverse ethnic groups. Indeed, it might not have been overt in the classroom situation and the researchers observed that about a quarter of white pupils had black friends and over half of the white students interacted on a friendly basis with black students. But in the second part of this bipartite research a somewhat different finding emerged. In this investigation an attempt was made to measure stereotypes by employing a 'forced choice' questionnaire administered to 81 teenagers in eight multiracial schools, and a 'free choice' questionnaire given to 155 teenagers from the same classes. On the forced choice questionnaire the adolescents were asked to rate items on six traits (e.g. clean–dirty) on a five-point scale in relation to 10 different ethnic groups including the white British. On the free choice questionnaire the 14- to 16-year-olds were asked to describe the same 10 ethnic groups in their own words. On both evaluations West Indians were seen in a favourable light in relation to other ethnic groups. This, apparently, also fits with a similar finding by Stanton (1972) with another sample of secondary school pupils. Moreover, a study by D'Souza (1978) involving 113 white pupils of a similar age in multi-ethnic schools in five boroughs in London discovered that their attitudes towards West Indians were more favourable than those towards Asians, 70 per cent being positive and only nine per cent extremely negative.

It might well be the case that the proportion of ethnic minority pupils in these schools was an influential factor in attitudes and preferences, as indeed a study of 504 children in six primary schools revealed (Richardson and Green, 1971). Though these children in general preferred white to dark skin colour in their best friends, children in a school with the highest proportion (35 per cent) of immigrant children liked the coloured child most. (See also studies on nursery children by Jahoda *et al.*, 1966; Laishley, 1971.)

Age of pupils may also be influential on white children's perceptions of blacks as it appears that investigations undertaken by Milner with five- to eight-year-olds and also by Davey and Norburn (1980a) and Davey and Mullin (1980) with seven- to 10-year-olds indicate considerable white group preferences. In his investigations using dolls Milner discovered that the great majority of the 100 white children aged five to eight in his sample consistently favoured white figures and rarely preferred the black dolls. Whilst he recognized that these choices do not necessarily imply actual prejudice against blacks, he suggested that evidence from another section of the study on stereotypes did indicate that the white children held very negative feelings of rejection towards black figures. Some 63 per cent of the white children indicated that the black figures were both 'bad' and 'ugly', while a further 31 per cent made one or other of these assertions. Nevertheless, on the preference section of the test 17 per cent of the white English children indicated that the black doll looked like their best friend.

Similar ethnocentric results have been found recently for white children in a large-scale and well designed investigation with 512 children in 16 primary schools with varying proportions of West Indian or Asian pupils and equally divided between North and South. As part of a series of tests on a paired comparison test using photographs to assess attitudes towards different ethnic groups (Davey and Norburn, 1980a) the 256 white children put their own-race photographs in the top four positions, although on the remainder they ranked the West Indians above the Asians. However on a limited choice technique which required the children to share sweets the white children were far less fairminded than those children belonging to ethnic minority groups and consistently favoured other whites. Those who were generous to minority group children were even-handed between the two groups. Once again, the white children had a much greater tendency to assign favourable attributes exclusively to themselves on the stereotypes test and tended to be derogatory about both the other groups. Moreover, in a preference test (Davey and Mullin, 1980) involving the same children who were asked to choose from photos of black and white children 'which one would you most like to be?' 86 per cent of the white children preferred their own group. This finding obtained irrespective of the ethnicity of the group with whom they were in contact or of the size of that group relative to their own in a particular school. Indeed, it also transpired from a sociometric questionnaire administered to 238 children in schools where half the children were from another ethnic minority group that those who tended to choose their own race on the preference test, i.e. especially the white children, were also more likely not to name any other-race friends (p> 0.05), though generally in these schools only a minority wished to confine their friendships to their own group and 63.6 per cent of white children preferred to have some other-group friends. However, as the authors point out, racial preference for one's own group does not necessarily mean rejection of another's.

Other evidence, on *actual* friendship patterns, is adduced by the study of nine-year-olds in one borough in London by Pollak (1979). She found that 41 per cent of the 61 English children had black friends and that this proportion rose to 48 per cent when those white children who had no opportunity to meet black children were excluded.

The largest study to investigate actual and desired friendship patterns was undertaken by Jelinek and Brittan (1975). They investigated the friendship patterns of British, Indian, Pakistani, Kenyan Asian, Cypriot, Italian and West Indian pupils in a national sample from 13 primary and 12 secondary schools. Six hundred and seventy-seven pupils aged eight, 611 aged 10, 1,507 aged 12 and 1,505 aged 14 were asked two questions on actual friendship and a third on desired friendship in which they were asked to name up to three friends they would like 'to play with at school', 'to have as friends' and 'to go about with at school'. The researchers found that by the age of eight ethnicity strongly influenced choice of friends and that own-group preferences increased with age for both actual and desired friendships for all the ethnic groups. In terms of actual friendships in primary schools Asians preferred their own group to a greater degree than did indigenous pupils, but the reverse was true for desired friendships. Other findings for West Indian pupils have already been cited (pp.158–9).

Two other studies are worth mentioning in conclusion to this section on the attitudes of the peers of pupils of West Indian origin. First, a modest, but interesting study (Edwards, 1978) which involved an examination of the attitudes of 20 working-class pupils from a large comprehensive school in Reading and 20 middle-class pupils equally divided between girls and boys, towards tape recordings of several different accents. One of these tapes was of a

Barbadian girl, born in Britain, who spoke both in a working-class Reading accent and also in Creole. It is interesting to note that the working-class pupils viewed the West Indian accent less favourably, whereas the middle-class judges did not distinguish between the Creole and the working-class accent, suggesting they look upon both groups equally unfavourably or even possibly that they lack first-hand experience in telling the two apart.

Finally, Verma (1975), who administered a scrambled sentence test to assess hostility of teenagers in multiracial schools, found no evidence to support the view that racially mixed environments were likely to create tension, anxiety and hostility. Three hundred and nineteen pupils from four multiracial and four all-white schools were involved in the study. The multiracial schools had between 20 and 50 per cent immigrant pupils. In two of the multiracial schools Asian groups were considerably less hostile than white and West Indian pupils though, in one school, the West Indian pupils had a lower hostility score than their white peers, and in the remaining school the white group had a lower hostility score than those of other groups. None of the differences was significant and the hostility score from the multiracial schools did not differ significantly from that of the all-white schools.

In conclusion the general trend of this review would suggest that although it has often been pointed out that a concept of race and indeed racial prejudice can be acquired at an early age, the attitudes of white children to their black peers in the school context and their behaviour especially towards West Indians, rather than Asians, seem generally to be favourable. Although such attitudes may well be enhanced when there is daily opportunity for pupils of different ethnic groups to come into contact with each other, against this has to be set the predominant finding of the preference of white children for other white children, whether in actual or desired friendship, and for this ethnocentric preference to increase with age. However, ethnocentricity is not a characteristic peculiar to white pupils as Section 13, pp.157–61 on West Indian pupils' attitudes showed.

Teachers' expectations and attitudes

Over and above the quality of schooling, and the relationship which pupils enjoy with each other, teachers' attitudes and expectations may be directly related to pupils' attainments. Certainly it is well known that West Indian parents believe it to be the case that the performance of their children is very much affected by the expectations which teachers have of them. Strangely, although there has been a good deal of research in the United States on this question there has been very little undertaken directly in relation to pupils of ethnic minority origin in this country.

The American study which made people aware that teacher expectation could be an important factor in their child's performance was that by Rosenthal and Jacobson (1968) who claimed to have shown that manipulated teacher expectancies could become self-fulfilling prophecies. In their experiment they handed teachers lists of children, chosen at random, whom they said would make much or little school progress during the year. It appeared that at the end of this year they found the IQ scores of the younger, but not of the older pupils matched their predictions. When reported the study as a whole provoked severe criticism and most attempts at replication in the United States failed. However, a considerable amount of research evidence in the UK, including English longitudinal studies of streaming, reviewed by Pidgeon (1970), tended to support the conclusion that the interaction between the teacher and pupil, especially the teacher's expectations of a pupil, are important determinants of achievement. On the other hand, studies of different design have shown that most teachers are not swayed by test scores which run counter to the child's actual performance at school. Other studies of the relationship between teacher expectation and teacher behaviour (reviewed, for example, by Brophy and Good, 1974) show marked differences between teachers, some of whom respond positively to high achievers and some to low achievers, yet others showing no tendency in either direction. Further light is shed on a likely explanation by a study (Seaver, 1973) which demonstrated that if a teacher has taught two children from the same family and the older child had been a good student his expectations may well be favourable for the younger child also, although this was not found to apply when two different teachers taught the children, thus suggesting that there is a teacher expectancy effect. As the situation exists it is probably not possible to replicate studies undertaken in America since teachers are now generally aware of these findings. Overall it may be said that although the evidence points towards a real effect on the child's performance by the expectations of his teacher the influence may possibly not be as direct or determining as some of these studies have been taken as showing. (See also pp.55–9 for a further assessment of the effect of teacher expectation in testing contexts.)

In fact, the situation with respect to pupils of West Indian origin is rather more complex than this brief review has suggested. For as well as the possible effects of teacher expectation in particular school situations there is also the question of teachers' general attitudes to ethnic minority pupils. Although much is often made of this it is perhaps not particularly surprising to find that there has been comparatively little research on such a delicate issue. One major research however which involved a national sample of 510 teachers, 171 primary and 339 secondary, in 25 schools with 18 to 84 per cent ethnic minority group pupils (Brittan, 1976b) revealed that teachers held considerable and important differences of opinion about the various ethnic minority groups. However, there was a high degree of consensus of opinion concerning the academic and social behaviour of pupils of West Indian origin. More than two-thirds of teachers in the sample expressed agreement or disagreement on three items, thereby indicating unfavourable opinions of West Indians, with only very small percentages expressing the opposite point of view. Moreover teachers appeared to be more willing to make generalizations about West Indian pupils as a group, and on the basis of comments made on the questionnaire the researcher concluded that there appeared to be 'large scale stereotyping of "West Indian" pupils'. This was also indicated by informal replies by heads and teachers concerning the achievement and occupational potential of West Indians in the survey by Allen and Smith (1975). Similarly Tomlinson (1979) interviewed 30 heads in connection with ESN(M) assessment and found that they were prone to respond at length about West Indian pupils, but not Asian pupils, and to have generalized views about them. Heads had strong feelings that the learning process was slower for West Indian pupils, that they lacked long-term concentration and that they would tend to under-achieve and be remedial.

Thus, it is not possible to consider teacher expectation towards ethnic minority pupils in general. What is needed is much more specific evidence about what kind of attitudes teachers have in particular towards pupils of West Indian origin, and to what extent these attitudes are manifested in their behaviour to such pupils in the classroom. This is an area in which it is most difficult to disentangle cause and effect, for which comes first, behaviour or attitude? Another issue which a broad consideration of teacher expectation tends to overlook is that teachers are not just a uniform group but each teacher is an individual and teaches in his own style. This is the kind of reasoning which has led some researchers to make claims such as that of Aisthorpe (1976) who remarked that although there were 75 per cent West Indian children in his Manchester junior school there were no significant teacher expectation effects. Moreover, it is surely correct to observe that though there have certainly been many misclassifications of West Indian children who were poorly adjusted to the school situation as ESN, there have also been successful black pupils, many of whom, no doubt, have in the general run of things done better than their teachers might have expected.

Two black writers who provide somewhat anecdotal and descriptive evidence on the issue of teacher expectation would be certain to argue otherwise. Coard (1971), himself a teacher of ESN pupils, claimed that most black pupils who were being diagnosed as ESN were incorrectly assessed by their teachers who held biased views towards such pupils. He suggested that the teachers were biased in three ways: culturally, insofar as they misunderstood the linguistic differences between them and their pupils; socially, inasmuch as they were middle class and held different values and beliefs associated with their class; and thirdly, insofar as they failed to appreciate the temporary emotional disturbance which such pupils were undergoing as a result of removal from the Caribbean to the UK. He further claimed that the attitude of the teacher could also affect the performance of the black child not only by his low expectations but also by open prejudice and patronization which he maintained were a frequent feature of interactions between teachers and black pupils.

Another study by a black researcher which involved some observation in multiracial schools in London (Giles, 1977) also tended to support the view of Coard that stereotyping was both subtle and overt. Giles made contact with 15 out of 21 infant and junior schools in nine divisions of the ILEA and eight out of 13 secondary schools, selected for their sizeable percentages of West Indian pupils, and interviewed head teachers, some teachers and two groups of black pupils about their perceptions of life in their schools. Giles avowedly started from the premise that teachers' attitudes and perceptions are crucial in the education of black children. And yet he found that most heads felt that 'since the same quality of education was available to both black and white children from working-class backgrounds it would not be valid or fair to infer a relationship between the racial composition of disadvantaged schools and poor achievement and performance among West Indian pupils as a selected group' (pp.6–7). In his somewhat superficial description of the case study schools Giles noted a tremendous variety in their social and cultural environments and also in the major features of the heads' and teachers' perceptions. However, he made little attempt to draw comparisons between schools or to highlight the genuine concern and confusion which most of the heads and teachers seemed to express. The research and its conclusions have been thoroughly criticized by Jeffcoate (1977) and Kirp (1977). The latter points out that Giles seemed to have approached the research presuming teachers held discriminatory attitudes and having a ready-made conclusion and set of policy recommendations to fit this presupposition. Whereas he actually found that, in general, heads and teachers did not see that black children had any particular problems over and above their socially disadvantaged white peers. Hence they did not treat them differently on acount of their colour. On the other hand, Giles himself argued that pupils of West Indian origin had both a different class and cultural orientation. However he conceded that they were possibly less co-operative and more disrespectful. But he also claimed that teachers saw 'a disproportionately bigger margin of under-achievement among West Indian girls than among the white girls, due to social rather than cultural factors. Teachers also often cited the problem which black pupils experienced in learning to handle freedom and choice in a relatively permissive school atmosphere whilst often living in repressive home environments. This was particularly noticeable in comparison with the children who came from the fairly lax discipline of white working-class homes, hence causing a problem for teachers who were trying to operate two standards at the same time to take account of pupils' differing needs. Even these few observations, would, however, tend to suggest that teachers were indeed recognizing differences between black and white pupils and attempting to treat them appropriately. Yet, in general, they did not feel able to support a programme designed to address the special needs of West Indian students which would ignore similar needs among the indigenous white pupils who were also socially disadvantaged. Giles acknowledged this in the opening chapter of his book and also realized that

'no one policy statement regarding the goals for multi-cultural education could serve the needs of Britain or London as a whole since characteristics of different cultural and racial minorities vary from authority to authority and even within schools in some authorities. This situation makes study of multi-cultural education and recommendations for effective programmes an extremely complex and questionable endeavour if it were to be undertaken as a basis for policy recommendations for Britain as a whole.' (p.153).

Yet he nevertheless went on to do just that–in the form of a black studies programme.

Despite some obvious deficiencies in the study by Giles, it is important for indirectly highlighting the genuine confusion amongst teachers as to how to treat pupils of West Indian and other ethnic minority groups in relation to similarly socially disadvantaged white pupils. Yet this confusion is not new. Testimonies to it have been produced both by groups of teachers (see Report of a London Working Party of Teachers and Lecturers, 1974) and individual teachers, for example, Rogers (1973) who pointed to both the sensitivity and uncertainty with which many teachers approached the difficulties of organizing school life and teaching in schools with varied ethnic compositions. The confusion, simply expressed, seems to be as to whether a black pupil is to be assimilated into the school so that he is seen primarily as an individual sharing a common humanity, but having his own particular needs; or, whether he is to be seen as different, one black child among a group of black children with a different culture, and who requires different treatment by virtue of his membership of the black group. The issue seems to amount to whether differences are to be ignored or accepted and accommodated but treated largely as if they were absent, or, on the other hand, acknowledged and distinguished in such a way as to highlight them. As Rogers points out, such confusions have not been helped by changes in the policy orientation of different governments or by general lack of professional rationale. As long ago as 1973 she suggested that there was a need to identify and investigate the features of successful multiracial schools so that these could be more widely publicized as examples of good practice, but although attempts to carry out such an exercise have been undertaken (e.g. by the Schools Council/NFER Project Education for a Multiracial Society, 1973-6) descriptions of such schools have not yet been made publicly available, though it is understood that a summary of the evaluation report of the project is to be forthcoming in 1982 (see also Schools Council, 1981 for a preliminary summary).

Overall the evidence on teacher expectation and attitudes does not really permit firm conclusions as to whether teacher expectations for black children are a determining influence on their school life and performance. Whilst it is most likely that some teachers do have negative perceptions of and attitudes towards (some) black pupils, it would also appear that many teachers are sensitively and actively concerned to evolve a consistent and fair policy towards the treatment of their black pupils both in respect to continuity of school organization from year to year and in their daily interaction with children of West Indian origin in their classrooms.

Teachers' attitudes to multicultural education
Not surprisingly, there has been a proliferation of research in this area in recent years although, as a result of Miller's (1969) study which found that teaching designed to reduce racial prejudice actually increased it, there has been considerable trepidation about introducing race relations programmes as such into the curriculum for fear that inter-ethnic relationships would be harmed rather than improved. It might well be argued, however, that Miller's study which involved 1,340 male apprentices aged 15 to 20, who were attending courses in liberal studies as part of their day release studies and who were given between one and three hours of teaching about race, may well have been both an unrepresentative group from which to draw inferences with respect to school courses, and also may not have received such teaching for long enough. Nevertheless, the reaction resulting from such findings also co-incided with evidence which suggested that many teachers were reluctant to introduce teaching about race relations or multicultural education in general into the curriculum.

A national survey (Brittan, 1976a) which investigated by questionnaire the attitudes of 510 headteachers and heads of departments in 25 schools in England and Wales to aspects of the curriculum, role of mother tongues, school organization and the impact of a multiracial situation found that although teachers were unanimous in acknowledging the responsibility of the school to promote good race relations, at least a fifth of the teachers were opposed to the introduction of lessons on the culture and countries of origin of the immigrants into the curriculum, although two-thirds were in favour of such changes. More teachers in schools with high percentages of ethnic minority pupils were more in favour of a multicultural curriculum than those in schools with fewer ethnic minority pupils. However, there was a discrepancy in the opinions expressed, which was to some extent explained by some of the 2,000 comments made by the teachers over and above the questionnaire, in that only 46 per cent agreed with the statement 'schools should adapt their ways to accommodate different traditions of immigrant pupils' and one-third disagreed, particularly those teachers in secondary schools. Similarly, only 43 per cent supported and 35 per cent were against the introduction of lessons on race relations into the curriculum. Further details are also available in Brittan (1973b). Brittan (1976b) also indicates that whilst 71 per cent of the same sample of teachers felt that ethnic minority pupils enriched the school, the majority found working in multiracial schools more tiring, though not necessarily more satisfying. There was little recognition by teachers of the need for specialized teacher training or the kinds of curriculum changes which might promote good multiracial education. Giles's report (1977) as reviewed above (pp.196–8) revealed similar ambivalences amongst London teachers about the need for multicultural education.

Whilst it is difficult to tell from the preliminary publication of the summary and conclusions to the 1978 Schools Council project Studies in the Multi-ethnic Curriculum (Little and Willey, 1981) to what extent teachers' attitudes towards a multicultural curriculum have changed over the last few years, and whether they are really in advance of action, as is claimed, there is some indication that it is felt that a greater awareness of the multi-ethnic nature of British society should be reflected in the curriculum, although it is, not surprisingly, those teachers in secondary schools with high or medium concentrations of ethnic minority pupils who believe that all pupils, regardless of the ethnic composition of the school, should be educated for life in a multiracial society. Teachers in secondary schools with fewer than two and a half per cent ethnic minority pupils remain to be convinced of the relevance of a multi-ethnic society to their teaching. Yet 78 per cent of the 525 schools sampled believed special attention, possibly in in-service training, should be given to the problems faced by white children in schools with large numbers of ethnic minority pupils.

Finally, it is interesting to note one specific project which provides information on an attempt to introduce teaching on race relations into the curriculum. In the late 60s and early 70s as part of the Humanities Curriculum Project, Lawrence Stenhouse devised an approach to teaching about race relations in British schools which aimed not to stress the changing of attitudes but to increase understanding of race relations issues by means of specific curriculum innovations. Bagley and Verma (1975) who evaluated these teaching techniques found, none the less, that changes in attitude amongst pupils who had received such teaching had indeed occurred. Among 226 pupils, 76 of whom were immigrants, in London, the Midlands and the North of England, it was found that prejudice had decreased, sometimes significantly, after teaching about race relations. However, it was also noted that 43 per cent of white boys were found to be highly prejudiced when tested by the reliable Wilson-Patterson Conservatism Scale.

More recently, an investigation by Widlake and Bloom (1979) of an on-going project which is attempting to implement some materials for multicultural education devised by the Centre for Urban Educational Studies has also noted considerable opposition to such programmes in general. Although the numbers of teachers involved in Manchester were not given in this outline article, the researcher stated that when asked for opinions on a provocative statement attacking the need for multicultural education and suggesting the assimilation of ethnic minorities into English culture, though existing users of the CUES material were virtually unanimous in disagreeing with this statement, almost half the remaining teachers were prepared to agree with such an attack. Yet though this finding paralleled that of Giles (1977) the author does not stress the implementation of multicultural education, but rather the need to overcome the apathy and opposition of teachers to multicultural education.

Indeed, it would seem that, if such programmes are thought appropriate, – and it is of interest to note the Schools Council/NFER Project Education for a Multiracial Society came to the conclusion that it was desirable for all subjects to be permeated with a multicultural element – either in certain schools, leas, or indeed nationally, then there will be no point in attempting to implement

them unless programmes of teacher re-education are first introduced. Whether such a policy is either possible or desirable since it
appears to override teachers' professional and private attitudes, is,
of course, another question, but it does appear to have been
acknowledged by the National Union of Teachers who have recently advocated giving express attention to teaching in a multi-ethnic
society in all teacher training courses (1980). Since then the National Association of Teachers in Further and Higher Education have
argued that initial and in-service teacher training courses should
contain a compulsory multicultural element (1981) and the Assistant Masters and Mistresses Association has similarly called for
improved teacher training to take account of the needs of ethnic
minorities (1981).

Teachers' attitudes to language
Having examined teachers' attitudes to multicultural education and
noted the reservations which they express it is appropriate to turn to
the evidence which research has gathered about teachers' attitudes
to two particularly controversial aspects of the education of pupils
of West Indian origin, namely language and behaviour. (An evaluation of the influence of language on the performance, particularly in
reading of pupils of West Indian origin is given in Section 6,
p.60ff).

In a national survey of teachers' opinions on curricular changes
Brittan (1976a) found that 71 per cent of the 510 primary and
secondary school teachers questioned agreed with the statement
'the English spoken by most West Indian pupils requires special
attention for the pupils to benefit from an English education'.
However, 15 per cent of the teachers disagreed and a small number
of comments indicated fundamentally different attitudes towards
the language of pupils of Caribbean descent. Many of these suggested that speakers of Creole were linguistically deprived. On the
other hand, some teachers showed particular awareness and
pointed to the need to distinguish Creole and Standard English.
None, it appeared, made reference to the importance of Creole in
terms of cultural identity.

Edwards, in several articles has also noted that bidialectism as an
asset for cultural identification or self-esteem seems to have been
underestimated by teachers. In one small study (1978) she asked 20
student teachers to judge samples of speech. She found that student

teachers did not distinguish between working-class white speakers and two West Indian girls, but they did differ in their evaluation of a West Indian girl who spoke in a working-class accent and also in Creole, judging her less favourably when speaking in a West Indian accent. Edwards suggested that there was extensive stereotyping in these judgements and that little attention had been paid to individual characteristics. She also produced evidence to show that the teachers' evaluation of the girl when speaking in a West Indian accent was lower in terms of academic potential than when the same girl spoke with a working-class accent. Elsewhere Edwards (1979) has argued that teachers' attitudes and expectations with respect to Creole lead to low academic performance on the part of the West Indian child.

'The stereotyping process leads features of Creole to be stigmatized and to develop connotations of, amongst other things, low academic ability. The teacher is then more likely to allow the stereotype to determine her behaviour towards the child and low teacher expectation will very probably lead to low pupil performance. The child for his part, feels threatened, especially in the early stages, by comprehension difficulties. These and the teacher's behaviour towards him produce a state of linguistic insecurity and he is very likely to seem inarticulate as a result. This reinforces the teacher's preconceived ideas and so the cycle is perpetuated.' (pp.97–8).

As has also been noticed with respect to arguments about self-esteem, circular explanations appear to be common in this field. But they are really no more than hypotheses – albeit with a grain of truth.

Teachers' attitudes to behaviour

To judge by teachers' reports in general and some of the evidence reviewed in Section 11 (pp.135–41) black pupils would appear to be much more deviant than whites. As with teachers' attitudes to language, however, it is difficult to disentangle cause and effect. Does poor behaviour lead to lower expectation for achievement, for example, or does low expectation lead to poor behaviour?

In the ILEA Literacy Survey (Mabey, 1980, 1981) teachers rated West Indian pupils aged eight, and their parents, negatively. They thought only 25 per cent of the West Indians compared with 50 per cent of the indigenous pupils had good relationships with other pupils, teachers and attitudes to school work. Similarly, they felt that only half of the West Indian parents were interested in their children's schools and they thought that only three per cent of the West Indian children came from culturally stimulating homes. More specifically in relation to behaviour, the study by Brittan (1976b) which looked at aspects of school life in relation to pupils and teachers found a consensus of opinion relating to the academic and social behaviour of West Indian pupils. Seventy-five per cent of the 171 primary teachers and 78 per cent of the 339 secondary teachers disagreed with the statements 'West Indian pupils are usually better behaved than English pupils' and 'West Indian pupils tend to raise the academic standard of this school.' West Indian pupils were similarly regarded unfavourably in relation to the correction of their behaviour: 57 per cent of primary and 72 per cent of secondary school teachers agreed with the statement 'West Indian pupils resent being reprimanded more than English pupils do.'

One important study which investigated behavioural deviance of 2,043 10-year-old children in London (Rutter *et al.*, 1974) provides information on teachers' attitudes towards West Indian pupils' behaviour. The Rutter Behaviour Questionnaire, a reliable measure in which teachers are asked to rate a child in relation to 26 descriptions of behaviour, was employed. Forty-nine per cent of West Indian boys were judged by their teachers to be 'behaviourally deviant' according to the norms of this measure compared with 25 per cent of the English boys. Just over a third of West Indian girls were seen by their teachers as 'deviant' compared with only 13 per cent of English girls. Thus, a total of 41 per cent of the 354 black children in the study were judged deviant compared with 19 per cent of the 1,689 white children, a highly significant difference. Both boys and girls of West Indian origin were more often rated as restless, squirming, unable to settle, destructive, quarrelsome, not liked by other children, irritable, disobedient, telling lies, stealing, unresponsive, resentful and often bullying. In addition, black girls, but not boys, were likely to be judged solitary, miserable and fearful. It is also of interest to note that migration appeared to influence teachers' ratings of children as 'deviant' since 83 per cent of the children inaccurately categorized by birthplace were perceived as deviant compared with 30 per cent of those accurately classified. The researchers suggested that although the Rutter scale is meant as a screening device the teachers may be looking at black children in biased or over-dramatic terms. Yet in a follow-up study when a number of 'deviant' children were studied intensively the clinical interviews indicated some excess of acting-out behaviour in black children. Also to a large extent black and white parents' descriptions of their childrens behaviour was very similar, but quite different from that given by their teachers. Moreover, it is of interest that a clinically based interview with teachers indicated a much lower prevalence of behavioural deviance in black children. It remained the case, however, that many more black children were behaviourally difficult and rebellious in the school situation than at home where they appeared, on their parents' evidence, to be as well adjusted as their white peers. Once again, it is difficult to know whether it is the school situation which is causing behavioural difficulties, as certain writers have suggested (e.g. BPPA, 1978), or whether the standards of behaviour which teachers expect are different from those which parents are prepared to tolerate, especially in the home. In view of the alleged authoritarianism in the West Indian home the position would seem particularly difficult to unravel.

Green (1972) who describes in an MPhil thesis an investigation into the attitudes of 87 teachers from infant, junior and secondary schools in which there were large numbers of children from different ethnic groups, found that the experiences most frequently reported in terms unfavourable to West Indian children involved discipline, sulking, social behaviour, aggressiveness and resentment, in that order. The friendliness of West Indian children was most frequently mentioned in favourable terms during the free-response interviews which were individually conducted. Such favourable statements were most often made by teachers who were rated on an independent measure as tender-minded, radical, and having naturalistic attitudes. The researcher also found that older, more experienced, teachers who hold more senior posts of responsibility are more likely to be less racially tolerant.

In an ethnographical description of one fourth year in a multiracial school in the West Midlands Driver (1977) noted that although the staff made particular efforts to respond to what they saw as the special educational needs of their ethnic minority pupils, limits in their 'cultural competence' led teachers to take on authoritarian roles, especially when challenged, which was usually by boys of West Indian origin. The relative frequency of these events led such teachers to make critical judgements of West Indian boys whom they generally considered to be difficult. Driver found that there was a high inter-correlation on two rating scales for academic and social behaviour and that this was twice as high for the boys of West Indian origin. The researcher's interpretation was that teachers' assessments were therefore 'problematic' and he suggested that teachers' own difficulties and uncertainties in teaching in multi-ethnic classrooms focused on the West Indian pupils as a whole, and especially the boys in the fourth and fifth years.

In conclusion, it appears from research evidence that the attitudes of teachers, and hence probably their expectations, are likely to be of considerable influence on the performance of children of West Indian origin in schools. However, it should be remembered that many of the research studies reviewed here tap only crude measures of teachers' attitudes, sometimes on forced-choice questions which allow little variation in the pattern of response and no qualifications to be made. Yet teachers as a profession, as with other groups of workers, are a diverse group of people, with different personalities, attitudes and expectations. It is by no means to be assumed therefore that they are racialist when considered as a professional group. The reservations which many teachers seem to express on the implementation of a multicultural curriculum may well be for professional rather than racially biased reasons – no research yet appears to have assessed their reluctance in sufficient detail to say definitely. Moreover, several studies have pointed to the honest bewilderment and genuine concern and sensitivity which many teachers who have daily to deal with difficulties in teaching pupils of minority ethnic origin obviously feel. Doubtless, these are the teachers who are doing their best in this situation, often in the absence of practical guidelines. They are probably, too, the kind of teachers in whom many children of West Indian origin confide, for as Pollak (1979) found, West Indian children are just as likely to talk to their teachers as to their mothers about their concerns. It seems reasonable to expect that all pupils will achieve more and do better when their teachers are approachable and available as the study by Rutter *et al.* (1979) indicates. Again, it may be that the quality of the school, the whole ethos of school life, the hidden as well as the overt curriculum are more important for their effect on performance than teachers' attitudes in particular. No research has yet been sufficiently detailed to give anything like an adequate account of these more intangible qualitative factors. However, one or two individual descriptions, such as that by Smith (1973), have told how certain individual multiracial schools have approached the education of pupils of ethnic minority origin, by means of a close partnership and interaction between home and school.

Conclusions to Part 3
The foregoing examination of the relative influences of the home and school on the education of the pupil of West Indian origin has highlighted a number of central features in this mutually interactive process. Of these the most important appear to be the self-esteem of the West Indian pupil, the attitudes of his teachers towards him and the many contrasts between his life at home and his life at school. But equally important influences, especially on the nature of the attitudes of parents, pupils and teachers, and the degree to which they are held, may be a host of factors, such as personality, external circumstances and the quality of the interaction itself, as well as the ethos of the school–none of which have been adequately taken account of in the research literature.

Self-esteem is obviously a crucial and pivotal concept in understanding the position of pupils of West Indian origin in schools. It may be particularly affected by the organization and atmosphere of the school, but as an enduring trait it can probably be changed by counselling and favourable social situations. For true integration to occur it is necessary to promote cross-racial friendships and racial interdependence as well as strong measures of personal and group autonomy. That there are schools where such integration has occurred is known, but it is unfortunately those schools in which such integration has not taken place of which most is heard. In the author's opinion more detailed case studies of particular schools showing how institutional forces can promote or prevent true integration are needed. The success of the school as an agent of acculturalization and socialization seems to depend on a myriad of factors including the aims and attitudes of teachers, the affinity of parental attitudes with those of the school, the attitudes and aspirations of ethnic minority pupils and those of white British children and, not least, the attitudes of society as a whole. As Dipack Nandy (1971) has put it

'Whatever special strategies education for a multi-racial society may require, they will be ineffective except against a background of a more effective and humane strategy for education as such. . . . What is important is that there will be little hope of achieving equality of opportunity, tolerance and a respect for cultural diversity for minority groups in society if these virtues are lacking in social relationships as a whole.' (pp.10–11).

It is very much in this context that any attempts to change the attitudes of teachers, particularly in respect of the implementation of a multicultural curriculum must be seen.

It is the author's view that there is evidently a need for greater tolerance and understanding of the difference in perspectives between the home and the school. Just as greater efforts need to be made by teachers to understand the background of the pupils of West Indian origin in their care and in particular their upbringing and family life in this country, so West Indian parents need to know much more about teachers' professionalism and the responsibility which their children's teachers have for their charges. There is some evidence to suggest that if the special needs of pupils of West Indian origin could be spelt out then the home and the school could possibly work together to meet these needs. Certainly, teachers require the guidance of clearer and more coherent and consistent policy recommendations. Much more, too, remains to be discovered about the attitudes of parents of pupils of West Indian origin, and in the writer's opinion a programme of education for parents organized in conjunction with black community organizations such as the Black Parents Movement and the Caribbean Teachers' Association about the way in which education in this country as a whole and in particular schools is organized, might be of great benefit. More specifically, by this means attention might be given to the real differences which may exist between parents' and children's aspirations, so that with a greater knowledge and appreciation of the functions of the school West Indian parents may come to make a more sanguine assessment of the abilities and potential of their children and the possibilities and limitations of schooling. Similarly, a delicate balance must be attained between motivating West Indian children to succeed and avoiding giving them a false impression of what they can achieve. This may well be to walk a tightrope between over-aspiration and apathy.

It is somehow necessary for the school to find a way in which it can contribute to the process of instilling confidence in the pupil of West

Indian origin and pride in his own ethnic group, and yet also enable him to have a realistic appraisal of his position within society at large. This is a tremendously difficult task and cannot be achieved by the school's agency and education alone, for it is dependent very much on the values and attitudes of society in general and the social conditions of the times. Moreover, social changes may well have to be brought about through the efforts of black people themselves. However, the school has an important role to play, though its influence at various times and cumulatively may well be less than that of the home. But the importance of the school should not be underestimated insofar as it is is a microcosm of society and an instantiation of it. Indeed there are obvious ways in which the education system can make a start: by accelerating changes in the overt curriculum and examinations; the appointment of black school governors, and most importantly, by becoming more sensitive to the hidden curriculum, so that examples of tolerant, encouraging and respectful attitudes and behaviour can set a tone and pattern and thereby lay the foundation for harmonious relationships between black and white in future years.

Part Four

Overview

Section 15: Research Methodologies

Since this has been primarily a review of empirical research on the education of pupils of West Indian origin it is appropriate to devote some attention to an appraisal of the research methodologies employed in the studies which have been considered, before turning to an overview of the general conclusions which can be drawn from the findings of such researches and recommendations for future practice. Criticisms will be related to the following aspects of research: design, sampling, assessment and interpretation and evaluation. Some of the criticisms advanced, whilst related specifically to this particular field of research in multi-ethnic education, are also relevant to educational research in general.

Design

First, it is fair to point out that there are a relatively small number of of research investigations of any size and importance central to the study of achievement of pupils of West Indian origin on strictly academic measures. The types of research methods employed can be basically divided into two categories: psychometric and analytic or descriptive. Both of these approaches are fairly well represented throughout the literature and it may well be that they have a certain complementary validity, although strict comparability is not in order. It will have been noticed that this research review concentrates on evidence provided by the more psychometric type of investigation. Psychometric research has a quantitative, numerical basis, tends to have a statistical bias and to employ tests whose validity and reliability have been established on a white population, as well as occasionally a few tests devised when required for special purposes.

The investigations reviewed have used varying types of research design sometimes with control groups against which experimental groups can be compared. However, these have often been inadequately matched or matched only for one or two variables such as age and social class and, for example in clinical studies, have sometimes not employed a separate group of 'normal' pupils of West Indian origin. However, attention since the early studies at least and especially perhaps in the early and mid-70s has been given to distinguishing between pupils of West Indian origin born in this country and those who are themselves migrants. An exemplary tripartite study which focuses on this distinction is that undertaken by Rutter and his colleagues in 1970 (Rutter *et al.*, 1974; Rutter *et al.*, 1975; Yule *et al.*, 1975). This investigation is also notable insofar as it drew comparisons by means of group and individual testing – a distinction to which insufficient attention has been paid in this field – though another series of studies (Davey and Mullin, 1980; Davey and Norburn, 1980a and b) show what can be achieved by individual testing of a relatively large number of pupils. To a limited extent such a comparison was a subsidiary part of the major survey on literacy undertaken by the ILEA (Little *et al.*, 1968; Little, 1975; Mabey, 1980, 1981), and this important research also embodied longitudinal measures on a cohort which enable particularly interesting conclusions to be drawn over time. There is a need for more studies of a deliberately longitudinal kind. That by the National Child Development Study, though it has the merit of having a national random sample, unfortunately contained relatively few pupils of West Indian origin and their numbers in the samples tested at different ages were variable.

Several more descriptive studies have also been included in this review of research, but it seems fair to say that in this field they tend to be less illuminative than anecdotal. This is possibly because the reports appear to be both more emotive and heartfelt. Often it is unfortunately the case that such authors seem to pick and choose evidence from the psychometric studies to support their own case in a particularly obvious way, so that it becomes a relatively easy matter for those of alternative persuasions to discount their arguments by those of opposing tendency.

Sampling

Although there are evident difficulties in undertaking research in this particularly sensitive field, it is unfortunately the case that sampling procedures were often far from rigorous. Studies on the whole tended to include disproportionately small numbers of pupils of West Indian origin, though in many cases this was the result of necessity or chance rather than deliberate research design. As a consequence studies of 40 or 50 pupils of West Indian origin are common and in fact the norm even when larger numbers of white pupils are included. Studies involving over 100 pupils of West Indian origin are relatively rare, especially when undertaken by individual researchers, as opposed to those surveys with institutional backing which have already been mentioned. Many smaller scale studies instituted by single researchers in connection with higher degree theses have only involved about 20 pupils of West Indian origin, though these studies often have an unusual interest and usefulness inasmuch as they sometimes employ specially designed assessment materials and show a particular appreciation of local conditions and patterns of performance (e.g. Aisthorpe, 1976). However, both of these features make such studies difficult to replicate, although their value should not be underestimated.

Most of the research investigations undertaken have been carried out in London either involving surveys of whole cohorts or schools in individual boroughs which appear in general to have indicated results similar to those found for the whole authority (ILEA). Other investigations have been undertaken in the other main centres of West Indian population, in particular Birmingham, and to a lesser extent Manchester, and where certainly known allusion has been made to these locations in descriptions of the studies. Indeed, it may well be the case that there are different factors operating in these urban environments as compared with those in the metropolis, but there is insufficient research evidence to draw any firm conclusions here. As has been pointed out (Collymore, 1980) most West Indians live in inner urban areas and hence some research investigations which have included West Indian pupils attending schools in suburban locations may give a somewhat unrepresentative picture.

As a consequence of the type of research design employed generally very few studies have been able to compare both performance at junior and secondary school age directly. Indeed, by far the majority of studies have sampled junior school populations.

Whilst this is undoubtedly a crucial stage of schooling, it is nevertheless a pity that so few studies of attainment and achievement looked
at secondary school populations since they assume an even greater
significance when it is realized that the pupils of West Indian origin
now in those schools are the first generation to have experienced
full schooling in this country. Moreover, few studies gave sufficiently detailed information on or adequately sampled different types of
school, such as single sex, mixed secondary modern or comprehensive, and studies often failed to differentiate between those with
small or large numbers of pupils or high and low percentages of
ethnic minority pupils on the school rolls.

It appears that records kept both at lea level and within schools
are often insufficiently detailed to provide information on the place
of birth of pupils of West Indian origin. In the absence of such
records researchers have often had to rely on teachers' estimates
(sometimes, indeed, e.g. Driver, 1980a and b, in retrospect) for the
identification of their samples, and those estimates may well be
inappropriate (Bagley, 1975b; Rosen and Burgess, 1980a). However, Rutter *et al.* (1975) have shown that these teacher estimates
are often subject to bias (especially in the case of behaviour) since
teachers tend to attribute the place of birth to the West Indies if this
is not known, and misclassification may well result. Such a matter is
of obvious importance when studies attempt to differentiate between children born in this country and those born overseas.
Furthermore, details on mixed parentage are very rarely indicated.
Hence, there is even less available evidence on island of origin or
rural/urban background and it is unlikely that such information is
readily available from schools.

Assessment

In view of the discussion of problems associated with assessment in
Part 2 (pp.49–59) it is not necessary to enter into a detailed
criticism again here. It will serve to reiterate a few main points.
Criticisms tend to relate to two main areas of testing: the test
materials and the testing situation. It is now widely appreciated that
until recently inappropriate materials have been used for testing
pupils of West Indian origin, among other ethnic minority groups,
on IQ, reading, and to a lesser extent mathematics, as all these
assessment materials involve some cultural biases. These materials
are all readily used in assessment within schools for placement in

streams or sets as well as in connection with transfer procedures, though little attention has been given in these contexts to the degree of misclassification which may have resulted. By contrast, the use of materials for the assessment of educational sub-normality have provoked much criticism. Once again at the culmination of schooling the validity of examinations as a publicly certificated form of assessment for ethnic minority pupils has received scant consideration.

There is, moreover, in the literature a notable confusion of the concepts of ability, potential and attainment which these test materials are used to assess. As Bagley *et al.* (1978) have argued, it is time to employ a broader concept of cognitive functioning and it is to be hoped that the recently available tests of learning ability (Hegarty and Lucas, 1978) which utilize a different process of assessment based on ability to learn, will go some way towards meeting a long-standing need.

Other criticisms have centred round the testing situation including the colour of the tester, the context in which the testing takes place and the expectations of the teacher. Detailed consideration of these criticisms has been taken account of elsewhere (pp.55–9, pp.183–9 and pp.193–207). It seems fair to say that whilst there is insufficient evidence from research undertaken in this country on the first two factors, there may well be more reason to support claims of adverse teacher expectation.

Despite the improvements which awareness of likely effects of assessment materials and testing context have brought about, new techniques of greater sensitivity and complexity are still required. Relatively crude measures of social variables continue to be employed within research design and far greater consideration needs to be given to the process variables of upbringing, parents' attitudes and school quality.

Interpretation and evaluation

It has been argued in this review that background data should be seen as part of the integral information taken into account by research in this field as it seems more than usually important to consider West Indian subjects in the round. The quality of social and demographic information influences the value of the results of the research to a major extent. Nevertheless, inadequate descriptions of background details are often supplied in research reports in this field and sometimes, moreover, even the data are presented sketchily. In addition, hypotheses are frequently not specified, neither are the premises and standpoints of the researchers involved. Frequently speculations are adduced as explanations and from time to time, as has been shown, statistical interpretations are in error and conclusions are sometimes drawn which are not justified on the basis of the evidence supplied.

The politically charged context in which research enterprises are often undertaken is infrequently adverted to, though the influences can be considerable, as in the case of research by D'Souza (1978) who mentions that at the particular time when his research was undertaken racial tension happened to bring the West Indian and Asian communities closer together, thus affecting the results of his attitude questionnaire. Close reading of texts also reveals the natural personal biases of researchers, though these are rarely explicitly stated. It is interesting to note that sometimes, however, deliberately or otherwise, such predilections do seem to give rise to the placing of emphasis on conclusions which are not necessarily indicated by an otherwise scrupulous presentation of evidence.

Another factor is the distinction which needs to be drawn between statistical significance and educational significance when findings are reported. What has been referred to as 'significant' in the text has usually meant statistically significant and though this may indeed also be of educational interest, the two concepts should not be conflated. Statistical significance, by definition numerically based, has, even when it employs such potentially useful techniques as cluster analysis, still to be interpreted and evaluated. In so doing it is essential to remember the human beings, and their interaction within the educational system, to which such numbers relate.

Regrettably, with some exceptions (notably work by Bagley and Rex and Tomlinson) researchers have failed to devote sufficient attention to information available from other disciplines which would complement their research on educational matters. A lack of interdisciplinary co-ordination is indeed a feature of educational research in general, which tends to have a natural bias towards psychology. In the particular case of research into pupils of West Indian origin anthropological and social-psychological evidence is distinctly relevant, but has been underestimated, and the philosophical questions arising particularly obviously in connection with the development of a multicultural curriculum or positive intervention in education have also largely been ignored (for an exception see Hegarty and Lucas, 1978).

It is also interesting to trace how on relatively slight evidence and indeed even negative wording (see for example, Little *et al.*, 1968) a number of research interpretations–in this case that performance of pupils of West Indian origin would improve with length of schooling or stay in this country–which have subsequently become almost mythological, have been erroneously perpetuated. It is possible, too, that other evidence which is somewhat slight or anecdotal, for example, that on the disadvantages associated with child minding and the lack of appreciation by West Indian parents of the importance of toys, play and parent-child interaction for young children, also falls into this category. Moreover, as has been seen in the case of the reporting of Driver's research (1980a and b), precipitant or sketchy publication in even the more reputable journals of the popular press can lead to some distortion of the actual evidence and encourage false impressions to circulate in the field.

Yet these criticisms must not be seen as intentionally too harsh, for it is obviously much easier to criticize reports of research than to undertake it, especially in such a controversial field. Research into the education of ethnic minority pupils is indeed a relatively new field of study, with a number of extra dimensions and especial difficulties over and above those normally associated with educa-tional research in general. Though considerable advances in under-standing have undoubtedly been made, research, of its nature, looks backwards or, at least, relates to the recent past, and it is necessary for methodologies both to become flexible in approaching a rapidly changing multi-ethnic situation and also to be more rigorous in terms of design and evaluation.

Section 16: General Conclusions

On the basis of the foregoing review of research what conclusions is it permissible to draw? Undoubtedly, the picture is complex, with minor inconsistencies, more important ambiguities and even con-tradictions at almost every turn. Notwithstanding these niceties there is an overwhelming consensus: that research evidence shows a strong trend to under-achievement of pupils of West Indian origin on the main indicators of academic performance. Pupils of West Indian origin perform less well on measures of IQ, verbal and non-verbal reasoning, reading and mathematics, and are more likely to be found in the lower streams of ordinary schools, in much higher proportions in ESN schools and there appears to be evidence that they suffer stress in the school environment. During the period of 15 years or so covered by this review of research a number of explanations have been advanced to account for the continuing under-achievement of pupils of West Indian origin in British schools and these will be briefly examined after a final consideration of research evidence on performance in subject areas in comparison with school peers. Two concluding sections of this report broach the questions of educational strategies (Section 17, pp.232ff) and further research (Section 18, pp.240ff) which are suggested by this review.

There are four main ways in which to evaluate the educational performance of pupils of West Indian origin: by an examination of differential performance within the group of West Indian pupils as a whole; a comparison of pupils of West Indian origin with pupils from other ethnic minority groups; a comparison of West Indian pupils with their white peers drawn from similar social class backgrounds; and a national comparison with white peers. It is proposed to consider each of these comparisons briefly in turn.

Just as the performance of an individual pupil in one subject area may not be as good as that in another subject, so the performance of one individual belonging to a group may vary considerably from that of another pupil of the same ethnic group. Although there is a firm trend for pupils of West Indian origin to under-achieve, the research reviewed has also testified to a great variation in performance throughout this group of pupils, (see, for example, Little, 1975) and has warned of the danger of generalization with respect to pupils of West Indian origin who often appear, particularly with respect to behaviour, to present a series of contradictions (see, for example, Schools Council, 1970). An appraisal of the performance of pupils of West Indian origin in British schools as a group therefore shows that they are not universally under-achieving, though in general the majority are not performing as well as might be expected. Despite the overwhelmingly depressed nature of the research findings it is possible to glean incidentally and from time to time, for example with respect to information on streaming, 11-plus transfer or examination passes, some indication that there are indeed some pupils of West Indian origin who might be termed (high) achievers. Whilst it would have been pleasing to have been able to counterbalance the overall negative findings of the research evidence of under-achievement with many examples of good performance, it is unfortunately still the case that those black pupils who do achieve are seen as exceptions and singled out for special citation (see Holberton, 1977; Jeffcoate, 1977; Richmond, 1978) or referred to in more or less anecdotal evidence. One study, Bagley *et al.* (1978) does, however, embark on a categorization of potentially distinctive features associated with pupils of West Indian origin who are high achievers for their group. The researchers in this study found that relatively high performance on a reading test correlated with such factors as pupils with a favourable attitude to school as a medium of achievement, a positive ethnic self-image and having parents who are highly critical of English culture and the English educational system. These children tended to come from homes where parents were bilingual (in Creole and Standard English) where the parents were well educated, and where the family lived in adequate material circumstances. Those children who performed relatively badly on the reading test tended to have associations with the converse set of circumstances.

Though this taxonomy tends to focus on the home, it is interesting to note that Holberton (1977), on the basis of first-hand experience of school environments, has put forward a descriptive portrait of black West Indian achievers and under-achievers which correlates very highly with the evidence suggested by statistical analysis of research data. He suggests that the achiever

'finds home a place where he can follow interests and hobbies; has grown-ups who are prepared to spend time with him; wants to stay on at school to see how far he can go; prefers university or college to employment at school leaving; receives the support of his parents in these aspirations; has parents who do not mind an argument about some things; does not feel unfavourably compared with other children; and does not spend a great deal of time with his peers' (p.18).

In the same article Holberton suggests that there are some schools which appear to be better at promoting successful partnerships with pupils of West Indian origin and in achieving a balance between traditional subjects and culture-specific subjects, underpinned by respect arising from genuine cultural awareness. It is in this kind of school, it appears, that the conditions which are conducive to the successful achievement of pupils of West Indian origin are to be found, but, as yet, research has not been able to set forth an adequate description of the particular and special conditions which such a school exhibits. Instead the research evidence has focused on the conditions which surround those children who performed relatively poorly, not necessarily because of low potential, but more often because of lack of opportunity and propitious home and school environments. Though the evidence of low performance is indeed substantial, there are contra-indications in the literature and it may well now be high time to consider not only ways in which the performance of pupils of West Indian origin relative to that of their peers may be improved, but also to promote a more positive research approach by looking more closely into the reasons for the success of some West Indian pupils who perform well not only in relation to their own group but to their peers as a whole.

Though time constraints did not permit it to be a function of this research review to compare in detail the performance of pupils of West Indian origin with their peers from other ethnic minority groups, reference has from time to time been made to pupils of Asian origin who have been involved in the same research investigations under review. It is noticeable that although these Asian children have similarly experienced difficulties of immigration or being second-generation immigrants and have likewise had to contend with racial prejudice on account of colour, they have, nevertheless, in the majority of cases in those research investigations reviewed, been found to perform better than pupils of West Indian origin. (See for example, Little *et al.*, 1968; Mabey, 1980, 1981; and the parallel research involving Asian and Glaswegian children (Ashby *et al.*, 1970), using a more extensive range of measures of ability and attainment, which found that there was an improvement in performance of immigrants with length of stay and that long-stay Asian immigrants performed better on attainment tests than Scots, and Asian boys better than girls.) During recent years it has therefore come to be recognized that ethnic minority pupils cannot be considered as a composite group since each ethnic group has different needs and abilities. It has been postulated (Little, 1975) that the differences are determined by such factors as parents' reasons for coming to the UK, the viability and transferability of a culture which is independent of British culture, social background variables which include class and colour, and the nature and intensity of the cultural conflict between the 'majority' world of the school and the 'minority' world of the home. In a later deliberation the same author (Little, 1978) suggested that possible reasons for differences in educational performance between pupils of West Indian origin and pupils of Asian origin were both the extra effort which had been made to accommodate children of Asian origin in schools, particularly with respect to language teaching arrangements, and the differential effect of the two cultures on the two groups' attitudes. He and others have observed that Asian children tend to come from homes with their own distinctive language and culture which places a particular value on learning and encourages self-improvement. By comparison the West Indian culture is more a variant of the dominant British culture and yet often disparaged by that culture, a response which is in itself likely to have discouraging results.

In view of these considered observations it is not surprising when turning to compare the performance of pupils of West Indian origin with that of white pupils, even those of similar social class background living in the same neighbourhood and attending the same schools, to find that pupils of West Indian origin are still performing relatively badly, although their white peers are by no means achieving the same standard as a nationally representative group of white indigenous children (see, for example, Payne, 1974; Little, 1975; Phillips, 1979; Essen and Ghodsian, 1979; Mabey, 1981). Depressing though it is to relate, it appears inescapable that by any standard of comparison the pupil of West Indian origin is underachieving.

It will be recalled that one purpose in undertaking this review of research (p.7) was to examine the education of pupils of West Indian origin with respect to a number of variables, namely, sex, age, length of schooling, size of school, geographical distribution, and island of origin. Accordingly, the following summary will be presented of the trends indicated by research on these variables.

First, research evidence suggest that there is a fairly strong tendency for West Indian girls in general to perform better on all measures, but especially on reading, than West Indian boys (see e.g. Yule *et al.*, 1975; McEwen *et al.*, 1975). Some researchers have suggested that the tendency towards greater achievement of West Indian girls reflects the traditional roles assigned to them in West Indian community life; the usual self-reliance and independence associated with domestic responsibility characteristic of the role of the West Indian female as opposed to the male's concern with his reputation and social life. It is, however, fair to point out that the findings for West Indian pupils should be set in a more general context, since comparable research on indigenous white girls and boys consistently shows that girls, with their relatively earlier physiological maturity, out-perform boys on all verbal tests up to the age of 15, after which the roles are reversed. Nevertheless the serious under-achievement of many West Indian boys suggest that particular attention should be paid to devising educational strategies to help them, possibly, for example, by introducing role models as a means of increasing self-esteem.

The evidence relating to performance by age is not so clear-cut and tends to vary according to the subject area under consideration. However, an overall appraisal reveals that early pre-school involvement is crucial if a good foundation is to be laid for later schooling. Indeed, there are indications not only of an early decline in performance but also that it continues for longer when compared with the performance of the school population as a whole. For example, Pollak (1979) found that the same children investigated at the age of nine had not made up the gap in education in their pre-school years which was evident on their entry into school at five, during their first four years of schooling. Moreover, Mabey (1980, 1981) discovered that performance in the ILEA Literacy Survey was higher at the age of eight than at the age of 15. Whilst the label 'progressive deficit' should not be attached on the basis of the results of this one study, other findings do suggest that, although pupils of West Indian origin appear to make some progress during their schooling, and those who receive all their schooling in this country do so to a much greater extent than those who have only received partial schooling here, as a group they still do not in general attain the same levels of performance as their white indigenous peers (Yule *et al.*, 1975). Other, longitudinal, studies are required before a firm judgement can be made on this matter, but a few researches seem to suggest that in the case of language influences the age of seven to eight is crucial, although dialect influences may not become apparent, as far as comprehension difficulties are concerned, until the later age of 11 or 12 (see Edwards, 1976). However, the optimism expressed in a number of studies which were carried out in the 1960s, indicating that the achievement of pupils of West Indian origin would increase with length of schooling, does not appear to have been justified. Rather the evidence suggests that they start poorly and continue in the same way, if not actually deteriorating relatively in performance with increasing age.

Size of school was infrequently attended to as a variable in research design and no conclusions can be drawn as to its influence on performance. However, the number of ethnic minority pupils on school rolls has received rather more attention, though this has for the most part been incidental and not systematic. The consensus of research evidence suggests that the ethnic minority group concentration in a school does not appear to affect performance or attitudes, either of the ethnic minority group pupils or white pupils, except at the extremes of concentration, i.e. less than 10 per cent or more than 60 per cent. Although there appears to be no consistent association between the number of black children in a school and their educational performance (Little, 1975) other researches (e.g. Louden, 1978; Dawson, 1978; and Bagley *et al.*, 1979) have found a curvilinear or linear relationship with attitudes and increased self-esteem on the part of black children. Therefore for social reasons at least a reasonably balanced distribution of ethnic minority group pupils could be justified within a school.

It is not possible on the basis of research to date to ascertain variations in performance within this country by geographical location, nor according to island of origin of the West Indian pupil. When reports of researches have explicitly indicated the area in which they were undertaken this has been stated in the text of this research review. Not surprisingly in view of the concentration of pupils of West Indian origin in the metropolis, by far the greater number of research investigations have taken place in London. One study (Phillips, 1979), relating to performance in Birmingham 10 years ago, suggests that achievement levels were even lower in that area, yet by contrast smaller scale studies give an impression of slightly higher levels of performance in Manchester. However, these indications should all be regarded with the utmost caution as the populations sampled are not strictly comparable. Since much of the research has been undertaken in London it has therefore mostly been concerned with pupils of Jamaican origin, and there is a fairly consistent suggestion in the literature that, compared with children whose antecedents hail from other islands, Jamaican pupils perform less well (see Bagley *et al.*, 1978, for example). However, these implications are not based on systematic evidence, as reference to children with origins in other Caribbean islands, occasionally Barbados and Trinidad in particular, is only incidental. Whilst it is likely that it would be a complex operation to amass such information, it would be of possible educational interest to examine island of origin as a background variable in any research undertaken into pupils of West Indian origin and especially to look at the performance of those pupils of East Indian background, with its different traditions and social history.

At this juncture it may be useful to summarize in conclusion the evidence on attainment in subject areas, school placement, and school activities in relation to pupils of West Indian origin. The inappropriateness of IQ tests in the assessment of West Indian pupils has raised considerable controversy and the same considerations have been found to apply with respect to verbal and non-verbal tests. There is, perhaps, slight evidence that pupils of West Indian origin do better on drill, rote learning, concept learning and transfer tests, visual drawing, spelling, rote memory and listening abilities, but it is equally possible that these findings would be explained by the particular circumstances of researches. The controversy and confusion over the use of IQ tests to determine assessment for placement in schools for the educationally subnormal (see, e.g. Tomlinson, 1978) has served to highlight the inherent cultural biases resulting in what appears to be generally agreed to be a disproportionate number of West Indian pupils being placed in ESN schools.

Whilst tests of reading may in general be subject to similar testing biases in connection with the context of test administration, evidence from these sources is probably more reliable, although such tests naturally concentrate on use of language and associated linguistic abilities. Nevertheless, performance on reading tests for pupils of West Indian origin as a whole has been shown to be uniformly lower than that for their peers of similar age. It seems that there are serious and complex difficulties in the area of language associated with historical and contemporary social conditions which have not yet been sufficiently understood or even fully recognized. In the area of mathematics, too, the evidence of achievement is similarly low, though there are indications of comparatively better performance, especially by boys. It is notable that there appears to be very little evidence on the performance of pupils of West Indian origin in even mathematics or English from the age of 11-plus transfer to public assessment in CSE or GCE, let alone information on performance in other subject areas.

It is interesting and encouraging to note, however, that although pupils of West Indian origin appear to be generally placed in the lower streams of schools, this does not seem to prejudice their holding posts of responsibility and authority as prefects and librarians. Moreover, they have notable achievements in sport, music, domestic science, craftwork etc. Admiring reference is frequently made to such skills and accomplishments, but whilst these are not to be underestimated, as achievements in themselves and as foundations upon which to build both in terms of educational achievement and self-image and esteem, such aptitudes are not necessarily adequate compensation for poor academic performance.

How then can this achievement or, rather lack of it, be explained? At the outset it seems quite obvious that there is no simple aetiology of under-achievement for pupils of West Indian origin. Rather, the problem is multidimensional. Over a number of years the following factors, at least, have all been proposed as possible explanations: length of stay, length of education in this country, degree of identification with host community, island of origin, social background, one-parent families, emigration patterns, adjustment to educational practices, differences between home and school especially of discipline, inappropriate tests, the colour of tester, teachers' attitudes, teachers' expectations and language difficulties. Some of these have already been discussed, but it is not clear whether they have an additive or interactive effect. As Verma and Bagley put it in the Preface to their first collection *Race and Education Across Cultures* (1975), 'one of the factors hampering our understanding of inter-group relations is that we look for answers in terms of a unitary phenomenon. But the relations to be explained are manifested in such diverse ways, and are so complicated and subtle that we do not yet know all the factors involved' (p.vii). This caution still appears true, but it has not prevented a number of different emphases being placed on interpretations of research evidence, so that at different times over the last decade or so, and depending on the reason for examining the sample under study, a whole range of explanations have been advanced for the under-achievement of children of West Indian origin. Thus, their focus has progressively shifted from the child, who, it was speculated, would improve his performance with length of schooling in this country, (Little *et al*., 1968; Schools Council, 1970), but who was then found to suffer severe social disadvantages which were thought to explain his lack of improvement (Little, 1975, for example), to the school and particularly the supposed low expectations of teachers (e.g. Coard, 1971; Giles, 1977), and later (BPPA, 1978) the impoverished self-esteem which it was claimed children experienced as a result of prejudice in the school, and finally over the last few years a gradual awareness that language difficulties might have been seriously underestimated (highlighted by Edwards, e.g. 1976, 1979). Some consideration will now be given to assessing these various attempts at explanation.

The first point which should be made is that over the years, as is evidenced by the research reviewed in this book, some key factors in the education of pupils of West Indian origin have changed considerably. It should be recalled that the pupils themselves change, not just in their development through the course of schooling–a factor which tends to be minimized by longitudinal study–but also during the span of even a relatively small-scale research, for a child has to be seen not just as a passive respondent but as an agent in the dynamic process of his own learning. Moreover, there are constantly evolving sub-cultures among all communities changing both as a result of their interaction with each other and within each community itself. And the West Indian community, fragmented as it has often been shown to be, is no exception. These factors taken concomitantly, and the nature of research itself mean that investigations can only delve into what has obtained and cannot predict any future pattern of events. To this extent the hypotheses that performance would increase with length of stay or schooling, advanced on the strength of finding slight differences in performance between children who had been born in this country and those who had newly arrived from the West Indies, seem to have sprung rather more from common-sense rationalizations than a sound basis of research experience. Thus the claims of some early studies which suggested that the pupil in the West Indies would have been doing better than his age peer who had emigrated to this country gave rise to a number of arguments variously described as 'adjustment', 'transitional' and 'transplantation', which proposed that the process of migration itself and the upheaval which this involved, especially for those children joining families whom they scarcely knew, must account for their relatively low performance. It was therefore hoped that they would acquire the linguistic skills of a more Standard English and assimilate with as little fuss as possible into the British school system. Such an explanation was not merely confined to pupils of West Indian origin but adduced for all immigrant children, irrespective of what have later come to be seen as their special and differential needs. Yet, as Kirp (1977), for example, has pointed out, the concentration on such factors as newness, acquiring facility in language, social norms etc. in an attempt to account for initial schooling difficulties to which adjustment had to be made, was to omit any consideration of the fact of race, and in particular colour. Ironically, also, whereas many early reports concentrated on behaviour, mentioning the dull, quiet nature of many West Indian pupils–behaviour which was often to contribute to them being assessed as ESN–more recent reports point to markedly contrasting boisterous and ebullient behaviour. However, there is a sense in which, although these arguments which attempted to account for initial adjustment needs are no longer strictly appropriate insofar as an increasingly high proportion of West Indian pupils, even those passing through secondary schools, have had no direct experience of life in the Caribbean, the degree to which their achievement in school compares with that of their age peers can be seen from a sociological viewpoint as a reflection of the extent to which they have taken over British social norms or have continued to re-establish themselves by means of social practices which are modified versions of social patterns of life in the Caribbean. The extent to which such changes take place will of course be influenced greatly by the climate of race relations in this country and this is, in the writer's view, probably the single most important factor to influence not only the general social adjustment of West Indian people but also the educational opportunities of their children. No doubt there have been gradual advances in increased racial tolerance, but daily events and the discrimination still evident in housing and unemployment for example, show that much remains to be accomplished in the promotion of more healthy racial attitudes. Regrettably there is little direct evidence to demonstrate the significance of the climate of race relations as an influence on educational performance from research studies (but see D' Souza, 1978 and Davey and Norburn, 1980b). Such a factor does not appear to have been considered a sufficiently relevant variable to be assessed in past educational research, either perhaps because it has not been seen as specifically *educational* or because of difficulties in actually assessing it and its influence—which would indicate lack of interdisciplinary permeation, especially by sociological research.

Although length of schooling has been found to have a marginal effect on the performance of pupils of West Indian origin (see, for example, Mabey, 1980, 1981) social background factors which were a common major explanation for low performance in the early 1970s have been found to correlate to a larger extent with underachievement. Nevertheless, correlation, it must be remembered, is not causality. For although such factors as a historical background which includes the crippling conditions of slavery, traditionally poor levels of education, and currently low parental literacy, low economic status, high unemployment, overcrowding in housing, a higher proportion of one-parent and large families, and child minding, can explain some of the differences between pupils of West Indian origin and their national peers in terms of school achievement, they do not explain all of the difference. Comparisons with socially disadvantaged white children in EPAs have shown that pupils of West Indian origin are still performing at lower levels. Although some research (see, e.g. Vernon, 1965 a and b; Bagley *et al.*, 1978) has tentatively indicated that there appears to be an association between the child's performance and the cultural stimulus provided by his home, it is not quite clear whether this can be closely linked with social class, and whether the *same* relationship applies between ethnic minority groups and social and family indices with respect to educational attainment as it appears to with the white British working class population. Moreover, some of the questions raised in relation to the influence of social background factors on educational performance have yet to be satisfactorily answered in connection with the child from white working class origins. Thus, although more sensitive measures of social disadvantage might be able to 'explain' differences in educational achievement, a more positive educational approach would be to concentrate on the ways in which the school adds to or reinforces the problems associated with a deprived background.

The extent to which language differences and difficulties may impair educational achievement is an issue of complexity and sensitivity and an area in which comparatively little research has been undertaken. Although it is possible that pupils of West Indian origin suffer linguistic impairment from an early age because of lack of stimulation from toys and play and conversation and interaction with their parents at home, the way in which this may affect later development and school attainment is relatively unassessed. The main concentration of recent research on language has been on dialect interference with reading performance and comprehension. This research (Trudgill, 1975; Edwards, 1976, 1979) has confirmed the view of those linguistic anthropologists who have maintained that Creole is either a different language or at least a dialect form of Standard English with a radically different structure. The influence of Creole dialect tends to be felt even when pupils of West Indian origin are born in this country (Schools Council, 1970; Edwards, 1976). Moreover, with its origins as a language of resistance and social cohesion, it has central links with identity and status and hence self-esteem. This is what makes any attempt to introduce language programmes such a sensitive and controversial issue. Not only do pupils appear to take attempts by teachers to correct their speech as personal affronts to their self-esteem, it seems that many West Indian parents have the belief that they have already learnt Standard English, which has indeed been a major feature of their striving to attain their aspirations and ambitions in coming to this country, and hence do not see the need for special language teaching for their children. However, there is a sense in which not only other minority groups with different languages, such as Italians or Poles, have to acquire a facility in English in order to benefit from education in British schools, but so do children with other English dialects, albeit less extreme forms, who are expected to converse and communicate within a school environment in relatively standard, middle-class BBC English. Thus, whilst the cultural and historical associations with language and identity should not be depreciated, either in general or in the particular instance of a child's speech in school, there is an argument for not allowing the important issues of identity and self-esteem, linked as they are with questions of colour and race, to deflect from the main issue in educational terms, namely, that success within the British school system, and indeed to some extent within British society, requires a certain fluency and familiarity with Standard English. Rosen and Burgess (1980b, pp.131–2) sensitively discuss this issue but state that 'in many respects the school's response should be no different from its response to all vernacular speech' and as a result of their survey of languages used in London schools they advocate in-service training to assist teachers confronted by linguistic diversity. To this end also it would seem appropriate, as has been recognized and advocated by Government reports for many years, to institute supplementary language teaching in cases where individual pupils would benefit.

As has been mentioned, closely linked with the extent to which language difficulties can be used in explanation of under-achievement is the explanation which centres on self-image, self-esteem or identity. This explanation has been favoured by, for example, the local Redbridge study (BPPA, 1978) and the argument on which it is based runs something like the following: children of West Indian origin grow up in a hostile society which portrays black people in a negative fashion, the child then internal-izes these attitudes, develops a poor identity which can lead to a lack of confidence and reduction in motivation and hence poor perfor-mance. Though this is an attractive explanation for the black community, the research evidence is far from conclusive. As this review has indicated, such an argument is mainly based on one moderate-scale investigation in this country (Milner, 1975) and other smaller scale studies (see for example, Bagley and Coard, 1975). But Davey and Mullin's (1980) more recent research would indicate that whilst it may well be the case that, as these studies suggest, black children would prefer to have white skins and some rate white people more highly – which might well be a realistic appraisal in the context of a colour-conscious society – it does not necessarily follow that such consciousness generates low self-esteem nor, that this in turn will produce low achievement. Indeed, the view that black children do in fact have low self-esteem has recently been challenged by a significant piece of research by Louden (1978) and by Bagley and Young (1979), and in addition it should be remembered that several studies (e.g. Jelinek, 1977; Dawson, 1978) have demonstrated the favourable attitudes to school which West Indian pupils hold. Having said this, there does appear to be evidence to indicate that steps can be taken to facilitate the acquisition of a positive self-image by pupils of West Indian origin, mainly by instituting a multicultural curriculum which makes a feature of black history and important black people who can be seen as models for the promotion of black consciousness and cultural identity. What, however, is not yet clear is whether it is the content of such a curriculum which appears to increase self-esteem, whether it is the way in which such teaching is conducted, or even the very fact that increased interest is being shown in black pupils by their teachers. In this way education has a vital part to play for the pupil of West Indian origin. It must enable him to adjust to a new culture whilst respecting the valuable elements of the old, to find his position within his adopted society and to participate in it, thereby enriching it and establishing himself as a person in his own right with his own identity and purpose.

Both of the preceding explanations of under-achievement in terms of language and self-esteem have hinted at the factors of teachers' attitudes and expectations which are increasingly being postulated as important if not crucial influences on West Indian achievement. Coard (1971) and Giles (1977) are two West Indian writers who have advanced low teacher expectation and unfavourable teacher attitudes as an explanation of low achievement by West Indian pupils, but they have adduced little by way of empirical evidence above the level of anecdote. However, one small-scale study by Edwards (1978) does suggest that student teachers may have negative and lower expectations for black pupils, and a national survey of teachers' attitudes (Brittan, 1976b) indicates that teachers may well have negative attitudes towards ethnic minority pupils. Whether this is really the case on a large scale and to what extent it influences day-to-day contact and perpetuates the cycle of under-achievement by negative labelling and low expectation it is difficult to estimate. Yet it seems clear that both black parents and black children believe this to be the case. And such beliefs are crucial. No doubt teachers as a cross-section of society will to some extent reflect the attitudes prevalent in that society, but it is difficult to estimate whether such negative attitudes as they may have are more influential on children's performance in school than their parents' beliefs and expectations which are more consistently transmitted and from an earlier age.

Contrary to the opinions of many teachers (see for example Townsend and Brittan, 1972; Brittan, 1976b) West Indian parents do appear to be very concerned about the education of their children (Davey and Norburn, 1980b). Indeed, as an earlier section (p.142ff) attempted to show, their social and economic aspirations may be considerable and great emphasis is placed on education as a means of achieving them. To the extent that this occurs within a family the child of West Indian origin may well be put in a position of extreme tension between what must often be the conflicting expectations and demands of his home and school. It would not seem unreasonable to suggest that the reported expectations of West Indian parents have been unrealistic and that, bearing in mind the considerable disadvantages which many pupils of West Indian origin suffer, it would have been surprising if such achievements could have been attained within such a society in so short a space of time. Yet persistence and perseverence must be the watchwords for all involved in the education of pupils of West Indian origin. Heller (1969) has observed that all first-generation immigrants tend to be perceived by the host society as belonging to the bottom of the socio-economic scale regardless of status in their country of origin. Social mobility, it appears, depends on the value placed on education by the minority groups themselves and evidence from America suggests that greater achievement and success in education and hence social mobility is usually attained by the second- or third-generation immigrant.

Much has yet to be done to promote these ends. In the meantime how is it possible to view the largely second-generation of West Indian immigrants at present undergoing schooling in Britain? These children are the first generation of a new experience – of complete schooling in the UK. Yet many of them are an in-between generation, semi-lingual in Standard English, and caught between the differential aspirations of their parents and the expectations of their teachers in the diverse worlds of home and school. Pryce (1979) a West Indian who gives a somewhat existential account of racial alienation and the problem of identity perceives it thus:

'the school anglicizes him, installing in his psyche a preference for all the "white" values of the dominant society, yet that society continually defines him as inferior, and he can never seem to measure up to it. He seems destined to remain an outsider by the very same values that he has been taught to revere' (p.137).

Less dramatically, it seems fair to say that even many West Indian pupils who are adjusted are not yet belonging – they are caught between the home and the school. It is part of the school's function to assist in the process of coming to belong and to convert some of the problems and difficulties into pluses. The following section on educational strategies examines some ways in which this may perhaps be accomplished.

Section 17: Educational Strategies

Although in the writer's view it is obvious that only major changes in social conditions and the climate of race relations will eventually break the cycle of disadvantage experienced by under-achieving West Indian pupils, what specifically educational measures can be adopted to promote their increased performance? Since this review of research has intentionally and by definition played down curricular aspects of education it is perhaps at this point appropriate to consider in outline a number of educational strategies which have either been proposed from time to time or are already in practice.

Let it not be doubted that during recent years increased awareness amongst teachers and educators of the position of ethnic minority group children has brought about considerable curricular changes and radical alterations in the environments of many schools. Yet these changes have often come about as the result of piecemeal policies related to *ad hoc* situations. This is almost certainly due to the lack of direction which research has failed to give – with the notable exception of the early recommendation of special language teaching facilities – and, as a result, the lack of central policy initiatives. Although it is to be noted that Paragraph 25 of the DES Minutes of Evidence on Racial Disadvantage to the Race Relations and Immigration Sub-Committee (Great Britain, Parliament, House of Commons, Home Affairs Committee, 1980) states: 'For the curriculum to have meaning and relevance for all pupils its content and values must respect the cultural identity of each pupil and reflect the cultural mix of society as a whole', it is true to say, however, that there would be difficulties of implementation of any overall policy largely because of the autonomy of different sections of the education system – local education authorities, heads in their schools and teachers in their classrooms – combined with differences of perceptions and perspectives in relation to differential needs of children. Yet it can be argued that there is a case for a consistent policy which could be given time to be implemented, to take effect and to be thoroughly evaluated. There is, for example, much confused argument in the literature both about equality of treatment for black children and positive intervention programmes. If it is accepted that children's needs differ, it should follow that they should be treated in different ways, but the justification for such differential treatment, especially with respect to members of minority ethnic groups is not always clear. As Hegarty has pointed out 'it is important to distinguish however between differential provision which is judged necessary because of the occurrence of factors which happen to be associated with membership of a particular ethnic group and differential provision which derives from ethnic group membership *per se*' (Hegarty and Lucas, 1978, p.19). He argues that the differences must reside in individual children and not in their ethnic grouping and that these must be related to relatively fundamental educational goals which are, in turn, determined by aims of education. Such aims may be both context- and time-dependent, so that, although the case of positive discrimination could be seen as simply meeting the needs of individual children, this could also be a means of redressing social ills and compensating for the socio-cultural disadvantages of certain groups. Although it might be unwise to establish positive intervention as a permanent feature of the educational system, a case might well be made for temporary involvement on this basis. For example, this might be seen in the light of the immediate day-to-day circumstances of many teachers who appear to require guidance on the extent to which Creole dialects may be permitted in school and whether individual children need special language help. In this respect the research evidence seems to have been quite clear cut: that there is a real case for special language teaching for many pupils of West Indian origin, and it has been suggested that at the extremes of under-achievement formal methods may well be most appropriate. Indeed a black researcher (Stone, 1981) has recently proposed that schools should concentrate on the formal teaching of basic skills and knowledge in connection with black pupils as the way to increase their achievement.

Positive intervention in the case of establishing a multicultural curriculum has not gone unchallenged with respect to its implementation in schools with a predominantly white population. Teachers in such schools have often been reluctant (Brittan, 1976a) to consider changes in curricular structure as they have seen programmes which increased racial awareness as irrelevant, but neither have teachers in schools with a high percentage of ethnic minority pupils been more ready to change (Giles, 1977; Widlake and Bloom, 1979). Schools of this kind and also those in which considerable attempts were being made to introduce multicultural curricula were encountered by the Schools Council/NFER Education for a Multiracial Society Project, 1973–6. However, a CRC investigation (1977) discovered that black studies were in general little taught and more recently Nandy (1981) has reported that, contrary to popular belief, in 1975 black studies remained an aspiration rather than a practice as the number of schools in the ILEA which had introduced black studies in the early 70s was very small and the courses were 'fragmentary in character and hastily improvised in their implementation'. At about the same time Bagley and Coard (1975) found that, even where attempts had been made in junior schools, cross-cultural knowledge had increased on the part of black pupils but was still low. Despite this the most appropriate time for such teaching is perhaps in the primary school. There is, moreover, conflicting evidence both on the viability and on the effects of direct teaching of race relations (Miller, 1969; Bagley and Coard, 1975; and Bagley and Verma, 1975).

Although there does appear to be slight evidence of an overt improvement, it is not clear whether this is a lasting phenomenon. Ideally, of course, schools with mixed ethnic minority group and main group populations, at least, will attempt to give proportional and balanced attention to the needs of all groups and to make efforts to increase pupils' self-esteem through awareness of each other's culture. However, the initial findings of a recent survey set up by the Schools Council in 1978 to determine the extent to which leas and secondary schools had instituted multicultural education (Little and Willey, 1981) indicates that this is still largely an ideal. The summary and conclusions of the main findings from 525 secondary schools, 70 leas and 22 examining boards reveal a lack of implementation of previous policy statements and a need for clear guidance on objectives for multi-ethnic education from DES and leas at a local level. At present the researchers found a diversity of local initiatives corresponding to widely differing local situations. Although there was evidence that many efforts had often been made to permeate the curriculum with a multicultural element in schools with high or medium concentrations of ethnic minority pupils, current work required further support by leas. Heads reported contraints of time and resources so that the low priority given to such development meant that little activity to promote a multi-ethnic curriculum was taking place in schools with few ethnic minority pupils. In fact only 25 per cent of schools with fewer than two and a half per cent ethnic minority pupils claimed that their teaching reflected a multiracial society, and this was often not systematic in its approach.

Besides overt curricular intervention there are the less tangible but possibly longer lasting effects of the hidden curriculum to consider as well as the physical appearance of the school and its ethos. In this respect many insights from the field of moral education could profitably be brought to bear on multiracial school communities so that these may become more moral environments where there is both sensitive awareness to the diverse needs of other ethnic groups and also an emphasis on self-discipline and social confidence which in turn may well also lead to increased self-esteem. In addition it should be possible for teachers to devise more educational contexts in which pupils from ethnic minority groups can work closely together in a way in which pupils can take account of other characteristics of their peers and hence transcend ethnicity.

More recently, too, some (see for example, Rosen and Burgess, 1980a and b) have argued for a review of examination syllabuses and an increase in their flexibility for assessing a wider range of skills and knowledge, which may be particularly applicable in the case of pupils of ethnic minorities. Some teachers have made initiatives to introduce CSE Mode 3 syllabuses in, for example, Caribbean studies, and Rosen and Burgess have argued that it is possible to imagine a syllabus, for example in geography, which would include a fairly sizeable option on the Caribbean. Such syllabuses, they argue, 'would build concretely on the diverse experiences which our pupils bring to their schooling, they would enrich the curriculum for all children and they would provide a more realistic preparation for living and working in a multi-cultural Britain' (p.154). But as Thomas-Hope (1981) has pointed out, it is most important that Caribbean studies should be introduced systematically into British education if they are to be an effective part of the syllabus. More generally, the 22 examining boards, responding to a questionnaire from the Schools Council project Studies in the Multi-ethnic Curriculum, appeared to see no need to systematically review syllabuses to consider their relevance to a multi-ethnic society. In fact only one of the eight GCE boards and 14 CSE boards had done so, partly it seems since they had received few suggestions from teachers. Yet 40 per cent of the heads, half in schools with high concentrations of ethnic minority pupils, saw public examination requirements as a major constraint on the development of a multicultural curriculum. In passing, it is curious to note that research has not yet explicitly evaluated the effect of a multicultural curriculum on school achievement though there have been interpretations that its effect has been favourable (Driver, 1980a; Dawson, 1978).

Many different researches have recommended the setting up of various projects involved with the promotion of multicultural education. At present there is much evidence that many attempts at curriculum development work are being undertaken, but these efforts are often isolated and lacking a general rationale so that there are still many classroom teachers who remain baffled in their day-to-day work. Since it has not been the purpose of this review to make an explicit or comprehensive attempt to investigate lea provision it would probably be invidious to mention specific authorities, but Williams (1978) details some advances which have been made. Proposals have suggested the general establishment of multicultural teachers' centres, some of which already exist to provide teachers with resources and to assist them in developing materials which can be used in schools. In-service training, especially for curriculum development and language specialists, has been the practice for some time. Such specialists might be particularly concerned to develop skills to help second-stage language learners – as many West Indian children in fact are – with the language of specialized subjects, or at a later stage, to relate this to vocational training, as well as assisting those who need a more basic understanding of Standard English. Some boroughs, as in the case of Waltham Forest, (Johnston, 1978) have instituted supplementary services with explicit aims of language tuition and reinforcement of self-esteem. Other authorities have appointed inspectors and advisers for multicultural education, made particular efforts to recruit black teachers and are involved with teacher exchange schemes to the Caribbean through the offices of the League for the Exchange of Commonwealth Teachers (Mundy, 1973), and indeed exchange schemes involving pupils of West Indian origin in British schools who are enabled to visit the West Indies for the first time (see Spencer and Kellas, 1980). Further details about current provision are available from the 1980 DES Minutes of Evidence on Racial Disadvantage to the Race Relations and Immigration Sub-Committee (Great Britain, Parliament, House of Commons, Home Affairs Committee, 1980).

Thus, while it can be shown that in many schools and in many leas considerable attempts have been made to assist ethnic minority pupils, it might be argued that one aspect, namely home–school liaison, has been somewhat neglected. For instance, Little and Willey (1981) report that although the 525 secondary schools in their survey on the multi-ethnic curriculum stressed the need for better links with parents, only 11 per cent of the schools reported that they had home–school liaison teachers working with ethnic minority groups. This is perhaps disappointing since home–school relations have long since been recognized as crucial (see for example, Evans and Le Page, 1967) though the area is perhaps fraught with more than usual difficulties. Nevertheless, it is suggested that this is where the most important future work needs to be undertaken. In general heads have a particular role to play in disseminating information about their school, its aims, organization and teaching methods and perhaps particularly study skills, so that West Indian parents can come to have a better knowledge and appreciation of the attempts which the school is making in their child's education. Moreover, a much greater involvement of black parents and their resources in the life of the school should be encouraged, particularly their participation in school trips and journeys (see Pollak, 1979) and the recruitment of black parents as school governors. Indeed, a recently reported study by Davey and Norburn (1980b) indicated a mandate for multicultural education by parents with the implication that schools should take the initiative in getting parents to assist in establishing a realistic multicultural curriculum. It is also reasonable to suppose that this could be assisted generally by facilitating contacts between local West Indian communities and schools.

Three specific projects which aim to involve parents directly are worth noting here. The first (Cherrington, 1979) is as yet a proposal to establish a pre-school childhood centre in Rugby which would aim to involve closer integration of all educational services for pre-school children and their families. It is intended to develop the more usual type of playgroup or nursery school provision to stress individualized learning programmes which involve parents at every stage and which will be closely monitored and evaluated over a period of a year to assess both increased parenting skills and child development on the basis of an involvement of five mornings each week. This intensive approach would seem to enhance the role of the parent as the principal influence on the child's early education and development, and to assist in the parent's understanding and knowledge of the growth of the child so that she may identify and reinforce naturally occurring learning experiences in the home. Several writers (Pollak, 1979; Bushell, 1973; Kitzinger, 1978) have endorsed the necessity to approach the education of children of West Indian origin at a very early age, and research (Little, 1975) has indicated that this may be particularly important for the acquisition of vocabulary and other linguistic skills which may be a prerequisite for later educational achievement.

Secondly, a project which has already been undertaken has shown how parental involvement can markedly increase reading skills. The Haringey Reading Project 1976–9 (Tizard *et al.*, 1980) fostered collaboration between teachers and parents in assisting children's reading in two infant and junior schools. A total of 1,867 children in six multiracial schools serving a manual working class area were involved. West Indians formed one of the main ethnic groups and were well established in the area. Many of the parents who participated were non-literate or English speaking. There was a complex research design to cover the four years of the intervention although unfortunately results are not given separately by ethnic group. Every child in two randomly chosen top infant classes at two of the six schools, used to provide a baseline measure, was heard to read at home from books sent by the class teacher. Their performance was compared with a parallel group taught as usual at school, another group which received extra tuition and parallel control classes. A high level of collaboration between parents and teachers was achieved and established directly by the class teacher on an individual basis. It was conclusively shown as a result of many detailed assessment procedures that extra reading practice at home led to highly significant improvement in reading attainment, whereas extra teaching at school resulted in no significant improvement. Parents were particularly effective with those who at the outset of the intervention were failing to read. A variety of noticeable improvements in adaptation to school especially in terms of behaviour were also observed. Parents expressed satisfaction at the involvement and teachers continued to ensure the involvement of parents in other features of school life after the end of the experiment.

At a wider level the school can also be influential in community activities (see, for examples Smith, 1973; Housden, 1980, and a recent report (*The Times*, 11.9.80) of police officers taking part in a fourth-year curriculum exercise in a Birmingham school with the aim of establishing greater mutual understanding) though it is important that such projects should go hand in hand with more fundamental changes. One project is worth particular mention in this context. The Govan Project in Strathclyde, though not undertaken in connection with pupils of West Indian origin, has employed strategies which might well prove to be useful in liaising between schools and West Indian parents (Low, 1978). This project, which was concerned with disadvantaged children, attempted to ameliorate language difficulties by a greater involvement with their homes as well as encouraging community pre-school provision. Secondary school pupils who had recently left school, but who were not in higher education or employment, acted as assistant home–school visitors by relaying information and ideas from the central community project organization. It was found that they were sometimes in a better position socially to relate to the parents of the children still in the school and to increase direct co-operation. This and other undertakings which have all been tried in connection with Community Service Volunteers could all be considered as possible ways of increasing home–school liaison with West Indian parents, thus possibly obviating the need which currently seems to be felt by many West Indian communities to initiate their own supplementary schools, either for the provision of black studies or even basic schooling (though it is interesting to note that these do not appear to be supported by help from West Indian teachers (Gibbes, 1980) and, indeed have been inveighed against by a black researcher (Stone, 1981)).

Surely, the formal education system has a particular part to play in promoting racial harmony, integration and advance. Engaged as it is in the business of encouraging critical thinking and greater understanding, its members, teachers and pupils alike, should be sharing in the discovery of new knowledge and thereby growing together in mutual awareness, tolerance and respect. For if the school situation in which the black pupil learns is torn by discord and blighted by open prejudice how can he expect or hope for just deserts in society at large? Small wonder, then, that at risk as he may well be on all sides, with socially disadvantaged circumstances, cultural confusion, diminished job prospects and striving to find his own identity, he sees himself failed and shunned by the school too, and rebels to emphasize the only certainty left to him – his blackness. Yet this experience can be so different. If the school can rebuild the trust and confidence he needs, both by the example of its caring relationships and pattern of behaviour which it establishes through all aspects of the school's organization, such a pupil may become both self-confident and disciplined and have an accurate self-image, so that he may come to achieve, not only for himself, but thereby to enrich the life of the school with his breadth of cultural experience. In so doing the school will also have rediscovered its own particular educational viability so that it may at last be possible for the high hopes which many West Indian parents have for their children to be fulfilled.

Section 18: Further Research

Section 15 suggested several methodological improvements which could be made in further research undertakings and it is the function of this Section to make a number of specific recommendations for further research which would seem to be indicated from the author's appraisal of the research literature.

1. It may well now be opportune to institute a national monitoring exercise within the ambit of the Assessment of Performance Unit which would complement the Schools Council investigation, Studies in the Multi-ethnic Curriculum. Much of the research reviewed indicates that many leas and schools may not have accurate quantitative data on pupils of West Indian origin in their areas, yet it can be argued that any major future research into the performance and attainment of pupils of West Indian origin would need to be able to draw on a pool of such records. Moreover, any national monitoring exercise should ideally, as Bagley (1980) suggests, monitor pupil performance in relation to school ethos, socio-economic background, and ethnicity in each borough. The caveats expressed on p.12 should also apply.

2. A major in-depth investigation should be mounted to study and compare the relation between the performance of West Indian pupils, their family background and factors internal to schools. The emphasis in such a study would be on home-school interaction and type, size and atmosphere of school, necessitating carefully matched samples for detailed study,

focusing particularly on those children who were comparatively high achievers. In this way it might be possible to investigate further the kind of differentiating features pointed to by Bagley *et al.* (1978) with respect to the effect of family variables on differential performance and to divergent performance by boys and girls. The kind of research exemplified by Rutter *et al.* (1979) and also the ethnomethodological approach of Marjoribanks (1979, 1980) with respect to ethnic minority groups in other countries, might well be used as starting points. It would also be particularly appropriate to base these studies in towns in the Midlands and the North or to be able to compare results with a London sample. (Since this review was undertaken a project on factors associated with success in multi-ethnic secondary schools led by D. J. Smith started in autumn 1980 at the Policy Studies Institute. The research appears to be intending to embody these suggestions, but aims to concentrate more on school characteristics than home/school interaction.)

3. There is also a case for mounting an attitudinal study to try and ascertain in what ways colour and ethnicity affect the attitudes of teachers and conversely to look at the attitudes of pupils to teachers, and their perceptions of home and school differences, especially on the issue of differential expectation and aspiration which has been postulated. It is recognized, however, that this would be an extremely controversial and hazardous undertaking, and might be more appropriately carried out on a smaller scale perhaps as follow-up work to such studies as those by Thomas (1978) and Dawson (1978).

4. Mention has already been made under the heading of educational strategies (pp.237–40) of the need to pay greater attention to pre-school education for children of West Indian origin, and although there is a certain amount of research and development work currently in progress (e.g. Cherrington, 1979) a case might be made to undertake further research in connection with children of West Indian origin at this age.

5. In view of the dated nature of most previous research in this area, with the notable exception of that by Rex and Tomlinson (1979), there would also seem to be a case for further studies, though not of a specifically educational kind, which would examine the patterns of family life of West Indians in this

country, paying particular attention to medical, and social, i.e. housing and employment, aspects of living and differences between first-, second- and third-generation immigrants. A more systematic and longitudinal investigation would be especially useful as an indication of long-term trends of adaptation. Findings could profitably be related to research on aspects of educational performance.

Many and varied are the statements and claims made about the education of pupils of West Indian origin and it is often difficult to discriminate between expressions of opinion and statements of fact. It is hoped that this review of research inasmuch as it relates to the preceding 15-year period, a time of considerable though gradual change, has helped, even within the limitations of its purview, to elucidate some of the issues, empirical evidence and proposed explanations. Certainly a number of inconsistencies and ambiguities have been revealed, and, in addition, evidence has often been found to be inconclusive. When these factors are seen in combination with continual changes in the education system, the climate of race relations in society as a whole and patterns of development of the West Indian communities, the purpose of future research to delimit and define the positive conditions of home and school life which promote achievement of West Indian children must be acknowledged.

References

Citations marked* are particularly relevant and useful.

AISTHORPE, L. A. (1976). The black child in the primary school: attitudes and performance. BEd thesis, Manchester College of Higher Education.

ALLEN, S. and SMITH, C. R. (1975). 'Minority group experience of the transition from education to work.' In: BRANNEN, P. (Ed) *Entering the World of Work: Some Sociological Perspectives.* London: HMSO.

ALLEYNE, H. M. McD. (1962). The effect of bilingualism on performance in certain intelligence and attainment tests. Unpublished MA thesis, University of London.

ANASTASI, A. (1968). *Psychological Testing.* (3rd edn) New York: Macmillan.

ANDERSON, E. and THOMAS, K. C. (1979). 'The effect of colour of tester on performance in a group reading test', *J. of Res. in Reading,* 2, 1, 44–52.

ASHBY, B., MORRISON, A. and BUTCHER, H. J. (1970). 'The abilities and attainments of immigrant children', *Res. in Educ.,* 4, 73–80.

ASSISTANT MASTERS AND MISTRESSES ASSOCIATION. (1981). *Education for a Multi-cultural Society.* A Submission to the Committee of Inquiry into Ethnic Minority Groups. London: AMMA. March.

BAGLEY, C. (1971). 'A comparative study of social environment and intelligence in West Indian and English children in London', *Social and Economic Studies,* 20, 420–30.

BAGLEY, C. (1972). 'Deviant behaviour in English and West Indian children', *Res. in Educ.,* 8, 47–55.

BAGLEY, C. (1973). 'The education of immigrant children: a review of policy and progress', *Journal of Social Policy,* 2, 303–15.

BAGLEY, C. (1975a). 'On the intellectual equality of races.' In: VERMA, G. K. and BAGLEY, C. (Eds) *Race and Education Across Cultures.* London: Heinemann.

BAGLEY, C. (1975b). 'The background of deviance in black children in London.' In: VERMA, G. K. and BAGLEY, C. (Eds) *Race and Education Across Cultures.* London: Heinemann.

*BAGLEY, C. (1977). A Comparative Perspective on the Education of

Black Children in Britain. Paper presented to a seminar at Centre for Information and Advice on Educational Disadvantage, Manchester. Also reprinted in *Comp. Ed.*, (1979), **15**, 63–81.

BAGLEY, C. (1979). 'Self-esteem as a pivotal concept in race and ethnic relations', *Research in Race and Ethnic Relations*, **1**, 127–67.

BAGLEY, C. (1980). Submission to the Rampton Committee of Inquiry into the Education of Children from Minority Groups.

BAGLEY, C. (1981). 'Behaviour and achievement in ethnic minority children in a national, longitudinal survey.' In: VERMA, G. K. and BAGLEY, C. (Eds) (1981). *Self-concept, Achievement and Multicultural Education.* London: Macmillan.

*BAGLEY, C., BART, M. and WONG, J. (1978). 'Cognition and scholastic success in West Indian 10-year-olds in London: a comparative study', *Educ. Studs.*, **4**, 1, 7–17. Similar to 'Antecedents of scholastic success in West Indian 10-year-olds in London' by the same authors, in VERMA, G. K. and BAGLEY, C. (Eds) (1979). *Race, Education and Identity.* London: Macmillan.

BAGLEY, C. AND COARD, B. (1975). 'Cultural knowledge and rejection of ethnic identity in West Indian children in London.' In: VERMA, G. K. and BAGLEY, C. (Eds) *Race and Education Across Cultures.* London: Heinemann.

BAGLEY, C., MALLICK, K. and VERMA, G. K. (1979). 'Pupil self-esteem: a study of black and white teenagers in British schools.' In: VERMA, G. K. and BAGLEY, C. (Eds) *Race, Education and Identity.* London: Macmillan.

BAGLEY, C. and VERMA, G. K. (1975). 'Inter-ethnic attitudes and behaviour in British multi-racial schools.' In: VERMA, G. K. and BAGLEY, C. (Eds) *Race and Education Across Cultures.* London: Heinemann.

BAGLEY, C. and VERMA, G. K. (1980). Brimer Wide Span Reading Scores in Pupils Aged 14–16 Years in 39 English Secondary Schools. Unpublished paper.

BAGLEY, C., WONG, J. and YOUNG, L. (n.d.). A Comparative Study of Cognitive Style in 10-year-olds in Contrasted Educational Settings in England and Jamaica. Department of Sociology, University of Surrey. Unpublished.

BAGLEY, C. and YOUNG, L. (1979). 'The identity, adjustment and achievement of transracially adopted children: a review and empirical report.' In: VERMA, G. K. and BAGLEY, C. (Eds) *Race, Education and Identity.* London: Macmillan.

BARNES, J. (Ed) (1975). *Educational Priority: Curriculum Innovation in EPAs. Vol. 3.* London: HMSO.

BEETHAM, D. (1967). *Immigrant School-leavers and the Youth Employment Service in Birmingham.* London: IRR.

BHATNAGAR, J. (1970). *Immigrants at School.* London: Cornmarket Press.

BLACK PEOPLES PROGRESSIVE ASSOCIATION AND REDBRIDGE COMMUNITY RELATIONS COUNCIL (1978). *Cause for Concern: West Indian Pupils in Redbridge.* Ilford: BPPA and RCRC.

BLAIR, C. (1969). Verbal and Non-verbal Testing of Immigrant Pupils in Primary Schools. Unpublished manuscript.

BLOOM, D. (1979). 'The case for patois in schools', *Learning*, Mar/April, 49–51.

BOLTON, F. and LAISHLEY, J. (1972). *Education for a Multi-Racial Britain*. Fabian Research Series, No. 303.

BOYKIN, W. A. (1977). 'On the role of context in the standardized test performance of minority group children', *Cornell Journal of Social Relations*, 12, 2, 109–24.

BRITTAN, E. (1973a). 'Organization in multiracial schools', *J. Appl. Educ. Studs.*, 2, 1, 27–30.

BRITTAN, E. (1973b). The opinions of teachers in multiracial schools on aspects of multiracial education. Unpublished MSc thesis, University of Surrey.

*BRITTAN, E. (1976a). 'Multiracial education 2. Teacher opinion on aspects of school life. Part one: changes in curriculum and school organization', *Educ. Res.*, 18, 2, 96–107.

*BRITTAN, E. (1976b). 'Multiracial education 2. Teacher opinion on aspects of school life. Part two: pupils and teachers', *Educ. Res.*, 18, 3, 182–92.

BROPHY, J. E. and GOOD, T. L. (1974). *Teacher-Student Relationships: Causes and Consequences*. New York: Holt, Rinehart and Winston.

BROWN, J. (1970). *The Unmelting Pot*. London: Macmillan.

BUSHELL, W. (1973). 'The immigrant (West Indian) child in school.' In: VARMA, V. P. (Ed) *Stresses in Children*. London: University of London Press.

CHERRINGTON, D. (1979). Rugby Early Childhood Centre: Summary of the Proposal for its Establishment. Centre for Advanced Studies in Education. City of Birmingham Polytechnic.

*CLARKE, E. (1957). *My Mother who Fathered Me*. London: G. Allen & Unwin.

COARD, B. (1971). *How the West Indian Child is Made Educationally Sub-normal In The British School System*. London: New Beacon Books Ltd. for Caribbean Education and Community Workers' Association.

COLLYMORE, Y. (1980). 'Achievement and underachievement: are West Indian girls top of the class?' *West Indian World*, 8.2.80.

COMMISSION FOR RACIAL EQUALITY (1978). *Ethnic Minorities in Britain*. Statistical Background. London: CRE.

COMMISSION FOR RACIAL EQUALITY (1980). *Race Relations in Britain. A Register of Current Research*. London: CRE.

COMMUNITY RELATIONS COMMISSION (1973). Multiple Deprivation and Minority Groups. CRC/73/113. Mimeograph.

COMMUNITY RELATIONS COMMISSION (1974). *Unemployment and Homelessness: A Report*. London: HMSO.

COMMUNITY RELATIONS COMMISSION (1975a). *Ethnic Minorities in Britain. Statistical Data*. (5th edn) London: CRC.

COMMUNITY RELATIONS COMMISSION (1975b). *Who Minds? A Study of Working Mothers and Childminding in Ethnic Minority Communities*. London: CRC.

COMMUNITY RELATIONS COMMISSION (1976). Evidence on Education to the Select Committee on Race Relations and Immigration Enquiry on the West Indian Community. London: CRC.

COMMUNITY RELATIONS COMMISSION (1977). *Education of Ethnic Minority Children. From the Perspectives of Parents, Teachers and Education Authorities.* London: CRC.

COOPERSMITH, S. (1975). 'Self-concept, race and education.' In: VERMA, G. K. and BAGLEY, C. (Eds) *Race and Education Across Cultures.* London: Heinemann.

COUNCIL ON INTERRACIAL BOOKS FOR CHILDREN (1975). *Racist and Sexist Images in Children's Books.* London: Writers and Readers Publishing Co-operative.

CRAFT, M. and CRAFT, A. Z. (1981). The Participation of Ethnic Minorities in Further and Higher Education, Summary and Conclusion of a Report. Nuffield Foundation Study.

CRAIG, D. R. (1971). The use of language by 7-year-old Jamaican children living in contrasting socio-economic environments. PhD thesis, University of London.

CROFTS, D. (1978). The importance of context in the classroom language of English and West Indian children. Unpublished MEd thesis, University of Manchester.

CROSS, M. (1973). 'Education and job opportunities.' In: MOSS, R. *The Stability of the Caribbean.* London: Institute for the Study of Conflict.

DANIEL, W. W. (1974). *A National Survey of the Unemployed.* London: PEP.

*DAVEY, A. G. and MULLIN, P. N. (1980). 'Ethnic identification and preference of British primary school children', *J. Child Psychol. Psychiat.*, **21**, 3, 241–51.

*DAVEY, A. G. and NORBURN, M. V. (1980a). 'Ethnic awareness and ethnic differentiation amongst primary school children', *New Community*, **VIII**, 1 and 2, 51–60, Spring-Summer.

*DAVEY, A. G. and NORBURN, M. V. (1980b). 'Parents, children and prejudice', *New Community*, **VIII**, 3, 206–12, Winter.

DAWSON, A. (1978). 'The attitudes of "black and white" adolescents in an urban area.' In: MURRAY, C. (Ed) *Youth in Contemporary Society.* Slough: NFER.

DOVE, L. (1974). 'Racial awareness among adolescents in London comprehensive schools', *New Community*, **III**, 255–61.

DRIVER, G. (1977). 'Cultural competence, social power and school achievement: West Indian secondary school pupils in the West Midlands', *New Community*, **V**, 4, 353–9.

DRIVER, G. (1980a). 'How West Indians do better at school (especially the girls)', *New Society*, 17th January, 111–14.

DRIVER, G. (1980b). *Beyond Underachievement: Case Studies of English, West Indian and Asian School-leavers at Sixteen Plus.* London: Commission for Racial Equality.

DRIVER, G. (1980c). 'Ethnic pecking order.' Letter to *TES. TES*, 3324, 22nd February, p.18.

D'SOUZA, M. B. (1978). 'Intergroup attitudes in multi-ethnic schools', *Oxford Review of Education*, 4, 2, 149–61.
DUMMETT, A. (1973). *A Portrait of English Racism*. Harmondsworth: Penguin.
DUROJAIYE, M. (1971). 'Social context of immigrant pupils learning English', *Educ. Res.* 13, 3, 179–84.
EARLS, F. and RICHMAN, N. (1980). 'Behaviour problems in pre-school children of West Indian-born parents: a re-examination of family and social factors', *J. Child Psychol. Psychiat.*, 21, 2, 107–16.
EDWARDS, V. K. (1976). 'Effects of dialect on the comprehension of West Indian children', *Educ. Res.*, 18, 2, 83–95.
EDWARDS, V. K. (1978). 'Language attitudes and underperformance in West Indian children', *Educ. Rev.*, 30, 1, 51–8.
*EDWARDS, V. K. (1979). *The West Indian Language Issue in British Schools*. London: Routledge and Kegan Paul.
EDWARDS, V. K. and SUTCLIFFE, D. (1978). 'Broadly speaking', *TES*, 13th October, p.19.
*ESSEN, J. and GHODSIAN, M. (1979). 'The children of immigrants: school performance', *New Community*, I, 3, 422–9.
EVANS, P. (1972). *Attitudes of Young Immigrants*. London: Runnymede Trust.
EVANS, P. C. C. and LE PAGE, R. B. (1967). *The Education of West Indian Immigrant Children*. National Committee for Commonwealth Immigrants.
FETHNEY, V. (1972). 'ESN children: what the teachers say', *Race Today*, 4, 400–1.
FIGUEROA, P. (1974). West Indian school-leavers in London: a sociological study in ten schools in a London borough. 1966–1967. Unpublished DPhil thesis, London School of Economics.
FIGUEROA, P. (1976). 'The employment prospects of West Indian school-leavers in London, England', *Social and Economic Studies*, 25, 3, 216–33.
FITZHERBERT, K. (1967). *West Indian Children in London*. London: Bell & Sons Ltd. Occasional Papers on Social Administration 19.
FONER, N. (1975). 'The meaning of education to Jamaicans at home and in London', *New Community*, IV, 2, 195–202.
FONER, N. (1977). 'The Jamaicans: cultural and social change among migrants in Britain.' In: WATSON, J. L. *Between Two Cultures*. Oxford: Basil Blackwell.
FOWLER, B., LITTLEWOOD, B. and MADIGAN, R. (1977). 'Immigrant school leavers and the search for work', *Sociology*, 11, 1, 65–85.
GASKELL, G. and SMITH, P. (1981). 'Are young blacks really alienated?' *New Society*, 14th May, pp.260–1.
*GHODSIAN, M., ESSEN, J. and RICHARDSON, K. (1980). 'Children of immigrants. Social and home circumstances', *New Community*, VIII, 3, 195–205, Winter.
GIBBES, N. (1980). *West Indian Teachers Speak Out: Their Experience in Some of London's Schools*. Lewisham, London: Caribbean Teachers'

Association and Lewisham Council for Community Relations.
GILES, R. (1977). *The West Indian Experience in British Schools. Multiracial Education and Social Disadvantage in London.* London: Heinemann.
GLATT, C. A. and KING, G. D. (1975). 'Institutional racism and white racists: a socio-psychological view of race and educational development.' In: VERMA, G. K. and BAGLEY, C. (Eds) *Race and Education Across Cultures.* London: Heinemann.
GLENDENNING, F. (1971). 'Racial stereotypes in history textbooks', *Race Today*, 3, 52–4.
GOLDMAN, R. J. (1973). 'Education and immigrants.' In: WATSON, P. (Ed) *Psychology and Race.* Harmondsworth: Penguin.
GOLDMAN, R. J. and TAYLOR, F. M. (1966). 'Coloured immigrant children: a survey of research, studies and literature on their educational problems and potential in Britain', *Educ. Res.*, 8, 3, 163–83.
GRAHAM, C. (1968). *Social and Psychological Problems in the London Borough of Brent.* Brent Consultation Centre (Paper presented at a one-day conference on Adolescence).
GRAHAM, P. J. and MEADOWS, C. E. (1967). 'Psychiatric disorder in the children of West Indian immigrants', *J. Child Psychol. Psychiat.*, 8, 105–16.
GREAT BRITAIN. DEPARTMENT OF EDUCATION AND SCIENCE (1971a). *Potential and Progress in a Second Culture.* London: HMSO. (Education Survey 10.)
GREAT BRITAIN. DEPARTMENT OF EDUCATION AND SCIENCE (1971b). *The Education of Immigrants.* London: HMSO. (Education Survey 13.)
GREAT BRITAIN. DEPARTMENT OF EDUCATION AND SCIENCE (1972a). *The Continuing Needs of Immigrants.* London: HMSO. (Education Survey 14.)
GREAT BRITAIN. DEPARTMENT OF EDUCATION AND SCIENCE (1972b). *Statistics of Education – 1971. Vol. 1. Schools.* London: HMSO.
GREAT BRITAIN. DEPARTMENT OF EDUCATION AND SCIENCE (1973). *Statistics of Education – 1972. Vol. 1. Schools.* London: HMSO.
GREAT BRITAIN. PARLIAMENT. HOUSE OF COMMONS (1974). *Educational Disadvantage and the Educational Needs of Immigrants.* Observations on the Report on Education of the Select Committee on Race Relations and Immigration. London: HMSO. Cmnd 5720.
GREAT BRITAIN. PARLIAMENT. HOUSE OF COMMONS (1978). *The West Indian Community.* Observations on the Report of the Select Committee on Race Relations and Immigration. London: HMSO. Cmnd 7186.
GREAT BRITAIN. PARLIAMENT. HOUSE OF COMMONS. HOME AFFAIRS COMMITTEE. RACE RELATIONS AND IMMIGRATION SUB-COMMITTEE. (1980). *Session 1979–80. Racial Disadvantage. Minutes of Evidence. Department of Education and Science.* London: HMSO.

GREAT BRITAIN. PARLIAMENT. HOUSE OF COMMONS. SELECT COMMITTEE ON RACE RELATIONS AND IMMIGRATION (1969). *The Problems of Coloured School Leavers. 1968–69, Vol. 2. Minutes of Evidence.* London: HMSO.

GREAT BRITAIN. PARLIAMENT. HOUSE OF COMMONS. SELECT COMMITTEE ON RACE RELATIONS AND IMMIGRATION (1973). *Evidence – Education Vol. 3.* London: HMSO.

GREAT BRITAIN. PARLIAMENT. HOUSE OF COMMONS. SELECT COMMITTEE ON RACE RELATIONS AND IMMIGRATION (1977). *Report with Minutes of Proceedings and Appendices to Report. Session 1976–7: The West Indian Community. Vol. 1.* London: HMSO.

GREEN, P. A. (1972). Attitudes of teachers of West Indian immigrant children. Unpublished MPhil thesis, Nottingham University.

HARTMANN, P. and HUSBAND, C. (1974). *Racism and the Mass Media.* London: Davis-Poynter.

HATCH, S. (1962). 'Coloured people in school textbooks', *Race*, **4**, 63–72.

HAYNES, J. M. (1971). *Educational Assessment of Immigrant Pupils.* Slough: NFER.

HEGARTY, S. (1976). 'Fair play in testing?', *A.E.P. Journal*, **4**, 3, 20–3.

*HEGARTY, S. and LUCAS, D. (1978). *Able to Learn.* Windsor: NFER.

HELLER, C. (1969). *Structured Social Inequality.* New York: Random House.

HEPPLE, B. (1970). *Race, Jobs and the Law in Great Britain.* Harmondsworth: Penguin.

HILL, C. S. (1967). *How Prejudiced is Britain?* London: Panther.

HILL, D. (1968). The attitudes of West Indian and English adolescents in Britain. MEd thesis, University of Manchester.

HILL, D. (1975). 'Personality factors among adolescents in minority ethnic groups', *Educ. Studs.*, **1**, 43–54.

HILL, J. (1971). *Books for Children: The Homelands of Immigrants in Britain.* London: Institute for Race Relations.

HILTON, J. (1972). 'The ambitions of school children', *Race Today*, March.

HINDS, D. (1980). 'Why I don't want to be British', *The Guardian*, 5th September, p.8.

HOLBERTON, R. (1977). 'The first generation of a new experience', *ILEA Contact*, **6**, 23, 9th December.

HOOD, C., OPPÉ, T. E., PLESS, I. B. and APTE, E. (1970). *Children of West Indian Immigrants: a Study of One-Year-Olds in Paddington.* London: Institute of Race Relations.

HOPE, R. (1980). Quoted in *The Caribbean and West Indies Chronicle.* March 1980, p.21.

HOUGHTON, V. P. (1966). 'Intelligence testing of West Indian and English children', *Race*, **8**, 147–56.

HOUSDEN, R. (1980). 'Adventures in the neighbourhood', *TES*, 6th June.

HUNT, S. M. (1975). *Parents of the 'ESN'.* Manchester: National Elfrida

Rathbone Society.
INNER LONDON EDUCATION AUTHORITY (1967). The Education
of Immigrant Pupils in Special Schools for ESN Children. Report 657.
Unpublished Internal ILEA Report.
INNER LONDON EDUCATION AUTHORITY (1972). Literacy Sur-
vey: 1971 Follow-up Preliminary Report. ILEA 203. RS567A/72 Re-
search and Statistics Group.
JACKSON, B. (1979). *Starting School.* London: Croom Helm.
JACKSON, S. (1971). *The Illegal Childminders.* Cambridge Development
Trust.
JACKSON, S. (1975). 'Unsatisfactory child minding: the educational
implications', *New Community*, IV, 2, 211–15 Summer.
JAHODA, G., VENESS, T. and PUSHKIN, I. (1966). 'Awareness of
ethnic differences in young children: proposals for a British study', *Race*,
8, 1, 63–74.
JEFFCOATE, R. (1977). 'Looking in the wrong place', *TES*, 24th June.
JEFFCOATE, R. (1979). *Positive Image. Towards a Multiracial Cur-
riculum.* London: Writers and Readers Publishing Co-operative.
JELINEK, M. M. (1977). 'Multiracial education 3. Pupils' attitudes to the
multiracial school', *Educ. Res.*, 19, 2, 129–41.
*JELINEK, M. M. and BRITTAN, E. M. (1975). 'Multiracial education 1.
Interethnic friendship patterns', *Educ. Res.*, 18, 1, 44–53.
JENCKS, C. (1973). *Inequality.* London: Allen Lane.
JENKINS, D., KEMMIS, S., MACDONALD, B. and VERMA, G. K.
(1979). 'Racism and educational evaluation.' In: VERMA, G. K. and
BAGLEY, C. (Eds) *Race, Education and Identity.* London: The Mac-
millan Press Ltd.
JENSEN, A. (1969). 'How much can we boost IQ and scholastic achieve-
ment?', *Harv. Educ. Rev.*, 39, 1, 1–122.
JENSEN, A. (1971). 'Do schools cheat minority children?', *Educ. Res.*, 14,
1, 3–28.
JOHN, A. (1971). *Race in the Inner City.* London: Runnymede Trust.
JOHNSTON, S. (1978). 'The West Indian supplementary service', *Disad-
vantage in Education*, 10, 12, July/August.
JONES, P. (1977). An evaluation of the effect of sport on the integration of
West Indian schoolchildren. Unpublished PhD thesis, University of
Surrey.
KATZ, I. (1973). 'Alternatives to personality-deficit interpretation of
negro underachievement.' In: WATSON, P. (Ed) *Psychology and Race.*
London: Penguin Books.
KAWWA, T. (1968a). 'Three sociometric studies of ethnic relations in
London schools', *Race*, 10, 2, 173–80.
KAWWA, T. (1968b). 'A survey of ethnic attitudes of some British
secondary school pupils', *Br. J. Soc. Clin. Psychol.*, 7, 161–8.
KELMER PRINGLE, M. (1966). *Deprivation and Education.* London:
Longman.
KIRP, D. (1977). 'Wrong problem, wrong solution', *TES*, 24th June.
KITZINGER, S. (1978). 'West Indian adolescents: an anthropological
perspective', *J. of Adolescence*, 1, 35–46.

LAISHLEY, J. (1971). 'Skin colour awareness and preference among London nursery school children', *Race*, **13**, 1, 47–64.

*LITTLE, A. (1975). 'Performance of children from ethnic minority backgrounds in primary schools', *Oxford Review of Education*, **1**, 2, 117–35. See also 'The educational achievement of ethnic minority children in London schools.' In: VERMA, G. K. and BAGLEY, C. (Eds) (1975). *Race and Education Across Cultures*. London: Heinemann, which is very similar.

LITTLE, A. (1978). Educational Policies for Multiracial Areas. Goldsmiths' College, University of London. (Inaugural Lecture.)

*LITTLE, A., MABEY, C. and WHITAKER, G. (1968). 'The education of immigrant pupils in inner London primary schools', *Race*, **IX**, 4 April.

LITTLE, A and WILLEY, R. (1981). *Multi-ethnic Education: The Way Forward*. Schools Council Pamphlet 18. London: Schools Council.

LODGE, B. (1981). 'Training courses fail to attract Asians', *TES*, 20th March.

LOMAX, P. (1977). 'The self concepts of girls in the context of a disadvantaging environment', *Educ. Rev.*, **29**, 107–19.

*LOUDEN, D. (1978). 'Self esteem and the locus of control: some findings on immigrant adolescents in Britain', *New Community*, **VI**, 3, 218–34.

LOW, I. (1978). Strathclyde Experiment in Education: The Govan Project. Department of Education, University of Glasgow. Mimeograph.

MABEY, C. (1974). Social and Ethnic Mix in Schools and the Relationship with Attainment of Children aged 8 and 11. Centre for Environmental Studies, Research Paper 9.

MABEY, C. (1980). ILEA Literacy Survey. West Indian Attainment. Unpublished. Similar to:

*MABEY, C. (1981). 'Black British literacy: a study of reading attainment of London black children from 8 to 15 years', *Educ. Res.*, **23**, 2, 83–95.

McEWEN, E. C., GIPPS, C. V. and SUMNER, R. (1975). *Language Proficiency in the Multiracial School: A Comparative Study*. Slough: NFER.

McFIE, J. and THOMPSON, J. A. (1970). 'Intellectual abilities of immigrant children', *Br. J. Educ. Psych.*, **40**, 348–51.

McINTOSH, N. and SMITH, D. J. (1974). The Extent of Racial Discrimination. PEP. Broadsheet No. 547.

MACK, J. (1977). 'West Indians and school', *New Society*, 8th December.

MADGE, N. J. H. (1976). 'Context and the expressed preferences of infant school children', *J. Child Psychol. and Psychiat.*, **17**, 4, 377–44.

MANLEY, D. (1963). 'Mental ability in Jamaica', *Social and Electronic Studies*, **18**, 54–71.

MARJORIBANKS, K. (1979). *Families and their Learning Environments: An Empirical Analysis*. London: Routledge & Kegan Paul.

MARJORIBANKS, K. (1980). *Ethnic Families and Children's Achievements*. Sydney: Allen & Unwin.

MARVELL, J. (1974). 'Moral socialization in a multiracial community', *J. Moral Educ.*, **3**, 3, 249–57.

MAYALL, B. and PETRIE, P. (1977). *Minder, Mother and Child*. University of London Institute of Education Studies in Education 5. Windsor: NFER.

MILLAR, S. (1968). *The Psychology of Play*. Harmondsworth: Penguin.

MILLER, H. (1969). 'The effectiveness of teaching techniques for reducing colour prejudice', *Liberal Education*, **16**, 25–31.

MILNER, D. (1975). *Children and Race*. Harmondsworth: Penguin.

MUNDY, J. H. (1973). 'DES overseas courses to Jamaica: 1971 and 1972', *New Community*, **II**, 3, 237–40.

NANDY, D. (1971). Foreword to McNEAL, J. and ROGERS, M. (Eds) *The Multiracial School: a Professional Perspective*. Harmondsworth: Penguin.

NANDY, D. (1981). A Review and Assessment of Black Studies in London Schools. A SSRC report lodged with the British Library Lending Division.

NATIONAL ASSOCIATION OF HEAD TEACHERS (1980). *Educational Needs and Attainments of Pupils of West Indian Origin*. Haywards Heath: NAHT. (Evidence to Rampton Committee.)

NATIONAL ASSOCIATION OF TEACHERS IN FURTHER AND HIGHER EDUCATION (1981). The Written Evidence to the Race Relations and Immigration Sub-committee of the Home Affairs Committee of the House of Commons. London. NATFHE. January.

NATIONAL FOUNDATION FOR EDUCATIONAL RESEARCH (1979). *Register of Educational Research in the United Kingdom. Vol. 3. 1977–78*. Slough: NFER.

NATIONAL UNION OF TEACHERS (1980). *The Achievement of West Indian Pupils*. Union evidence to the Rampton Committee of Inquiry into the Education of Children from Ethnic Minority Groups. London: NUT.

NEW SOCIETY (1980). 'Report. The problems of black teachers', p.419, 27th November.

NFER PUBLISHING COMPANY (1980). *Catalogue of Tests for Educational Guidance and Assessment*. Windsor: NFER.

NICOL, A. R. (1971). 'Psychiatric disorder in West Indian school children', *Race Today*, 14–15, Jan.

OAKLEY, R. (Ed) (1968). *New Backgrounds: the Immigrant Child at Home and at School*. London: Oxford University Press.

OFFICE OF POPULATION CENSUSES AND SURVEYS (1973). *Young People's Employment Study: Preliminary Report. No. 1*. OPCS. Social Survey Division.

OFFICE OF POPULATION CENSUSES AND SURVEYS (1974). *Young People's Employment Study: Preliminary Report. No. 2*. OPCS. Social Survey Division.

OFFICE OF POPULATION CENSUSES AND SURVEYS (1976). *Young People's Employment Study: Preliminary Report. No. 3*. OPCS. Social Survey Division.

OFFICE OF POPULATION CENSUSES AND SURVEYS (1980). *Young People's Employment Study: Preliminary Report. No. 4*. OPCS. Social Survey Division.

OPPÉ, T. E. (1964). 'The health of West Indian children', *Proceedings of The Royal Society of Medicine*, **57**, 321–3.

PATTERSON, S. (1963) *Dark Strangers*. London: Tavistock Publications.

PAYNE, J. (1974). *Educational Priority. EPA Surveys and Statistics. Vol. 2.* London: HMSO.

PAYNE, J. F. (1969). 'A comparative study of the mental ability of seven- and eight-year-old British and West Indian children in a West Midlands town', *Br. J. Educ. Psychol.*, **39**, 326–7. MA thesis, Keele.

PEACH, C. (1968). *West Indian Migration to Britain. A Social Geography.* London: Oxford University Press for Institute of Race Relations.

PHILLIPS, C. J. (1979). 'Educational under-achievement in different ethnic groups', *Educ. Res.*, **21**, 2, 116–30.

PHILLIPS, D. (1977). Language Proficiency in a Group of First Year Junior Children in Manchester. Manchester: Manchester Polytechnic. Unpublished.

PIDGEON, D. (1970). *Expectation and Pupil Performance.* Slough: NFER.

PLESS, I. B. and HOOD, C. (1967). 'West Indian one-year-olds: a comparative analysis of health and service utilisation', *The Lancet*, 24th June.

POLLAK, M. (1972). *Today's Three-year-olds in London.* London: Heinemann.

POLLAK, M. (1979). *Nine Years Old.* Lancaster: MTP Press Limited.

PRESCOD-ROBERTS, M. and STEELE, N. (1980). *Black Women: Bringing it all Back Home.* Bristol: Falling Wall Press Ltd.

PRINCE, G. (1967). 'Mental health problems in pre-school West Indian children', *Maternal Child Care*, **3**, 483–6.

*PRYCE, K. (1979). *Endless Pressure. A Study of West Indian Life Styles in Bristol.* Harmondsworth: Penguin.

PURUSHOTHAMAN, M. (1978). *The Education of Children of Caribbean Origin: Select Research Bibliography.* Manchester: Centre for Information and Advice on Educational Disadvantage.

REPORT OF A LONDON WORKING PARTY OF TEACHERS AND LECTURERS (1974). 'West Indian children in London schools. What kind of teacher education is possible?', *Multiracial School*, **3**, 2, Autumn.

*REX, J. and TOMLINSON, S. (1979). *Colonial Immigrants in a British City. A Class Analysis.* London: Routledge & Kegan Paul.

RICHARDSON, S. and GREEN, A. (1971). 'When is black beautiful? Coloured and white children's reactions to skin colour', *Br. J. Educ. Psychol.*, **41**, 62–9.

RICHMOND, A. (1973). *Migration and Race Relations in an English City.* London: Oxford University Press.

RICHMOND, J. (1978). 'Jennifer and Brixton blues', *New Approaches in Multi-racial Education*, **6**, 3, 3–10.

ROBERTSON, T. S. and KAWWA, T. (1971). 'Ethnic relations in a girls' comprehensive school', *Educ. Res.*, **13**, 214–7.

ROGERS, M. (1973). 'Education in a multi-ethnic Britain: a teacher's eye view', *New Community*, **II**, 3, 221–9.

ROSE, E. J. B., DEAKIN, N., ABRAMS, M., JACKSON, V., PESTON, M., VANAGS, A. H., COHEN, B., GAITSKELL, J. and WARD, P. (1969). *Colour and Citizenship.* Oxford: Oxford University Press for The Institute of Race Relations.

ROSEN, H. and BURGESS, T. (1980a). Linguistic Diversity in London Schools: An Investigation carried Out in the English Department of the University of London Institute of Education. Mimeographed. Later modified and published as:

*ROSEN, H. and BURGESS, T. (1980b). *Languages and Dialects of London School Children. An Investigation.* London: Ward Lock Educational.

ROSENTHAL, R. and JACOBSON, L. (1968). *Pygmalion in the Classroom.* New York: Holt, Rinehart and Winston.

ROWLEY, K. G. (1968). 'Social relations between British and immigrant children', *Educ. Res.*, **10**, 2145–8.

RUTTER, M. and MADGE, N. (1976). *Cycles of Disadvantage.* London: Heinemann.

RUTTER, M., MAUGHAN, B., MORTIMORE, P. and OUSTON, J. (1979). *Fifteen Thousand Hours.* London: Open Books.

RUTTER, M. L. and MITTLER, P. (1972). 'Environmental influences on language development.' In: RUTTER, M. L. and MARTIN, J. A. M. (Eds) *The Child with Delayed Speech.* Clinic Studies in Developmental Medicine, No. 43, London: Heinemann/SIMP.

*RUTTER, M., YULE, B., MORTON, J. and BAGLEY, C. (1975). 'Children of West Indian immigrants – III, home circumstances and family patterns', *J. Child Psychol. and Psychiat.*, **16**, 2, 105–24.

*RUTTER, M., YULE, W., BERGER, M., YULE, B., MORTON, J. and BAGLEY, C. (1974). 'Children of West Indian immigrants – I, rates of behavioural deviance and of psychiatric disorder', *J. Child Psychol. and Psychiat*, **15**, 4, 241–62.

RUTTER, M., YULE, W., TIZARD, J. and GRAHAM, P. (1967). 'Severe reading retardation, its relation to maladjustment, epilepsy and neurological disorder', *Proc. First Internat. Conference on Special Education.* London.

SARGEANT, A. J. (1972). 'Participation of West Indian boys in English schools' sports teams', *Educ. Res.*, **14**, 3, 225–30.

SCHOOLS COUNCIL (1970). *Teaching English to West Indian Children: the Research Stage of the Project.* Working Paper 29. London: Evans/Methuen.

SCHOOLS COUNCIL (1972). *Concept 7–9.* Leeds: E. J. Arnold. Project on Teaching English to West Indian Children.

SCHOOLS COUNCIL (1981). *Education for a Multiracial Society, Curriculum and Content 5–13.* Information Centre, Schools Council, London.

SCIPIO, L. (1973). 'The black child in the British school system: a personal view', *J. Appl. Educ. Studs.*, **2**, 1, 19–23.

SEABROOK, J. (1980). 'A Jamaican tale of two sisters', *New Society*, 11.9.80.

SEAVER, W. B. (1973). 'Effects of naturally induced teacher expectancies', *J. Pers. Soc. Psychol.*, **28**, 333–42.

SECKINGTON, J. M. and REID, M. (1980). Youth at Work. A Report on an Experimental Advisory Service for School Leavers. Education Department, Royal County of Berkshire.

SIRIWARDENA, L. (1980). 'West Indian performance.' Letter to *TES*, 7th March.

SMITH, D. J. (1974). Racial Disadvantage in Employment. PEP. Broadsheet No. 544.

SMITH, D. J. (1977). *Racial Disadvantage in Britain.* Harmondsworth: Penguin.

SMITH, D. J. (1981). *Unemployment and Racial Minorities.* London: Policy Studies Institute. No. 594.

SMITH, M. (1973). 'The multi-racial school: a case study', *J. Appl. Educ. Studs.*, **2**, 1, 24–6.

SMOLINS, G. (1975). Reading and comprehension: a comparative study of some 8-9-year-old children of English and West Indian origin. Unpublished MA dissertation, Birkbeck College, University of London.

SPEARS, A. K. (1978). 'Institutionalized racism and the education of blacks', *Anthropology and Educ. Quarterly*, **9**, 2, 127–36.

SPENCER, D. and KELLAS, I. (1980). 'Some like it hot in little England', *TES*, 13th June.

STANTON, M. (1972). 'Pupils' views of national groups', *J. Moral Educ.*, **1**, 3, 147–51.

STEIN, C. (1980). 'Eysenck first with the evidence.' Letter to *TES*, 8th February.

STOKER, D. (1969). The Education of Infant Immigrants. A Report Prepared for the Schools Council Project in English for Immigrant Children. Leeds: The Institute of Education.

STONE, M. (1981). *The Education of the Black Child in Britain. The Myth of Multiracial Education.* London: Fontana.

STONES, E. (1975). 'The colour of conceptual learning', *Res. Intell.*, **1**, 2, 5–10. Also in VERMA, G. K. and BAGLEY, C. (Eds) (1979). *Race, Education and Identity.* London: Macmillan.

SUTCLIFFE, D. (1976). 'Hou dem taak in Bedford, sa', *Multiracial School*, **5**, 1, 19–24.

SUTCLIFFE, D. (1978). The language of first and second generations of West Indian children in Bedfordshire. Unpublished MEd thesis, University of Leicester.

TAYLOR, F. (1974). *Race, School and Community.* Slough: NFER.

THE TIMES (11.9.80). 'Black youths bear the brunt of unemployment.'

THOMAS, K. C. (1978). 'Colour of tester effects on children's expressed attitudes', *Br. Educ. Res. J.*, **4**, 2, 83–91.

THOMAS-HOPE, E. M. (1975). 'The adaptation of migrants from the English-speaking Caribbean in select urban centres of Britain and North America.' Paper presented to the Congress of Applied Anthropology, Amsterdam. Unpublished. In revised form as 'Identity and adaptation of migrants from the English-speaking Caribbean in Britain and North

America'. In: VERMA, G. K. and BAGLEY, C. (Eds) (1981). *Self-concept, Achievement and Multi-cultural Education*. London: Macmillan.

THOMAS-HOPE, E. M. (1981). 'The status of Caribbean studies in Britain', *Society for Caribbean Studies Newsletter*, pp.4–7, 18th March.

TIZARD, J., HEWISON, J. and SCHOFIELD, W. N. (1980). Collaboration between Teachers and Parents in Assisting Children's Reading. Project Summary. Thomas Coram Research Unit.

*TOMLINSON, S. (1978). 'West Indian children and ESN schooling', *New Community*, **VI**, 3, 235–42.

TOMLINSON, S. (1979). Decision-making in special education (ESN-M) with some reference to children of immigrant parentage. Unpublished PhD thesis, University of Warwick.

TOMLINSON, S. (1980). 'The educational performance of ethnic minority children, *New Community*, **VIII**, 3, 213–34.

TOMLINSON, S. (1981). *Educational Subnormality: a Study in Decision-making*. London: Routledge & Kegan Paul.

TOWNSEND, H. E. R. (1971). *Immigrant Pupils in England: the LEA Response*. Slough: NFER.

TOWNSEND, H. E. R. and BRITTAN, E. M. (1972). *Organization in Multiracial Schools*. Slough: NFER.

TRISELIOTIS, J. (1968). 'Psycho-social problems of immigrant families.' In: OAKLEY, R. (Ed) *New Backgrounds: the Immigrant Child at Home and at School*. London: Oxford University Press.

TRUDGILL, P. (1975). *Accent, Dialect and the School*. London: Edward Arnold.

TRUDGILL, P. (1979). 'Standard and non-standard dialects of English in the United Kingdom: problems and policies', *Intl. J. Soc. Lang.*, **21**, 9–24.

VARLAAM, A. (1974). 'Educational attainment and behaviour at school', *GLC Intelligence Quarterly*, **29**, 20–37.

VERMA, G. K. (1975). 'Inter-group prejudice and race relations.' In: VERMA, G. K. and BAGLEY, C. (Eds) *Race and Education Across Cultures*. London: Heinemann.

*VERMA, G. K. and BAGLEY, C. (Eds) (1975). *Race and Education Across Cultures*. London: Heinemann.

VERMA, G. K. and BAGLEY, C. (1979). 'Measured changes in racial attitudes following the use of three different teaching methods.' In: VERMA, G. K. and BAGLEY, C. (Eds) *Race, Education and Identity*. London: Macmillan.

VERMA, G. K. and BAGLEY, C. (Eds) (1981). *Self-concept, Achievement and Multi-cultural Education*. London: Macmillan.

VERNON, P. E. (1958). 'Education and the psychology of individual differences', *Harv. J. Educ. Res.*, **28**, 91–104.

VERNON, P. E. (1965a). 'Environmental handicaps and intellectual development: Part I', *Br. J. Educ. Psychol.*, **XXXV**, 1, 9–20.

VERNON, P. E. (1965b). 'Environmental handicaps and intellectual development: Part II', *Br. J. Educ. Psychol.*, **XXXV**, 2, 117–26.

VERNON, P. E. (1969). *Intelligence and Cultural Environment.* London: Methuen.

VERNON, P. E. (1975). 'Intelligence across cultures.' In: VERMA, G. K. and BAGLEY, C. (Eds) *Race and Education Across Cultures.* London: Heinemann.

WARD, J. (1978). 'An observational study of interaction and progress for the immigrant in school', *Educ. Studs.,* **4**, 2, 91–7, June.

WATSON, P. (1970). 'How race affects IQ', *New Society,* 16th July.

WATSON, P. (1973). 'Stability of IQ of immigrant and non-immigrant slow learning pupils', *Br. J. of Educ. Psychol,* **43**, 80–2.

WEINREICH, P. (1979). 'Cross-ethnic identification and self-rejection in a black adolescent.' In: VERMA, G. K. and BAGLEY, C. (Eds) *Race, Education and Identity.* London: Macmillan.

WEIR, K. (1980). 'The West Indian pupil in a junior school: testing their language ability', *Eng. Lang. Teaching J.,* **24**, 4, Summer.

WHITEHOUSE, R. (1973). 'The cultural background of West Indian children in relation to their educational aspirations', *J. Appl. Educ. Studs.,* **2**, 1, 10–18.

WIDLAKE, P. and BLOOM, D. (1979). 'Which culture to teach immigrant pupils?', *Education,* 14th December.

WIGHT, J. (1971). 'Dialect in school', *Educ. Rev.,* **24**, 1, 47–58.

WILES, S. (1968). 'Children from overseas', *Institute of Race Relations Newsletter.* February.

WILLIAMS, J. (1978). West Indian Children in Dudley. Dudley CRC. Mimeograph.

YOUNG, L. and BAGLEY, C. (1979). 'Identity, self-esteem and evaluation of colour and ethnicity in young children in Jamaica and London', *New Community,* **VII**, 154–69.

*YULE, W., BERGER, M., RUTTER, M. and YULE, B. (1975). 'Children of West Indian immigrants – II, intellectual performance and reading attainment', *J. Child Psychol. and Psychiat.,* **16**, 1–17.

Index

Please note that all topics refer specifically to West Indians unless otherwise stated